NOVELISTS IN INTERVIEW

Also by John Haffenden

John Berryman: A Critical Commentary
Viewpoints: Poets in Conversation
The Life of John Berryman

As editor

Henry's Fate & Other Poems, 1967–1972
by John Berryman
W. H. Auden: The Critical Heritage

NOVELISTS IN
· INTERVIEW ·

Martin Amis · Malcolm Bradbury · Anita Brookner
Angela Carter · William Golding
Russell Hoban · David Lodge · Ian McEwan
Iris Murdoch · V. S. Pritchett · Salman Rushdie
David Storey · Emma Tennant · Fay Weldon

John Haffenden

· METHUEN ·
LONDON · NEW YORK

First published in 1985 by
Methuen & Co. Ltd
11 New Fetter Lane, London EC4P 4EE

Published in the USA by
Methuen & Co.
in association with Methuen, Inc.
29 West 35th Street, New York, NY 10001

Photoset by Rowland Phototypesetting Ltd,
Bury St Edmunds, Suffolk
Printed in Great Britain by
Richard Clay (The Chaucer Press) Ltd,
Bungay, Suffolk

British Library Cataloguing in Publication Data

Novelists in interview.
1. English fiction – 20th century – History
and criticism   2. Authors, English – 20th
century – Interviews
I. Haffenden, John, *1945–*
823'.914'09   PR884

ISBN 0-416-37590-1
ISBN 0-416-37600-2 Pbk

Library of Congress Cataloging in Publication Data

Main entry under title:

Novelists in interview

Bibliography: p.
1. Novelists, English – 20th century – Interviews.
I. Haffenden, John.
PR882.N68 1985   823'.914'09   85-11434
ISBN 0-416-37590-1
ISBN 0-416-37600-2 (pbk.)

· CONTENTS ·

· ACKNOWLEDGEMENTS ·

I should like to thank Craig Raine for commissioning the William Golding interview when he was editor of *Quarto*, and Gillian Greenwood for first publishing a number of the other interviews in the *Literary Review*, and for her patient professionalism in keeping me up to the mark. I am grateful to the *Literary Review* for permission to reprint those pieces.

My warm thanks are also due to several persons who helped me in various capacities, especially Rupert Lancaster, Linda MacFadyen, Harriet Goodman, Sheila Turnbull, Jenny Morton, Serena Davies, Deborah Benady, Sophia Sackville-West, Janice Price and Belinda Dearbergh; and to British Rail for getting me there time and again on time.

· INTRODUCTION ·

The aims of interviewing literary authors are perhaps not wholly distinct from the aims of literary biography, except for the obvious fact that an interviewer cannot reach beyond what an author is prepared to present of his or her life and work. Leon Edel, in *Literary Biography* (London: Rupert Hart-Davis, 1957), approvingly quotes Sainte-Beuve's well-worn conviction:

> Literature, literary creation, is not distinct or separable, for me, from the rest of the man. . . . I may taste a work, but it is difficult for me to judge it independently of my knowledge of the man himself; and I will say willingly, *tel arbre, tel fruit.*

But Edel was surely unwary in citing such a candid but critically innocent declaration, especially when Sainte-Beuve speaks of being unable to 'judge' a work independently of a knowledge of the writer. Marcel Proust attacked what he called Sainte-Beuve's 'pinchbeck ideal' of trying to match the writer and the work: 'the writer's true self is manifested in his books alone,' he asserted in *By Way of Sainte-Beuve.* Many other writers have similarly and justifiably protested against any equation of their literary works with their personal experience and social selves. Salman Rushdie, for example, remarks in the interview in this volume, 'I think, like most writers, that I am most completely myself when I write, and not the rest of the time. I have a social self, and my full self can't be released except in the writing'.

In *Theory of Literature* (1949; 3rd edn, Harmondsworth: Peregrine, 1963), René Wellek and Austin Warren put forward the view that biographical study can 'help us in studying the most obvious of all strictly developmental problems in the history of literature – the growth, maturing, and possible decline of an author's art'. They also advisedly say what obviously needs to be said again and again: 'The whole view that art is self-expression pure and simple, the transcript of personal feeling and experiences, is demonstrably false . . . the artist may "experience" life differently in terms of his art.' The literary biographer can obviously be a menace when he or she reads creative work for factual information about an author's life. That is not to say that authors may not speak about their lives and experiences, their views and aesthetic principles, their ways of working and what writing means to them. It is natural and not improper for readers to feel, as Julian Barnes (or perhaps I should say his character Geoffrey Braithwaite) writes in his splendid recent exercise in critical fiction, *Flaubert's Parrot* (London: Cape, 1984): 'But if you love a writer, if you depend upon the drip-feed of his intelligence, if you want to pursue him and find him – despite edicts to the contrary – then it's impossible to know too much.'

If it is true, as Henry James asserted in his story 'The Real Right Thing', that 'The artist was what he *did* – he was nothing else', it may be equally true to say that writing is the major action of the artist's life. Must we presume that novelists' commentaries on their works are bound to be 'rationalizations' or even misinterpretations simply because they are extraneous? Leaving aside the question of judgement, since it would be unnecessarily pious to take any literary work at the author's own valuation, I believe it is invaluable for authors to tell us about their materials and methods, and about what they had in mind. Any understanding of the creative process, or what Leon Edel properly calls the 'fashioning consciousness', is useful to the act of criticism.

My endeavour in undertaking these interviews is therefore to ask the novelists how they interpret the intentions and meanings of their individual works – with reference to specific novels including William Golding's *Rites of Passage*, Russell Hoban's *Riddley Walker*, Iris Murdoch's *The Philosopher's Pupil* and Salman Rushdie's *Midnight's Children* and *Shame* – and about the ideas and visions that inform those works. Arising out of the explication of individual achievements are questions concerning the novelists' convictions about the function of fiction, as well as some discussion of cultural context and of narrative modes including realism, postmodernism, allegory and fable. My role in asking the questions combines the critic and the reporter. I have tried to resist imposing my views on the interviewees, or in any sense putting words into their mouths, but there is actually little danger of that: the novelists are well able to dispute or refute opinions with which they disagree. Furthermore, while a literary interview is above all else a service to the writer and his or her works, and a service to the reader, I have not felt it necessary to be slavish to the writers' statements. What I have always carried in mind and applied to the novel are T. S. Eliot's remarks about the status of the poem:

> The poem's existence is somewhere between the writer and the reader; it has a reality which is not simply the reality of what the writer is trying to 'express', or of his experience of writing it, or of the experience of the reader or of the writer as reader. Consequently the problem of what a poem 'means' is a good deal more difficult than it at first appears. (*The Use of Poetry and the Use of Criticism*, London: Faber, 1933)

Poets and novelists alike would surely agree with Eliot's sense of the matter. Finally, and on a basic level, the interviews may at least speak to Samuel Johnson's sense of natural human curiosity as he expressed it in *The Life of Milton*: 'who does not wish that the author of the *Iliad* had gratified succeeding ages with a little knowledge of himself?'

Yet some schools of criticism regard it as a radical nuisance – a wet playtime – for authors to comment on their own work. They require authors to be at best non-existent, at least mute and indifferent. 'The author should die once he has finished writing', Umberto Eco writes in *Reflections on 'The Name of the Rose'* (London: Secker & Warburg, 1985). 'So as not to trouble the path of the text.' Unfortunately not all authors will obligingly offer themselves to that wormy circumstance. Eco's pert pronouncement is in line with what has become an orthodoxy of recent critical theory, the insistence on the semantic autonomy of the work of literature. At least since W. K. Wimsatt and M. C. Beardsley's essay on 'The Intentional Fallacy' (1946),[*] critics have widely agreed that a work of art is self-existent and independent, not to be evaluated or 'judged' by reference to an author's comments on it: 'the design or intention of the author', Wimsatt and Beardsley wrote, 'is neither available nor desirable as a standard for judging the success of a work of literary art.' The novel or poem or play has abandoned the author who produced it. 'Critical enquiries are not settled by consulting the oracle' – the author.

But when Wimsatt and Beardsley went on to remark that it would not be a proper critical enquiry to ask T. S. Eliot whether or not he had Donne or Marvell in mind when he wrote 'The Love Song of J. Alfred Prufrock', William Empson – a critic committed to intentionalism in all its aspects – wrote in the margin of his copy of their book, *The Verbal Icon*: 'the poet may mean more than he knew – easily may not want to tell. No reason for not asking.' Empson both refused to legislate against the privileged status of the author as someone who might offer useful information and allowed for unconscious intentions. More recently, Morse Peckham has argued simply, 'If you are puzzled by what someone is doing, asking him what he is trying to do is such an obvious step that no smart argument could possibly talk us into thinking it foolish,' on the understanding that:

[*] *Sewance Review*, LIV, Summer 1946; reprinted in W. K. Wimsatt and M. C. Beardsley, *The Verbal Icon*, Lexington, Ky: University Press of Kentucky, 1954. It is now conveniently reprinted in an invaluable volume edited by David Newton-De Molina, *On Literary Intention* (Edinburgh: Edinburgh University Press, 1976), together with a number of the other essays to which I refer later in this introduction: Morse Peckham, 'The Intentional? Fallacy?'; W. K. Wimsatt, 'Genesis: A Fallacy Revisited'; George Watson, 'The Literary Past'; Alastair Fowler, 'Intention Floreat'; and E. D. Hirsch Jr, 'In Defense of the Author'. More good grist can be found in Frank Kermode, 'Appendix: The Single Correct Interpretation', *Essays on Fiction 1971–82* (London: Routledge & Kegan Paul, 1983).

a man's view of his intentions is likely to change in the course of his work and in retrospect; he may work better than he knows; and, in short, his 'intentions' as invoked in this context seem to be mere retrojections in time of his perform-ance. ('The Intentional? Fallacy?')

The author may certainly harbour *arrière-pensées*, and of course speaks retrospectively about his or her work, but that does not make an *a priori* and possibly cynical case for excluding from consideration the author's every statement.

In a later essay on this subject ('Genesis: A Fallacy Revisited'), W. K. Wimsatt writes,

the closest one could ever get to the artist's intending or meaning mind, outside his work, would be still short of his *effective* intention or *operative* mind as it appears in the work itself and can be read from the work.

Aim is obviously not achievement, and at first glance it seems persuasive to argue that the phenomenon of the text is less fallible than the 'generator of the utterance' (as some critics nowadays term an author). During the course of one interview some years ago, however, William Golding remarked first, 'I feel that what I meant is then written', and shortly afterwards, 'if there *is* meaning to the books, then it's gone by the time you've written it' (quoted in Jack I. Biles, *Talk: Conversations with William Golding*, New York: Harcourt Brace Jovanovich, 1970). What the apparent contradiction points to is that the text as phenomenal object or fact includes and is the achievement of a 'progressive intention', as George Watson has sensibly explained it: 'because a man alters his intention in the course of action, it can hardly be said of him that he is acting other than according to intention' ('The Literary Past').

Ian McEwan, in the interview below, takes care to point out that 'when you finish a piece of work you rapidly forget all the confused alternatives that existed along the way, and you imbue it with intention'. The honest admission that any artist might wish to clarify for himself his own accomplishment, and that to isolate one originating intention is to speak *ex post facto*, is not to deny the instructive value of the artistic process. An author arranges words to the end of communicable meaning, though it might well be the case that the meaning remains obscure to the writer and even at odds with any meaning another reader might derive from the construct. But at least the relative verifiability of 'progressive intention' should be distinguished from the final significance which an author or another reader may discover. An interesting case in point is David Storey's observation about his play *Mother's Day* that 'All my intentions were totally disconnected from what I was actually writing', since he is talking about the tension between intuitive writing (or perhaps unconscious intention) and designed meaning. When Fay Weldon says about her novel *Puffball* that it 'now seems to me a very complex book, far more complex than when I wrote it, a pattern of opposites and contradictions and polarizations', she has discovered for herself significance after the event, a significance which is certainly open to negotiation with any meaning constructed by another reader.

A good part of my brief in the interviews below was accordingly to question the authors about what Alastair Fowler has called 'realized intention' (*Kinds of Literature*, Oxford: Clarendon Press, 1982), and about just how they came to realize their intentions. Fowler has perceptively written that:

> abandoned early intentions can still, after they are altered, leave traces, unintelligible in terms of the final intention but not irrelevant to criticism. . . . Much of the connection between various states of intention will naturally be hidden within the psychological adyta of the writer. But other sequential relations – chronological, logical, linguistic – are not only available, but evident. ('Intention Floreat')

For sound critical and scholarly reasons, Fowler's full argument proposes that we should respect the author's awareness of meaning, at least at the first level of enquiry, because we 'must acknowledge the privileged status of the particular set of words intended by the author':

> The lexical string expresses, in fact, the writer's grammatic and semantic intention, and in turn it binds the recipient to understand one specific communication, in contrast to count-

less others. . . . Respect for the text of an author seems to constitute *de facto* recognition of the privileged status of his intention. . . . The reason for insisting on intention is that without it the work disappears altogether. ('Intention Floreat')

The interviews printed here go a long way, I think, to prove that the novelists are altogether aware of 'progressive intention' – the struggle to proclaim the meaning of what the imagination possesses (as Wallace Stevens rendered it in his poem 'Credences of Summer'). David Lodge, for example, remarks that he was 'led inexorably to use a dominant, intrusive voice' in *How Far Can You Go?* His material, that is to say, made formal requirements of the critical author which were not beyond his recognition and control. Salman Rushdie similarly discovered his best available strategy in writing *Midnight's Children*, as part of the process of gaining control of the novel. Perceiving the importance of escaping from autobiography, he shifted from a third-person narration to a first-person narration in order to realize the character of his central protagonist. 'The moment of control happens, if I'm lucky,' he says about his writing, 'at the end of the first draft.' David Storey works to control his writing by the means of 'objective' narrative. His determination to write according to creative intuition may be taken as an aspect of selective intention: 'the theme has got to come out of the material.'

Such examples largely endorse the view that intention cannot be simplistically regarded as a 'single entity' – merely an originating or prescriptive idea – but that, as Alastair Fowler argues, 'Intention means different things at different stages of composition' ('Intention Floreat'). Fowler is equally correct to point out that 'intention' must be seen to have numerous aspects and phases: practical, generic, semantic, unconscious.

In an interview published elsewhere, Iris Murdoch has said:

I think out matters of symbolism and I'm very careful about names and so on; thus, the chances are, if there is something fairly telling in the book, then, that is something I intended. I feel there is a *small* area of conscious activity of this kind. . . . I should be surprised, in fact, if anybody pointed out anything of this sort in my own work which I wasn't conscious of, but I wouldn't rule out the possibility of there being an area of this kind. It isn't very profitable to look at. . . . Sometimes, one notices later on various things one has done, things which were done instinctively at the time. The total situation is thoroughly set up and you are thoroughly imagining it; then, many of these effects can happen automatically. (Quoted in Jack I. Biles, 'An Interview with Iris Murdoch', *Studies in the Literary Imagination*, XI, Fall 1978)

Iris Murdoch works to control her material, but she acknowledges the possibility that some intentions may be reflex or unconscious – presumably generated by what she calls in the present volume 'the fire of a personal unconscious mind'. When David Lodge remarks that 'Because my fiction aims to have at least a basis of recognizable representation of the real world, it will reflect the limitations of my own character and experience', it may be that he is speaking not strictly of the unconscious but of acceptable self-presentation: an aspect of the relationship between the author's self and his work which he is prepared to recognize. Malcolm Bradbury makes a thematic factor of what he terms his sense of 'personal incapacity', so translating self-awareness into a point of meaning. Ian McEwan, on the other hand, values 'that rather mysterious or unreflective element that is so important in fiction' – the element which pertains to what Alastair Fowler calls 'psychological adyta'; so does Martin Amis when he refers to what he finds amoral, unconscious and god-given in his writing. Salman Rushdie remarks that in his novel *Shame* the character of Sufiya 'more or less made herself up'. 'I think it's unusual to be frightened by one's own creations, but she did make me worried about her.' It may no longer be clear to him just when that mysterious character was adopted as part of his design or intention, but it seems likely that his next remark is an explanation after the event: 'unresolved ambiguity was obviously at the heart of her.'

K. K. Ruthven, in his lucid and illuminating book *Critical Assumptions* (Cambridge: Cambridge University Press, 1979), draws on an attractive distinction (which he in turn takes from an article by Allan Rodway and Brian Lee) between purposeful 'intention' and purposive 'purport', the latter term signifying the meaning of the literary work regardless of what the author may have considered to be his primary intention in writing it. Minimizing the importance of an author's 'original meaning', however, to insist upon the purposiveness and thus the autonomy of the resultant work is to disallow the author's intelligence and deliberation with regard to 'progressive intention', the author's developing awareness of communicable intent. Even Russell Hoban's declaration that he refuses to write 'clockwork novels', and his remark that 'I don't really impose any structure', do not indicate that he is ignorant or careless of the resultant structure and meaning of the works he finally signs. The same would be true of Emma Tennant's comment that 'It is a question of hitting or finding the correct method to resolve the thing that you are lucky enough to receive: the right method will resolve the thing that has suggested itself.'

The deconstructionist critic Paul de Man, in an essay entitled 'Form and Intent in the American New Criticism' (*Blindness and Insight*, 1971; 2nd edn, London: Methuen, 1983), has taken issue with the New Critical decision to change 'the literary act into a literary object . . . similar to that of a natural object'. He argues that the effort to see a work of literature as one thing – to reify it – leads to criticism which, far from establishing the unity it predicates, discovers itself in a vortex of ambiguity and irony. What de Man concludes, however, so far as I understand his drift, strikes me as taking delight in a kind of one-sided interpretation of Byron's lines –

> The beings of the mind are not of clay;
> Essentially immortal, they create
> And multiply in us
> ('Childe Harold's Pilgrimage')

– since he posits 'the intentional structure of literary form', as he calls it, a form which is 'never anything but a process on the way to its completion'. 'It is constituted in the mind of the interpreter as the work discloses itself in response to his questioning. But this dialogue between work and interpreter is endless.' Such an appetite for the pleasures of postponement yet again demands that the author dismount from the see-saw in order to leave the interpreter in sole possession of the game. 'Considerations of the actual and historical existence of writers are a waste of time from a critical viewpoint', de Man writes almost parenthetically. Why the author should be so resolutely dismissed is not clear to me. E. D. Hirsch, Jr spotlights the least that should be said: 'The meanings that are actualized by the reader are either shared with the author or belong to the reader alone' ('In Defense of the Author').

Good authorship is at once good criticism. T. S. Eliot's remarks about 'critical poetry' apply equally well to 'critical fiction':

> The critical mind operating *in* poetry, the critical effort which goes to the writing of it, may always be in advance of the critical mind operating *upon* poetry, whether it be one's own or someone else's. I only affirm that there is a significant relation between the best poetry and the best criticism of the same period. (*The Use of Poetry and the Use of Criticism*, London: Faber, 1933)

In Eliot's terms, what I have asked the novelists in this volume to do is principally to turn their critical minds *upon* their novels. The nature of their responses shows, I believe, that it is to a certain extent possible to recover the critical mind operating *in* fiction.

Vladimir Nabokov, a consummately self-conscious artist, brilliantly anticipates and incorporates the critical mode in this passage from *Transparent Things* (London: Weidenfeld & Nicolson, 1973), which plays with an author, a narrative voice, a character named Hugh Person and a novelist called R.:

> All his life, we are glad to note, our Person had experienced the curious sensation (known to three famous theologians and two minor poets) of there existing behind him – at his shoulder, as it were – a larger, incredibly wiser, calmer and stronger stranger, morally better than he. This was, in fact, his main 'umbral companion' (a clownish critic had taken R.

to task for that epithet) and had he been without that transparent shadow, we would not have bothered to speak about
our dear Person. . . . He did not heed his shadow, and
fundamentally he may have been right. We thought that he
had in him a few years of animal pleasure; we were ready to
waft that girl into his bed, but after all it was for him to decide,
for him to die, if he wished.

Not every author chooses so overtly to manifest the critical
mind in the novel (John Fowles's *The French Lieutenant's Woman*
(London: Cape, 1969) is to my mind a self-importantly laboured
experiment by comparison), but – as I hoped to discover by
asking questions in such quarters – the authors I interviewed are
thoroughly aware both of their artistic convictions and of their
critical craft. Whether they are talking about modes and genres,
or realistic and reflexive devices, their observations convinc-
ingly urge other readers to disappropriate any convenient critical classifications of their works. Areas of Emma Tennant's
work are popularly labelled 'fantastic', for example, but in the
interview she articulates good reasons for shunning the term in
favour of 'metaphor'. Angela Carter and Salman Rushdie share
the view that what may seem purely fantastic in their fictions
(according to the common definition) should be taken as, to use
Rushdie's description, 'a method of producing intensified images of reality – images which have their roots in observable,
verifiable fact'. Malcolm Bradbury self-discriminatingly points
out that in *The History Man* 'realism intruded into abstraction
and tragedy intruded into absurdity'. Rushdie further explains
how his novel *Shame* consciously uses allegory, fable and myth,
but without the orthodox implications of those modes. All such
comments go to show that the authors are intensely deliberative
about just how, when and why they exploit or violate the
conventions they make their own. All of them demonstrate, as
Salman Rushdie felt while writing *Shame*, that an author is
necessarily and knowingly both the writer and the reader.

Among more general questions, the novelists offer several
suggestions for seeing fiction as essentially a comic form. The
scope of comedy is virtually limitless, as V. S. Pritchett ex-

plains: 'comedy is diverting to the mind; it sharpens the judgement, it doesn't take received ideas very willingly, it inspects, and it has a natural verve.' To my mind, such considerations serve to connect the comic impulse with many observations on the moral and truth-seeking import of 'style'. While Fay Weldon finds it tempting to 'trivialize' by being funny in fiction, it is otherwise possible to see a consensus which aligns the vitality of comedy with the serious aims of liberation (in many senses). Making things funny often goes hand in hand with the purposes of ridicule. In so far as comedy can be anti-authoritarian, it functions as the enemy of 'unexamined ideologies of behaviour' (Brookner), as a mode of escape from ideological systems (Bradbury). That area of intrinsic seriousness in comedy is surely the reason why Salman Rushdie is moved to conjoin 'comedy and tragedy', Iris Murdoch 'truth and happiness', David Lodge 'satire and romance' and Anita Brookner 'zest and virtue'.

Further to the question of comedy, the implicit dialogue that I hoped to negotiate between the novelists finds some common ground in considering the larger purposes of the novel, where the status of authorial authority is radically put in question. Far from feeling that the novel is a vehicle of confidence and certainty, the novelists commonly state that it functions only as an *attempt* to understand and explain experience. William Golding and Russell Hoban, for example, try to express in their works what they find to be inexplicable in life, and many of the other novelists join voices in regarding the novel as a mode of enquiry, never of surety. For Anita Brookner, the novel examines a 'moral puzzle'; for Fay Weldon, a 'proposition'. Constantly challenged by the world, the contemporary novelist places little faith in his or her ability to 'shape the world' (as William Golding puts it). However, if the diseases of modern life are insecurity and estrangement, of living and crying for help in what Golding terms 'the ambiguous century', that cry can be met with the *energy* of art to which all the novelists testify. Art is 'a pleasure which is uncontaminated', Iris Murdoch affirms.

Julian Barnes valuably advises the reader of *Flaubert's Parrot*:

Do not imagine that Art is something which is designed to give gentle uplift and self-confidence. Art is not a *brassière*. At least, not in the English sense. But do not forget that *brassière* is the French for life-jacket.

V. S. Pritchett expresses the same sentiment – without Barnes's playfulness but no less bracingly – in the interview in this volume: 'art shows what is keeping people alive.' Although interviews end without concluding the topics under discussion, all questions and answers inevitably prompt further questions in lively minds. Alastair Fowler has written in his essay 'Intention Floreat', 'Conceding authorial privilege means giving the author the first word, not the last'. But it is at least proper for the novelists here to have the last word when they are formally interviewed.

I chose the fourteen novelists in interview because of my interest in their individual achievements, which may have some elements in common but are different in just as many ways, and certainly not with a view to exemplifying a particular trend or theory of the contemporary novel. My aim was to bring together in one volume discussions with a wide range of authors in Britain today, not to offer an easy forum but to engage them in sustained questioning about creativity and their achieved works of art. I should add that what I wrote in my previous collection of interviews, *Viewpoints: Poets in Conversation* (London: Faber, 1981), is equally true of this volume: the length of each interview bears no relation to any judgement of relative merit or importance – only to the circumstances of the day and the time available for each recording. Given the great number of writers of prose fiction in England, it was obviously impossible to be comprehensive without creating an unmanageable book. In limiting it to fourteen interviews, I am only too well aware and sorry that I could not include other novelists whose work I find stimulating and valuable, but just as no critical weighting is implied by the proportions of each interview here, so I had no intention that any critical inference should be drawn from my omissions.

No interview can hope to elicit all the answers, since dialogues of this kind are limited to subjects and areas of which the interviewees are willing and able to give account. If writing novels is a mode of exploration, the most I could attempt was to press the novelists further to explore themselves and their works – without thinking that I knew better. It may be that the novelists will disagree with some of the views I have put forward in this Introduction, or indeed with the headnotes to the interviews, for which they are in no way responsible. Novelists are still only human, even if their novels are turned into texts.

The proof of a question is in the answer. If I have missed opportunities to challenge or follow up certain points, I must take responsibility for lack of skill and understanding. A useful interview is a willing co-operation between interviewer and interviewee, however, and I should like to offer my warmest thanks to the novelists for their courtesy and patience, and for giving more and better of themselves than some of my questions may have deserved. This book is dedicated to them.

· MARTIN AMIS ·

Some journalists, it seems, like to see in Martin Amis the public bumptiousness they find in his father, Kingsley Amis, as though they can hardly bear to believe in his filial attack of major literary talent. When I met him, in September 1984, he was sighing with disbelief at the shamelessly silly profile that had appeared in a recent issue of *Time Out*.

His novels, with their witty treatment of a sick society, arouse as much hot critical debate as the personality fostered by the media. *The Rachel Papers* (1973, winner of a Somerset Maugham Award), *Dead Babies* (1975), *Success* (1978), *Other People: A Mystery Story* (1981): inimitably Martin Amis – as is his ambivalent dissection of video-game addiction, *Invasion of the Space Invaders* – his novels depict brutally unreasoning energy and obsession with all the outrageous funniness to be wrung from cultural absence.

Born in 1949, he gained first-class honours in English at Exeter College, Oxford. He has been fiction and poetry editor of *The Times Literary Supplement*, 1974, as well as literary editor of the *New Statesman*, 1977–9, and he is now a Special Writer for *The Observer*. He runs a working pad – a flat in a solid and gabled Victorian edifice – in Westbourne Park, that outland of North Kensington, a crow's mid-course between Wormwood Scrubs and Paddington. Outside the front door a small but thriving fig tree obtrudes Martian-green tongues; upstairs, the flat looks as if it has just been burgled ('I paid my cleaning lady £70, and she's gone off on holiday'). An 'Eye of the Tiger' pinball machine rears in a corner of the kitchen; the curtainless sitting-room houses a wall of hardback novels, TV set, video, a scroll-armed sofa, the heavily and neatly revised manuscript of a new story entitled 'The Time Sickness', and here and in the study there rises a tide of working books while other papers bulk in the bidet. Local kids scream in a playground next door: 'Riot lessons', my host jokes, and fetches me coffee and a generous drop of the hard stuff. He is kitted out for tennis, and in due course rushes out to his car – a small, black, beaten-looking model – to meet the match suggested by his gear.

His latest novel, *Money* (1984), is a linguistic *tour de force* about corruption and self-victimization; it is savage and compelling, and 'terribly, terminably funny', as W. L. Webb called it in *The Guardian* (27 September 1984). Anthony Burgess has written, 'It is a brilliant and frightening novel, grim, accusatory, damnably efficient and totally devoid of such outworn properties as charm' (*The Observer*, 30 September 1984). Ian Hamilton justifiably guessed that it may turn out to be 'one of the key books of the decade' (*London Review of Books*, 20 September–3 October 1984), and Emma Tennant greeted it with a similarly noble compliment: 'Martin Amis has written a book that should rank with *Lolita*. In this world impoverished by money he has discovered extraordinary verbal richness' (*Literary Review*, November 1984).

* * *

'Early acclaim won't harm a writer if he has the strength, or the cynicism, not to believe in that acclaim': that's what you wrote about Norman Mailer, and you must have been speaking from experience. Which was it in your case?

My belief is that everything that's written about you is actually secondary showbiz nonsense, and you shouldn't take any notice of it. Partly because it is likely to be wrong, but mainly because you have to be thoroughly obstinate about what you're doing. The whole body of response that you get as a writer has little to do with the actual writing. One of the most obvious and well-set-up enemies of promise is the aggregate of what is written about you.

Because it makes a feature of your personality or social conduct?
That's right. It's also amazing how naively people think you respond to criticism: they think that you read the critics and suddenly start doing things differently, whereas in fact you are often a year into the next novel by the time its predecessor comes out.

Money is set in 1981: was it begun then?
I started it in 1980. It could have been set any time, but the conjunction of the Royal Wedding and the riots in 1981 seemed a natural timetable for the book. I also thought it amusing to write an historical novel about something which actually happened only the other day.

Most of the profiles written about you describe you as having enormous self-consciousness and self-conceit. Does that trouble you?
I don't know if I've always felt like this – I've articulated it to myself just recently – but actually I don't care what anyone says about me: I can't remember being upset by any review or profile, and this attitude communicates itself to people who interview me. Some take more violent exception to it than others. The embarrassing truth is that what you want is a readership, and you have to achieve it by this clumsy, accidental method of becoming well known, which has nothing to be said for it apart from getting you a readership. I am constantly aware that the only life I have in the common imagination – which is a working definition of fame – is always likely to prick up unpleasant things. Basically, it seems, in this area of 'early acclaim', no one *wants* to think well of anyone; all the impulses are working the other way, and I fall into that trap again and again. I am accused of manipulating the media, of being an adroit self-publicist, but I can only say that if that's what I'm doing I am making a very bad job of it.

Would you confess to the cliché of being fascinated in your writing by what you deplore?
In my writing, yes, I am fascinated by what I deplore, or I deplore what fascinates me: it's hard to get it the right way round. But another equally reliable cliché is that you feel completely distinct as a writer and as a person. The writing takes place in this odd capsule where I work, which is the only place it

happens. Certainly one has had a taste of the John Self life in *Money*, a taste of all kinds of possible lives, but it isn't what you are thinking all the time: it is just what happens when you go to your study.

*In one or two places – particularly in a profile of Gloria Steinem you wrote – you've disputed the notion that the style is the man, but in an article on Angus Wilson (*Atlantic, *May 1984) you wrote, 'the relationship between a writer's life and work, while not direct or unwavering, is there on the page, detectable in imagery as much as in content.'*

Joan Didion wrote, '*Style is character*', and I said that style is not character; if it were, everyone would write as self-revealingly as Didion does, and not everyone does. Style is everything and nothing. It is not that, as is commonly supposed, you get your content and soup it up with style: style is absolutely embedded in the way you perceive. On the other hand, it is something you are given anyway, and I think writers are only aware of having a talent when it does a lot of the work for them, when they encounter a huge difficulty and find that their talent solves it after a couple of days: it takes on some of the work-load. That's what style feels like, too. It's the sort of amoral, god-given area of writing, the bit you don't have to work at, although you are terrifically careful of working at it once it's there on the page. I simply say the sentence in my head until it sounds right. No matter how many times I go through books, I always find rhymes and chimes and bad rhythms that make me start. As Northrop Frye has said, you are the midwife rather than the mother: you want to get the book into life in as undamaged a state as possible. You have done all the things which professionally you should do to it, and if it is alive it wants to be rid of you too – of all the feeding-tubes of the ego, as Frye said – because otherwise the ego will pop in and start tidying up when the book has actually gone dead on you.

I wonder how much the business of plotting a novel matters to you, particularly when you often seem so possessed by the central characters of your books? Money *might well have worked simply as a scathing chronicle of John Self's degeneration through drink and sex and power, whereas you introduce the twist of having him undone by the manipulator, the phoney Fielding Goodney. It might strike one as a trick ending when the bulk of the novel has given us perhaps too few suggestions that Goodney is the antagonist.*

It has been said already that the plot is almost a distraction in this book, but I think it's important that Fielding Goodney is like an artist. I don't understand it fully yet, but I'm sure it all has to do with that idea. Everyone in the book is a kind of artist – sack-artists, piss-artists, con-artists, bullshit-artists – and perhaps this leads on to something I will understand and write about later. There is a type of person who is a handsome liar, a golden mythomaniac, who lies for no reason, without motivation. It's a great affront to the novel, because A. C. Bradley and that whole school of humanistic criticism tell us that people behave for reasons, whereas – if you read *The Sun* every day, and keep your wits about you in the street – you see that motivation has actually been exaggerated in, and by, the novel: you have something much woollier than motivation.

The Martin Amis character in Money *suggests that motivation must now be seen as something more inward and neurotic.*

Yes, motivation has become depleted, a shagged-out force in modern life.

In Money, *however, the reader has seen too little of the character or thoughts of Fielding Goodney even to feel concerned about whether or not he has motivation. We may be amused or disturbed by the trick or gimmick of the plot, but he is presented more or less as a suave ideal in John Self's eyes.*

Yes, 'ideal' is right: he is meant to seem like an absolute given, like Quentin in *Dead Babies.* He embodies confidence, which is at last in my novels identified as a psychopathic state. The last chapter says that confidence is a wildly inappropriate response to present-day life. Fielding Goodney is meant to embody and show the weakness of such a state of mind. In *Other People*, which has a sort of menacing narrator-figure, I say that 'some people have fear and some people have confidence, whereas actually no one has confidence – the most confident people you know have no confidence.' But that wasn't quite right: there are all sorts of executive confidence and performing confidence. But I'm talking about deep confidence. *Panic* is actually the appropriate response to life. I remember telling my father three years ago that the plot of *Money* would all be based on a totally unexplained confidence trick which I meant to be as bald and brutal as possible – absolutely unexplained – and I think that's quite a good analogy for money.

To what extent do you think of your novels as presenting metaphors for a whole society? You have written that William Burroughs's drugged world is meant to suggest 'the image of the whole world as a structure of addiction and controls', which you called 'the radical falsification line', but the world of your novels is ridden with sex and alcohol and exploitation too.

Burroughs is surely extreme. All writers must falsify. I remember coming across the phrase 'radical falsification' when writing about Keats as an undergraduate: I loftily said of 'Ode to a Nightingale' that the world *isn't* just a matter of hungry generations treading you down. I suppose what fascinates me about drink and sex is that they are the magical area of ordinary life: the area where people behave very strangely and yet go on being themselves.

You are on record as having said that you're 'obsessed by down-and-outs and the griefs of ordinary people', and yet you mostly go for extremism rather than ordinariness. In a way that some readers might find cynical you heighten everything to the point where it is burlesqued . . .

Burlesqued and therefore domesticated. Horrible things aren't horrible in novels, because you have this intermediary which is writing, style, and everything which gives pleasure in a novel. It really is a haggard old paradox. Why do you feel good at the end of *King Lear*? Because some sort of purgation has happened? The idea of purgation has never interested me as a directive. You feel good at the end of *Lear* because *Lear* is great poetry.

Does display or exposure interest you more than purgation?

There's a beautiful paragraph in Nabokov's *Lectures on Literature* which appeals to me:

> The turning of the villain into a buffoon is not a set purpose with your authentic writer: crime is a sorry farce no matter whether the stressing of this may help the community or not; it generally does, but that is not the author's direct purpose or

duty. The twinkle in the author's eye as he notes the imbecile drooping of a murderer's underlip, or watches the stumpy forefinger of a professional tyrant exploring a profitable nostril in the solitude of his sumptuous bedroom, this twinkle is what punishes your man more surely than the pistol of a tiptoeing conspirator. (London: Picador, 1983, p. 376)

So it isn't a set purpose to make this life look frightful. It is, to the writer, self-evidently frightful. On the other hand I feel very sympathetic to all my characters, even the villains and buffoons.

With respect to your own novels, it can, I think, raise an uncomfortable paradox in the reader's mind that you can write with a Nabokovian writerly relish and at the same time keep up the indignation usually expected of the satirist.

I'm never sure that what I've been writing is satire. *Money* is a sort of dramatic monologue, but Self never actually *says* anything intelligent in the whole book. At one point he asks Martina Twain why she likes him: '"Why?" Because I'm so twentieth century. "Why?"' It's important that he doesn't actually *say* 'Because I'm so twentieth century', since all his quoted remarks are fumbling.

He sees himself as a representative figure?

He suspects that he is, yes. Another example is when he reads in the newspaper about that girl who is allergic to the twentieth century – all modern fabrics make her roar with rejection – and he thinks, 'I'm addicted to the twentieth century'. I do mean him to be a consumer, and he is consumed by consumerism, as all mere consumers are. I also mean him to be stupefied by having watched too much television – his life is without sustenance of any kind – and that is why he is so fooled by everyone; he never knows what is going on. He has this lazy non-effort response which is wished on you by television – and by reading a shitty newspaper. Those are his two sources of information about the planet. On four or five occasions his mind stretches to thinking about Poland, and he always sees it as a sort of soap opera: he wonders about Danuta Walesa, for example, and hopes she's had her kid OK.

One central feature in your novels is your enormous involvement with the nature of language – particularly perhaps in Other People *– which I don't think critics have sufficiently observed. You seem to suggest that the world is not only defined and decoded by language but also that language does actually reify the world: we can't perceive or conceive anything except for the way we think in language.*

The thing I feel best about in *Other People* is the question of cliché. Every time someone uses a cliché it becomes sinister, because the girl takes it literally. When an old lady sees that Mary is barefoot in the street, she says, 'You'll catch your death', and Mary says, 'Will I?' She is not inured to cliché as we all are. The things that get said in clichés are really poetic, menacing, mystical, and it was a set purpose for me to try to get that across. I don't know if I settled down to put over anything about language in *Money*, although I was dealing with the question of whether or not it is a genuine difficulty to have a stupid narrator while not being interested in writing a novel that is realistically stupid. I would never – not even in a short story – want to impersonate a stupid person, because I would always want to write at full stretch. Realism is a footling consideration. And yet I think that what I write about my characters' thoughts is realistic. V. S. Pritchett is a great poet of the creed that ordinary people have beautifully tangled, expressive, mystical thoughts, and there can be no more interesting quest for a writer than to examine that. In Pritchett, this is an act of faith.

I think some readers might confuse what can be said and what can be thought.

Yes, though for the writer it is a very handy distinction. I learned from Saul Bellow's *Henderson the Rain King* that you can have a great dolt of a character who says completely realistic things like, 'Thanks, Prince. I wish you all kinds of luck with your rain ceremony, but I think right after lunch my man and I had better blow', after a beautifully long, complicated paragraph about all his warring responses and yearnings. Apart from anything else, that is very poignant, because of course ordinary, unbookish people can't give any shape to what they think. It perhaps ties up with the desire everyone has to be an artist of some kind, but how can they be? You can only be an artist if you've been up to a point lucky with your background and put in years of reading; you can't step off the factory conveyor-belt and do it.

But it can lead to what might be taken as an unstable register of language, or at least to a sort of incongruity. John Self's indirect thoughts are given in diction and images which he could never actually manage, for example, and I think Alan Hollinghurst pointed out that in Other People *the character Mary could not think of cars as 'dare-devil roadsters'. How do you square that with your supposedly ironic authorial stance towards the demeaning attitudes and responses your characters often express? Is it a way of at once fulfilling the artistic expectations of readers and inviting them to collude with artless jerks?*

I give them too much, you think? I suppose irony and realism aren't as interesting as the stuff itself, which one helplessly calls life. It is indiscipline of a kind, I suppose, that I won't sacrifice local effects for some overall effect, but I do think ordinary people are capable of these things. I am absolutely with Pritchett in the idea that the most extraordinary, magical thoughts are in people – but of course they are like the jewel and the flower in Gray's 'Elegy': they don't exist because they are never brought out. I always feel that it's a marvellous generosity on Pritchett's part for him to equip ordinary lives with beautifully expressed thoughts, but I know there is an analogy for those thoughts in them.

It's all part of the suspension of disbelief in a novel, do you think, a sort of fiction of self-expression?

Yes. I haven't thought about it programmatically, but I do think people's thoughts are infinite and dormant.

The only novel you've written where irony wasn't required, it seems, was The Rachel Papers, *where Charles Highway is in a way a self-ironist. He has a literary self-consciousness which in other novels you might reserve for the authorial voice. He says about Rachel, for example, that her 'character was about as high-powered as her syntax' – and of course he is shamingly right: she is a sorry girl who tells lies – and he refers the reader to Angus Wilson's idea that he himself might be suffering from 'adolescent egotism'.*

Yes, the only twist I was conscious of giving to the adolescent novel – the genre to which *The Rachel Papers* belongs – is that

9

Charles Highway is a budding literary critic, whereas the narrators of such novels are usually budding writers. During one particularly painful and messy episode with Rachel, for example, he says 'But these are matters for the psychologist, not for the literary critic'. He is a nascent literary critic, with all the worst faults of the literary critic – that comfortable distance from life. The only come-uppance he gets is from the university tutor who interviews him towards the end. Reading the book again after five years I saw with pleased surprise that the tutor was an author-figure, because all my other books have author-figures. He scolds Charles for his misuse of literature. Charles is a crude case of someone who tries to turn literature to his own advantage – using Blake, for example, to seduce girls. Critics do this too, in a sense, the bad ones.

The tutor says 'Literature has a life of its own, you know'. Would you go along with the idea that whereas the novel traditionally adjudicates right and wrong and punishes bad characters, literature actually offers false models for life, which is in reality more messy and less exact?

That's certainly true. In a comic novel the rejected heroine would usually be given some good lines – lingering to set the record straight – but in *The Rachel Papers* Charles Highway says on the last page, 'She left without telling me a thing or two about myself, without asking if I knew what my trouble was, without providing any sort of come-uppance at all'. You can see the whole process of meting out apt punishments or improbable conversions becoming rather strained even in the nineteenth century, and indeed in Shakespeare when the comic festivities need to be hurriedly assembled at the end of *Much Ado* – where frightful shits are allowed to marry quite nice girls, just because it's a comedy and everyone is getting married. Among the many mysterious processes under way in this century is a breakdown of genre, so that comic novels can take on quite rugged stuff. It seems clear to me – now that I can look back on my work – that what I am is a comic writer, and that comedy is a much looser form than it once was. It no longer follows the Shakespearian model where comedy means a rejection of the older society – the older generation with its hidebound laws and prohibitions, as in *As You Like it* – and happy endings after complication: a comic shape which is still there in Jane Austen and Dickens. *Lucky Jim* shows the maturing comic form on its last page, where Dixon has got the girl and the Welch family appear: 'Dixon drew in breath to denounce them . . . then blew it all out again in a howl of laughter.' He's noticed that the Welches have one another's hats on, and his laughter – not his denunciation – is the deliverance of comedy. You don't punish, you laugh.

Yes, you've written elsewhere that comedy gives us 'a world where the greatest sins are folly and pretension'; but in your novels you are often dealing with corruption and crime – which might require a moralistic impetus.

It is all a lot more ragged now. Look at my father's last two mainstream novels: they're still in the shape of comedy, but they take on very sensitive, painful matters. You are bound to come up with something odd when as a comic writer you write about things which are only in comedy to be defeated. But they aren't defeated, as life constantly shows us. I think the novel is moving more and more closely to what life is like – not the same thing as realism – and that is why it's so autobiographical at the moment. I am not a particularly autobiographical writer, but I notice that the only thing you trust is something you have been through. It doesn't mean that you set things down as they happened, but the idea of the imagination romping free doesn't quite make it any more.

In Money *you anticipated that problem, I think, by including a me-persona, 'Martin Amis', so that nobody might identify you with your hero, John Self, indulging a wet, drunk fantasy.*

I was wondering whether I did put 'me' in there because I was so terrified of people thinking that I was John Self. But actually I've been hanging around the wings of my novels, so awkwardly sometimes, like the guest at the banquet, that I thought I might jolly well be in there at last. Also, every character in this book dupes the narrator, and yet I am the one who has actually done it all to him: I've always been very conscious of that, and it is perhaps an index of how alive and unstable my characters are to me. I learned this lesson from writing *Dead Babies*, since I kept on coming across people, usually women, who were so tender-hearted and so full of generous belief in characters that they couldn't bear to finish the novel – because they knew that terrible things were going to happen to the character Keith Whitehead. At the time I used to think, 'It's only *Keith*! Who cares what happens to *Keith*?' This guy is carefully divested of every possible reason for being liked, and yet people really do care about his character. I wrote about Keith with a sort of horrible Dickensian glee, and it never occurred to me that his unlovableness could awaken love.

You do admit to schadenfreude, *or a sort of gleeful superciliousness, when you are dealing with such a character?*

Absolutely, yes, and in *Money* I say that the author is not free of sadistic impulses. But it isn't real sadism, because I don't believe in Keith in the way some readers do. It's double-edged: I do believe in him in some ways, but not in the same way that I believe in real people. The glee might be creative glee of an irresponsible kind.

Some readers might carry away the notion – if I can put it crudely – that the logic of what you write points to the idea that the ugly are unsatisfactory people . . .

Unacceptable, inadmissible? No. It is funny that what assails me most strongly when I walk the street is the thought, 'Pity the plain', which I say to myself again and again. And by 'plain' I mean a lack of luck, conspicuous disadvantage. I have a huge amount of sympathy for them: I think the plain are the real livers of life, the real receivers; they have great vividness. My feelings are always the opposite of dismissal of those people.

And yet you can treat them on the page with novelistic ruthlessness.

It's perhaps because of the intoxication caused by the sense of freedom you have as a novelist: there is no limit to what you can do. The antecedent for me appearing in this book, by the way, is a novella I started writing – between *Dead Babies* and *Success* – in which I was to be the central character: I was going to summon Charles Highway from *The Rachel Papers*, Andy Adorno from *Dead Babies*, and Gregory from *Success*, and put things right with them; but that novella didn't work out. I wondered how something so self-indulgent could be such murder to write, and I soon abandoned it.

You do tend to polarize your characters into misfits on the one side and the suave degenerates – such as Quentin in Dead Babies *and Gregory in* Success *– on the other.*

Yes, I know. *Other People* was praised for showing my escape from all these obsessions, but I've emphatically returned to them in *Money*! When I started writing this book I knew there was no getting away from the fact that I was returning to those old things, and perhaps I've finished with them now. I found myself in the first chapter writing about a tennis match between someone who was strolling around and hitting top-spin fore-hands and a sort of wheezing, farting, vomiting, flailing misfit: I could see that I was at it again! I suppose it does all stem from social shames and adolescent horrors . . .

Do you think there's a connection between the self-abuse of your pathetic, misbegotten characters and the self-delight of the writer?

Again it's something one is loth or helpless to explain. Perhaps I can't go on like this much longer, but on the other hand I don't think writers need more than two or three subjects. I've recently been reading a lot of Graham Greene – who is perhaps too paradigmatic in this connection – and he says the same things again and again. It's a Renaissance Man who has three things to 'say' about life; usually it's one or two things.

Self-abuse in your novels – whether it's sexual or alcoholic self-abuse – is often connected with a low intelligence quotient.

Well, the character of Jamie in *Other People* is intelligent, and he does it. I think drink – and all that it includes as an idea in a novel of mine – is more of a painkiller than a quest for a good time, since it so obviously doesn't result in a good time. 'I never meant me any harm,' says John Self, after a heavy night. Drinking is fleeing from real sensations, insulating yourself; it's a reality-softener for people for whom the world is too sharp.

Do you recognize in yourself a puritanical streak? After all, you do believe in innocence – simple innocence and criminal innocence – and in corruption.

I have strong moral views, and they are very much directed at things like money and acquisition. I think money is the central deformity in life, as Saul Bellow says, it's one of the evils that has cheerfully survived identification as an evil. Money doesn't mind if we say it's evil, it goes from strength to strength. It's a fiction, an addiction, and a tacit conspiracy that we have all agreed to go along with. My hatred for it does look as though I'm underwriting a certain asceticism, but it isn't really that way: I don't offer alternatives to what I deplore.

I am clear about the moral transgressions and even the occasional strengths and steadfastnesses of my characters, but I don't ever feel the need to point them out. I may be just a victim of what I take to be the nature of moral thinking in our time, which is actually lazy. At one point in *Money* John Self thinks, 'What is this state, seeing the difference between good and bad and choosing bad – okaying bad?', and he decides – though I don't know if I spelt this out in the final draft – that it's a state of corruption. A certain sort of perverse laxity about oneself, moral unease without moral energy. I think people do and always will have moral awareness, but the executive branch is weak at the moment; and perhaps I reflect or connive at that in not sorting out reward and punishment.

There is a moral reckoning in Success, *I think: as Terry gains confidence and power, so his moral stock bottoms out.*

Yes, it is definite in that book: Terry kicks tramps. Among all the comments made about my work my favourite is what a girl remarked to me after reading *Success*: 'I liked the bit where you kicked that tramp.' There are a lot of tramps in my books. John Self in *Money* ends up as a tramp, and yet I feel that it's my first happy ending. I would hate like anything to be a tramp, but it felt right for him, and there is a possibility that he will not be all right. I don't know if you noticed, but the only semi-colon in the book appears in the last sentence, which is meant to be a mighty clue to the idea that he is slowing down . . . because at one point he has said that he wants some semi-colons in his life. He wants to slow down and look at the scenery.

What I'm really saying is that every writer thinks he's in the forefront of breakdown and collapse. Money is the strongest manifestation of all sorts of modern crap; you can't start thinking clearly until you've got over money, and the only way John Self is going to get over money as an idea – since he has no culture and has never read anything – is to be divested of it. That's probably why it felt like a happy ending to me.

You've written that the novelist's fatal disease is ideas, and yet you do use ideas in your novels – ideas about the spurious nature of money, about obsessionalism, and even perhaps about ontology in Other People . . .

I really mean Ideas with a capital I; but I'm not sure that it's true anyway since Saul Bellow, for instance, incorporates ideas very vitally in his novels. There are no rules for the novel, and I keep on being reminded of what a wonderfully lax and capacious form the novel is. I do think it's a slight humilation for an imaginative writer to serve ideas; it is much better just to be alive to how ideas filter through into daily life, rather than to have controlling theses.

Do you feel at all obliged to be a psychologist in writing novels, or are you much more concerned with behaviourism?

It's an *ex post facto* business deciding that question, if it is a real distinction. I think my novels are behaviourist rather than psychological. Writing novels is a kind of high anthropology. It is terribly difficult for a writer to know what he is up to, since so many decisions are already made before he sits down to write – like the selection of material, which I believe is not a conscious choice on the writer's part. It's as unconscious as the deeply mysterious business of a novel arriving – when you suddenly feel a little twitch. The only thing that appeals to you about that twitch or idea is that you can write a novel about it; it has no other appeal, and you might even deplore it, but there it is. All that part of it is completely amoral, unconscious, and god-given. I think Leavis said that the selection of material is a moral decision, but it's not a decision; it's a recognition.

What you are also very conscious of, I think, is the business of foregrounding style. Everything you write bears the strong stylistic presence of the author, with very deliberate rhythms and cadences, even when in Money *you describe New York police cars as 'pigs' cocked traps ready for the first incautious paw' – a phrase which begins with the jangling dissonance of that cluster of consonants and then shades into an iambic rhythm with internal rhyme.*

Style is serving something else, which is I suppose a voice. When you're writing you run it through your mind until your tuning-fork is still, as it were. I think I might well be a frustrated poet in some ways; I can't write poetry.

Yes, I suppose my question is really about the authorial poetry or lyricism of what you write, whatever the material.

I might be a better novelist if I could write poems too, in order to separate the two. My father's last remaining taunt to me is, 'I don't seem to see a new book of poems by you . . . when you are going to produce a new book of poems?' He says it in a sort of puzzled, teasing voice – because he is both. I think what he dislikes about my prose is overkill, as he would see it, because he has got the other channel to follow and I haven't. I have tried like mad to write poetry, and I have written two published poems – but they were really chopped-up prose, not a different vein. On the other hand, I think prose is a beautiful medium, and can take anything you care to put into it.

But are you ever conscious of surrendering human insight for the sake of stylistic sheen?

I would certainly sacrifice any psychological or realistic truth for a phrase, for a paragraph that has a spin on it: that sounds whorish, but I think it's the higher consideration. Mere psychological truth in a novel doesn't seem to me all that valuable a commodity. I would sooner let the words prompt me, rather than what I am actually representing.

Although even well-informed readers might properly expect the style to serve the subject – not the 'message', I mean, but the content?

I'm not conscious of any great tension there; I don't feel that I'm short-changing the truth by writing at my highest level of energy, although I think it sometimes exhausts the reader. My wife-to-be felt completely exhausted and had to go to bed after reading the first twenty pages of *Money* – partly because of the behaviour of the chap – but I think it's rather good to exhaust the reader. I don't mind. Do the readers good. Teach them.

In your critical essays you have insisted on disinterestedness or distance in novel-writing – the idea that real life and concerns must be refashioned to make a work of art – but I wonder if sometimes your own novels don't come near to betraying that standard by dint of your passionate, lyrical infusion as author?

I don't think so. The reason why you can't put real people into novels, even real authors, is because they don't fit: the fiction itself would be making all sorts of demands on them, and people aren't like that – they aren't meant to fit into novels. Similarly, the style is a radical reworking of impressions; if there's enough style it does have a radical effect on perception. Writing a novel always feels to me like starting off in a very wide tunnel – in fact it doesn't look like a tunnel at all, since it's marvellously airy and free at the beginning, when you are assigning life to various propositions – but finishing off by crawling down a really cramped tunnel, because the novel itself has set up so many demands on you. There is so little room for manoeuvre by the end that you are actually a complete prisoner of the book, and it is formal demands that cause all these constrictions: the shape gets very tight by the end, and there are no choices any more.

I think readers can often feel defeated by the riddle of Other People. Among other critics, I think, Paul Ableman said that the end of the novel left us with what he called 'the shoddy enigma of an author's refusal to clarify his meaning rather than the authentic one of a mystery too profound for clear expression'. Could you take this opportunity to provide a little explication?

There is a consistent but not a realistic explanation of the book. In fact, only Ian McEwan 'got' the book, as it were, and I must admit to failure here – because I thought readers would understand by the end. The simple idea of the book – as I point out several times in the text – is, why should we expect death to be any less complicated than life? Nothing about life suggests that death will just be a silence. Life is very witty and cruel and pointed, and let us suppose that death is like that too. The novel is the girl's death, and her death is a sort of witty parody of her life. In life she was Amy Hide, a character who was privileged in all kinds of ways and made a journey downward through society – as some very strange people do: downward mobility is largely a new phenomenon, and it's a metaphor for self-destruction which some people seriously do enact – and therefore her life-in-death is one in which she is terrifically well-meaning and causes disaster. In her real life as Amy Hide she was not well-meaning, and brought disaster on herself. The Prince character, the narrator, has total power over her, as a narrator would, and also as a demon-lover would. At the very end of the novel she starts her life again, the idea being that life and death will alternate until she gets it right: she will go through life again, she will meet the man at the edge of the road, she will fall into the same mistakes . . . but actually I wanted to suggest on top of everything else that she would in fact get it right this time. There is another complicated layer which has to do with the fact that in the Amy Hide life the Prince character was as automaton-like as she was, and didn't realize what was going on; in the death he *does* realize what was going on, and at the end he doesn't any more – he again becomes an actor in this life. The idea is that you are on a wheel until the point where you can get off purely by behaving well – by meaning well *and* doing well.

So the narrator and Prince are the same voice – I think I picked up one clue in the fact that the narrative voice and Prince describe squats in the same terms: 'People are serious about living together' – and I'm glad you confirm the identification.

Yes, and as narrator and as murderous demon-lover he has equal power to knock her off: they are exactly analogous.

In one sense, I suppose, it's an epistemological novel – being concerned with how we know anything – which matches your consuming interest in punning and the place of language in interpreting the world.

Yes. As you know, it was said to be a Martian novel, although I began it a year before Craig Raine's Martian poem appeared. The *donné* for me was the chance to describe the world as if I knew nothing about it, and perhaps it did fall prey to a rather elaborate set of metaphysical notions. It is not an ideas-novel in the sense that I believe in reincarnation or anything of that sort; it's just a way of looking at life.

Can you respond to Alan Hollinghurst's comment that 'The Martian technique . . . celebrates the phenomenal suggestiveness of things, but bring it to play on a human subject and the wit of the writer can seem to be achieved at the expense of the human subject's witlessness. . . . Amis elides authorial free-ranging intelligence with the restricted reactions of the protagonist, and it is often hard to see where one becomes the other.'

But what is the human subject? It's only something that I have presented. There is what I can call the human fallacy, when human interest consumes a reader: the idea being that people have to be cared for and protected and given full justice in the novel, but who says? I might offend human concerns, but I am offering the concern: characters have to come at my evaluation of them. It's a perfectly understandable fallacy, and very moving. I say in *Money* that the reader, while he is reading, is a sort of author-*manqué*; the reader has this power to believe and create life, and if what happens to the characters – in whom he's invested so much feeling – offends him, then he says that it's the fault of the novel. He is not reading in a disciplined way, but in a human way. Such responses are not calculable by the author.

That sort of fallacious reading derives, of course, from the expectations of realism.

Yes; I have enough of the postmodernist in me – although I hope that I'm on the humorous wing of postmodernism – to want to remind the reader that it is no use getting het-up about a character, since the character is only there to serve this fiction.

Prince says about Amy Hide that she was 'cruising for a bruising' – implying a masochistic tendency in this particular girl – and you are on record as saying that you originally wanted the character to be a man but found that it had to be a woman, 'because women are acted upon'. Were you suggesting anything about the passivity or victimization of women in general?

The Amy Hide character, though not the Mary Lamb character, is a certain sort of recognizable fringe female character one does come across. I suppose I do believe in types, and she is a type, but there's no larger idea about women in there. She is so totally defenceless at the beginning of the novel that I had to deprive her even of physical strength, so it had to be the weaker sex – less able to protect herself, more damageable.

There's a curious sense in which her naive life-in-death parodies the promiscuity of her real life: she gives and takes cuddles and comfort from everyone, as though she's enacting the idea of free love in all innocence.

Yes, she puts the character Alan, for example, through torment by having no history of understanding sexual tension and jealousy. The scene was designed to give maximum torment to Alan: it was the sort of thing she would have done deliberately as

Amy, but now she does it out of innocence. The question really is: if life is so witty, why isn't death witty?

She does develop considerable sensitivity.

Yes, she is sensitive – terrifically sensitive to breakage – but she gets it all wrong – and at the end she is defeated by emotional passivity in a man, Jamie, which opens up some sort of terrible hole in her. She realizes that her power 'to make feel bad' is the only power she has. I do think it's the basic strategy – a woman 'sulking' is the common word for it, but it's much more complicated than sulking – it's how women assert themselves, by being unhappy. Since it's such hell being with an unhappy person, the man has to make it right. It's equally self-punitive, and I don't think it's used cynically. I think men are confused about women by not understanding this more mystical life that they have. One of the things that baffles me about my father's view of women – which he's turning to very good use in his writing but which doesn't make any sense in exposition – is that he thinks their crying is a sign of emotional immaturity. But it's not a sign of anything. Women wake up crying when they've had bad dreams: it's a nearer, more available response than the crying of a man, who knows that something's really up when he's about to cry (or knows that he's being temporarily mawkish). A woman's repertoire of emotions is richer. It's not emotionally immature to cry in your sleep and wake up crying, it's obviously something else entirely. V. S. Pritchett seems to me extraordinarily feminine in his writing: 'I paid the bill. She stood in the doorway while I brought the car round, with that way women have of pretending not to be there' – I think that's beautiful, but I don't know what it means. It seems to me a marvellously rich and mystical idea, but to women (I've asked them about it) it's just a way of standing. For Pritchett to have access to all that feeling is a great gift. As an artist he is exceptionally pure.

Did you feel that your feelings about women and about yourself developed in writing Other People?

I think I was probably less of a male chauvinist when I finished it. Whenever you go into something, all the automatic responses gradually slip away. It was educative for me, I think.

Do you feel any need to justify what some readers may consider to be pornographic scenes in your novels? In your profile of Gloria Steinem you recorded her view that pornography is part of the conspiracy of 'anti-woman warfare', and you went on to suggest that it might be better to see it as 'mere weakness and chaotic venality'. This question may relate to certain heavy passages in Money: *do you feel yourself to be something of a male apologist in respect of pornography?*

I think the feminists have got a very strong argument against pornography, but I don't think it's a civil-rights issue. Many women take pornography as an organized attack but it isn't that: it's just a nasty way of making money for all the people who are in it. Non-coincidentally, the industry is strongly criminal. Pornography is certainly insulting, but there's nothing crusading or even coherent about it. I think there is a sub-text for women's objections to pornography – I asked Germaine Greer about this, and she denied it hotly – which is that it excludes women, and women don't like what excludes them. It excludes them because men go off with it and masturbate, and I think that's a strong subliminal reason for women's objections to it. The best argument against pornography is that it's obviously bad in *itself*. Not corrupting necessarily; just bad.

There are certainly one or two pornographic scenes in *Money*, and they're there for the effect they have on the narrator: he has no resistance to pornography, or to any other bad thing. It's very easy for me to decide that I don't write pornography, because I'm sure that one of the definitions of pornography would have to be that the creator of pornography is excited by it, and I'm not excited by anything except by how I'm going to arrange the words. All definitions, by the way, would have to include the element of money.

You somehow managed to make John Self in Money *both obnoxious and endearing, but could it not be said that in creating the excitement of his vulgar and meretricious career you are inviting readers to indulge their bottom-line impulses and erotic drives?*

If his erotic drives were stronger, then presumably pornography wouldn't have such easy access to him. Pornography isn't really erotic, it's carnal; it's a frippery for the jaded, and jadedness is again an enemy of eroticism. John Self likes everything that's bad – that's the trouble with him – he has no resistance, because he has no sustenance, no structure. Pornography is one of his many symptoms, if you like. The crucial pornographic scene is when he is seduced, as it were, by his then stepmother, Vron. That's his nadir in the book: everything has collapsed, so why not do the worst thing? Then he is beaten up, and told that his father isn't his real father; so it had to be the worst possible sex. The artistic objection is the only objection. But it seems to me that it's John's worst moment, and the idea of pleasure isn't in that scene at all: isn't he in fact getting the lesson of pornography? It never occurs to me that the reader could find such a scene titillating, because that's just not what I'm thinking about. Perhaps I should be thinking more about whether the reader will be finding it offensive and therefore, in a sense, good. Exciting.

You could say that it's good as a form of comic excess, but then someone else might judge that it all goes to demonstrate your sense of frailty about anything you might have to say about more complex responses . . .

Because I have to pile on all this vulgar stuff? Well, obviously, vulgarity is something that interests me a lot, and people may not want to give me the benefit of the doubt, but one risks that. I never reproach myself for it, and I think that those are the sorts of criticism you have a duty to ignore.

You don't plant moral signposts in your novels, but there remains the danger that you might appear to connive at the sicknesses of contemporary society.

All evil-doing is neurotic and mad, and the connections with what it is about the world that makes people transgress are, I think, getting woollier all the time. I think television is the great source of crime now. Gratuitous crime, for example, is more or less a modern phenomenon; crimes are less obviously crimes of need or desperation. So it's harder work trying to fathom what has gone so wrong to make people transgress in increasingly extraordinary and horribly energetic ways. A novelist has to take a reading of the world, and that is what happens in all the novels that interest me. Just what is going on here? It sounds banal, but it's an absolutely vital question for the novelist. It's the highest investigation. Yet it's always best to trust the artistic impulse; I don't have a strong contrary impulse to go around assigning moral statuses to characters. The point is that you have to make it as vivid and intense as you can, and let the reader choose. Style is not neutral; it gives moral directions.

You include two strings of literary allusions in Money: *to* Othello *and to Orwell's* Animal Farm *and (perhaps slightly less)* 1984. *How important were those allusions in your planning of the novel, and do they in fact amount to a mythic structure in your mind? Or are they just curlicues?*

I asked Saul Bellow if *Augie March* had a mythic structure, and he said that it just had a patina. You don't want to be fondling the elbows of thesis-candidates. There is a strong Shakespearian theme in *Money*, and it's impossible not to think of Shakespeare as a sort of writer-god. John Self's interpretation of *Othello* is that Desdemona is being unfaithful, because fifty pages earlier he's seen a pornographic film which uses the same plot – plus graphic infidelities. Shakespeare is the model or taunting embodiment of what he's excluded from, and Fielding Goodney's relation to John Self is really that of Iago. Though Self, of course, isn't Othello – he's Roderigo, the lecherous spendthrift and gull. When Goodney fights with him, he appears to say, 'Oh damn dear go . . . Oh and you man dog'; later on the Martin Amis character tells Self that the words might have been 'O damn'd Iago, O inhuman dog' (this is the best line in the play and says everything about Iago), at which point John Self thinks Martin Amis is talking about his own car! ('He drives a 666, a little black Iago.') Martin Amis says, 'Fascinating. Pure transference', because at that moment Fielding Goodney had thought he himself had been betrayed, whereas in fact he had been the betrayer.

I'm not a great Orwellian, but I wanted *Animal Farm* because of the animal imagery in my book, and I thought it would be wonderfully funny if someone could read *Animal Farm* just thinking it was an animal story and not an allegory.

Did you have any sense of Fielding Goodney being a type of O'Brien, persecuting this victim of modern society, John Self?

The wised-up operator, the one who knows all the uncomfortable truths: there was a glimmer of that, but it doesn't have particularly wide emphasis. The point of it is that John Self's education is under way, but he still sees himself as on the O'Brien side, whereas in fact he isn't: he's a victim. He likes the sound of classless Oceania, and he sees himself as an idealistic young corporal in the Thought Police, but the reader suspects that he's more of an occupant of Room 101.

Is John Self a nihilist, and would it not have been logical for him to have died at the end of the book?

He does end up dead in a way – outside the novel, outside money and *Money*, in endless and ordinary life. To describe him as a nihilist is stretching it. What he lives through may be a sort of nihilism, but he has no informing ideology of the way he lives.

What do you feel you've learned from your father's writing?

The most obvious thing is the English tradition of writing about low events in a high style, which is the tradition of Henry Fielding. I think I've inherited and haven't had to work much at ear – although it's not as good as my father's – the importance of rendering the way people speak as exactly as you can: that is quite easy, in fact, because you don't contrive it, you listen to it.

Can you read his books in a way that is divorced from your relationship to him?

When I first read him it was like talking to him, but now I'm much more conscious of the art in what he writes.

William Empson once remarked that the point of art is just to be good art, whereas another writer will insist that art has to do with discovering form. Do you think literature has a function?

I would say that the point of good art is remotely and unclearly an educative process, a humanizing and enriching process. If you read a good novel, things must look a little richer and more complicated, and one feels that this should eat away at all ills. The only hope is education, and one is vaguely – though not centrally – involved in that process of education.

· MALCOLM BRADBURY ·

Malcolm Bradbury is Professor of American Studies (in a Programme he was responsible for setting up) at the University of East Anglia, Norwich, where he has taught since 1965. Born in 1932, he was educated at the University College of Leicester, Queen Mary College, London, Indiana University and the University of Manchester; before East Anglia he taught at Hull University and (with David Lodge) at the University of Birmingham. He has also held visiting appointments at Oxford and Zurich. He has published four novels – *Eating People Is Wrong* (1959), *Stepping Westward* (1965), *The History Man* (1975) and *Rates of Exchange* (1983) – as well as stories and parodies, and plays both for radio and for television.

> I have found writing for television, and so learning its systems and technicalities, one of the largest influences on my practice as a novelist. If the writing of fiction is a complex technical inquiry into all the strategic relations of language – of subject–object relations, angles of vision, the formation and decomposition of predictable codes – then the development of that inquiry has been much advanced, for me, by the elaborate lore now commonplace in films. (*The Times Literary Supplement*, 18 November 1983)

Bradbury's first two novels took a liberal and comic view of the academy, and earned him a high reputation as a parodic wit in the English social-realist tradition. While those novels narrate the activities and observations of 'confused but concerned moral agents', his long-laboured later fictions, *The History Man* and

Rates of Exchange, confront deeper problems both of the comic mode and of the historical situation which puts unsustaining liberal values under pressure. 'I have a moral agony going on in my guts about what it is that we actually are as human beings', he has said in a profile by Ronald Hayman (*Books and Bookmen*, April 1983). 'I do start out with a comic conception, but I must end up with a tragic one, because my subject is the classic one of what's happened to humanism.'

The History Man gives witness to the meretricious career of Howard Kirk, a sociologist whose radicalism is self-serving and triumphant. The book's narrative distance accentuates both the comedy and the tragedy of the plot which Kirk visits upon his subjects – family, friends and students. Valentine Cunningham, writing in the *New Statesman* (7 November 1975) properly explained the character of Kirk: 'His quasi-Marxist quest constantly to preside over history's cutting-edge denies earlier models of humanity (and fiction) any chance of validity.' Bradbury himself commented elsewhere that Howard Kirk is 'in a trap. We're all in a trap. A secular world, where there's nothing to live on but history and fashion' (*Evening Standard*, 24 December 1975). He was later to say 'I'm basically a manic–depressive. . . . I was depressed the whole time I was writing *The History Man*. It's certainly my bleakest book. . . . Howard Kirk wanted to turn style into quality. Of course he's a fantasy version of some aspects of myself, and in some ways he's quite the opposite. The parties Elizabeth and I give are certainly a deep disappointment to everyone who comes because they're not like Howard's' (*The Sunday Times*, 1981).

Two of the notable critical books Bradbury published while writing *The History Man* in part gloss the threat that sociology seemed to pose for the 1970s. In *Possibilities* (1973) Bradbury pointed out that '*homo sociologicus* is the role player', while *The Social Context of Modern English Literature* (1971) urged resistance to the falsehood of 'a definition derived primarily from perceiving society first and man in it second':

Today writers are constantly urged towards commitment, which usually means direct identification with some prevailing ideological system. . . . Such systems are often the selfish vulgate myths . . . of sectors in the society who, seeing the historical process as the only thing that matters, seek in the long or short run to monopolize it. In short, they have little to do with the free run of ideas; indeed it becomes the case that you monopolize history through ideas, by selectively describing it. (p. 255)

At the outset of 1984 Bradbury still wished for the future, 'May we have imagination instead of politics, aspiration instead of history. A pretty vain hope, I think' (*The Times*, 31 December 1983 – 6 January 1984).

Rates of Exchange again gives comic shape to the possible tragedy of contemporary history. As Julian Rees has written of the novel, 'Eighties Man' is portrayed as 'Humorous in his confusion but tragic in his hopelessness. Bradbury shows him groping for identity in a world that defies comprehension' (*Literary Review*, May 1983). D. J. Enright has described the book as 'a terribly sophisticated *écriture*, and a simple tale of innocence abroad' (*The Listener*, 21 April 1983), but – as Bradbury explains in this interview – any such division of areas of interest formed no part of his authorial intention or approach.

Malcolm Bradbury married in 1959, and has two sons. The family home is an elegant Victorian house approached by a gravel drive; to one side of a stone-flagged entrance hall is Bradbury's bright and busy study, which is occupied by a pair of modern typewriters and neat stacks of books and papers. Pipe and matches in hand, Bradbury settles himself into one of the sitting-room sofas, beneath an eerie portrait of himself by John Bratby; he asks me just one question about the proposed scope of the interview (which took place in October 1984), and then applies himself to my questions with rapt professionalism, interrupting himself only to snicker in a way quite like Charles Hawtrey.

In struggling to negotiate formal problems and moral perspectives, Bradbury's novels positively measure up to the definition of what Raymond Federman has termed 'surfiction': 'the

kind of fiction that constantly renews our faith in man's imagination and not in man's distorted vision of reality – that
reveals man's irrationality, rather than man's rationality' (*Surfiction: Fiction Now and Tomorrow*, Chicago: Swallow Press,
1975). In *The Times* (23 June 1984) Bradbury has characterized
George Steiner's literary–cultural endeavours in these terms:
'He has always seen literature as fundamentally part of the world
of human ideas, as a metaphysical, a moral and an historical
presence' – a description which could equally well apply to
Bradbury's own vision of the pursuit of literature.

* * *

*I understand that you spent part of your childhood in Sheffield during
the war, when the Luftwaffe bombed the city. The experience left you
feeling terrified and helpless, you've recorded. I wonder if you could
connect that experience with a remark you've also made about yourself:
'I probably have a desire for security, for reassurance, which is expressed
in rather deviant fashion in my work'? Do you feel that your wartime
childhood left a deep imprint on you, and did it contribute to what you
consider the fundamentally tragic view in your work?*
Yes, I was actually born in Sheffield. My father worked for the
railway, the LNER: he began as a booking clerk, but he moved
to London into the advertising side of railways – posters and
station design – based at Liverpool Street, a station in which I
spend a lot of time these days. So we lived in suburban London
from about 1934 to about 1941, when his department was
moved out of London. My mother, brother and I went back to
the family in Sheffield, where we lived in an area near a
railway-carriage works and steel-works, which was heavily
bombed. There was terror by night and disturbance by day;
schooling was interrupted, and we moved from school to school
all over the city. It was very terrifying, and I do believe that
children of my age who were in such bombed cities were very
much affected by the experience. Perhaps that is why I felt a
shock of recognition on just reading J. G. Ballard's *Empire of the
Sun*, which is about a childhood that was far more war-scarred
than mine was. I think children of that generation did go

through a very disorientating time which has all sorts of effects on their emotional perceptions later in life, and for a writer this is often expressed in the form of style. Although Ballard's style in his novel is very reiterative, it is an interesting go at seeing how the mind of a child that loses its domestication begins to work. For me that's almost the strongest part of that book.

Your first two novels, Eating People is Wrong *and* Stepping Westward, *work with a comic social-realist and humanist tradition, while your later novels,* The History Man *and* Rates of Exchange, *though still sustaining an ostensibly comic mode, tread in more disquieting and serious shoes. Do you feel confident that your most recent books move in a morally enhancing direction?*

I think I've lived in a very familiar contradiction that I find expressed in a lot of post-war literature. The generation that came into the universities in the 1950s was given a perception of literature as a moral entity – largely through F. R. Leavis, of course – and there is no doubt that Leavis in turn represented the flavour of a period. At the end of the war it seemed that all sorts of evils had been defeated, and when the question arose of how democracy and new history should express itself, moral values became part of the foreground of the argument about the future. There is no doubt that writers like Saul Bellow caught the tone of that argument marvellously well: he began to tease out the question of the nature of the responsibility of one human being for another, with all the authority of a Jewish writer writing after the holocaust. British writers started to explore the question of what moral claims might be exercised through the society of post-war British life, which was itself seen to be cleansed and remoralized by the Welfare State. Above all, writers began to ask what values the peace must now be prosecuted for. That search for a moral equation was very understandable, and until the late 1950s it was expressed in moral terms far more than in political terms. I am still extremely sympathetic to those attitudes, and a good deal of my sense that fiction matters is derived from them. But in the end I came to see that what seemed to be moral issues could actually be interpreted in all sorts of other ways.

It now seems to me that the morality that was being pursued

in Britain in that post-war period was curiously confining, a revival of a kind of cautious puritanism. So many of the values that came to be associated with it are probably best illustrated by the interpretation that Leavis gave of D. H. Lawrence, a writer who very much influenced me at that time. Leavis's Lawrence was homespun and puritan, my Lawrence was far more radical and daring and essentially 'modern'. So a quarrel gradually developed between myself and this moral interpretation. It has been further complicated by the fact that when you study this period backwards, you can see how much it was implicated with a kind of dangerous political conservatism: many of the people who ostensibly argued the case on moral grounds were actually arguing their way towards things like McCarthyism. As time went on, what seemed to be a pure argument about standards of behaviour and life-enhancement became increasingly politicized, so the issues grew more complicated.

It seems to me that the writer is always compelled to assert form as history. You try to pursue the form of the novel, and you may believe in a tradition, which for writers in the 1950s was often roughly in the form of Leavis's Great Tradition. But the result of that portrait was that eighteenth- and nineteenth-century forms of liberal fiction – giving images of the relationships between the individual and society, and images of a decent life – had been over-stabilized, and now were being repeated by writers in the 1950s. Historically that repetition is essentially false, I think, since in style there is an historical imperative. Style is deeply affected by the grammatical and presentational perceptions that come to you from the language of your own culture, and from the language of the *philosophies* of your culture. So the moral issue was for me partly crossed with the existential issue, since existentialism provided a very different kind of argument about morality from Leavis's view of things.

As history moves on, do you mean, it requires new styles – adaptations of cultural expression – to meet its changes?

Writing a novel is essentially a form of enquiry; it has logical, intellectual and aesthetic imperatives built into it from the debates that surround it. In my view it is impossible for a writer merely to regard form either as a sequence of technical skills or as a pure object. It is historicized, but I would explain the historicization not in Marxist terms but in terms of an obligation for the novelist to be thinking in his or her culture – here and now – with a special responsibility for language. Language itself is perpetually reshaping.

In many of your critical writings you have insisted on the moral and humanistic potential of the novel, but you are also on record as saying that you delight in what you've called the ideological evasiveness of anarchic perception. For better or worse, I think, your readers still like to see you as a comic writer, and of course you connect the notion of 'anarchic perception' with the nature of comedy. Comedy itself can often function as a mediation between cultural chaos and fictional order, but do you feel that your concept of 'ideological evasiveness' is really rationalizing a weak position? Is your evasiveness actually disingenuous, and are you in fact far more sure of your cultural and ideological stance than that phrase would suggest?

Not disingenuous; it's fairly considered, I think. As far as my practice as a writer is concerned – which is in the end far more interesting to me than my practice as a critic – I do believe that writing is very largely made out of contradiction. It is precisely the sense of entering the world of inconsistencies that makes one think that one is entering the drama of fiction. The quest for a subject, the quest for a form, arises precisely from a willingness to explore those areas. Comedy is certainly a classic example of a mode of writing which functions according to laws of primary inconsistency, as it were. What I perceive to be comic is that ambiguous area between the authentic and the unreal. The individual might have the conviction that he is speaking from the heart of self, but then comedy might ask, is there really a self? Part of the drama of creation is a willingness to work at odds with oneself.

I know that you have felt seriously interested in the critical progress of postmodernism and its basis in a changing epistemology. Strategies of defamiliarization are clearly at work in The History Man *and* Rates of Exchange. *But then you've also written a delightful piece in* The Observer – *significantly perhaps on 1 April 1984 – on* La fornication comme acte culturel, *by Henri Mensonge, which argues that what you called the 'privileging' of fornication is illusory nonsense, the 'historyless idealization' of transcendent sex. Sex is nothing sacred, that piece has it, just an ordinary exchange of discourse. It seems to me that in some curious way such a demystifying challenge does actually reflect what I take to be the enquiry into the illusoriness of 'received reality' you make in* Rates of Exchange. *But* La fornication comme acte culturel *obviously makes the claims of deconstruction overreach themselves in a preposterous way.*

Henri Mensonge was of course invented, for April Fool's Day, and he is the logical outcome of deconstruction in my view. That piece was a parody, and parody usually serves for me the same sort of procedure as fiction: that is to say, it tends to allow me to come close to questions of authenticity and what people perceive to be the real truth, while at the same time preserving that ironical, questioning and sceptical protection.

Deconstruction is fascinating precisely because it pushes this question of authenticity to the limit. It could be said that all deconstructionist writing is meta-parody, and that what it parodies is discourse itself. The result is that many of the things which we think to be verifiable and true − because they're spoken or written − are questioned at their linguistic source. This applies equally to cultural and emotional exchange. I identify with that, because I think it is part of the gesture I make as a writer. For the early-twentieth-century author the nature of the argument about what was authentic in language was very different: it was still possible to believe that there was a transcendent symbol of some sort. Even if there was a death of the word, it was possible to argue, there was something beyond the word to which you could break through − if you could organize language in the right way. It was only discursive or metonymic language that was in a trap; if you could create the new metaphor, the symbolist transcendence, then you could come out at the other end of the problem. Now, at the end of the twentieth century, that argument has been robbed of its authenticity. The whole question of what is authentic and what is inauthentic does seem to be philosophically crucial, and the crucial nature of it has been put firmly at the point of language − which is precisely what writers deal with. In that sense, the writer has the potential to be a major intervener in the late-twentieth-century historical situation.

What is fascinating about deconstruction is that it has deconstructed itself: it has finalized all the possibilities, it has gone to the very limits of the refusal to authenticate. For a writer that leaves a crucial question, because the classic form of the novel has to do with the authentication of its matter. The great critics of deconstruction are *writers*, writers who have a real signature – Derrida, Foucault, Barthes. For me the important thing is that deconstruction is conducted by such writers as a drama in which Roland Barthes, for instance, finally wants to retrieve Roland Barthes. The game in play is therefore a game of profoundly enquiring ambiguity; the writer's game.

In my more recent fiction, there is a way in which – having persistently felt trouble with my sense of the real, my sense that there are moral perceptions and a true experience that I want to express – I am asking questions about how fiction may reach towards truth. Of course fiction has always existed as some form or another of this particular type of enquiry. All art is imitation, and all imitations are deceits. So the value of art as continuous human enquiry is precisely the realm of ambiguous imitation: the recourse that all imitation has to some idea of the real – there must be a thing imitated, if one uses the word 'imitation' – along with an assertion of its own deceit. Once art becomes a communal activity, it deals with a deceit that is agreed upon; there is a community of deceit.

Yes, you've said elsewhere that you are sceptical by nature. What you're now saying, I take it, is that your novels incorporate not only scepticism about the fact of writing itself – that it is simultaneously deceiving and undeceiving – but also about yourself as an author with any pretensions to convey moral sureness?

Yes, a common modern problem. There's a fairly characteristic evolution in my writing from a more or less realistic form of writing – where I'm writing familiar and domesticated provincial portraits of the culture: scenes from provincial life – to another kind of writing in which I find myself being pushed harder and harder away from those techniques of domestication and habituation, in order to feel that I'm getting somewhere.

Like many postmodern writers, I did begin in the context of realism, which is inescapable. Many experimental fictions will willingly assert that trace: *Ulysses* insists on its mimetic aspects before it begins to destroy them. In my career there is obviously a very strong mimetic trace. I remain interested in the idea of fiction as a realistic moral enquiry; but at the same time I've become more and more concerned with those elements in language and those elements of social and historical crisis which threaten it.

Your gut instinct would still be a nostalgic one, nostalgic for that humane and realist mode?

I think that's true. But it seems to me that the argument in structuralism and deconstruction has its own historical situation. The historical situation shows the exhaustion of two philosophical systems, both of which have the same eighteenth-century sources and a political form: Marxism and a Benthamite liberalism. Both of them are fundamental historical causes of our situation. Capitalism and communism appear to be the historical materials which are in contention, and both depend on such highly exhausted philosophies that I perceive our situation as being *fin-de-siècle*. Deconstruction seems to me to be a form of late-twentieth-century decadence, a certain type of devolved intellectual exhaustion, and I can't fully acquiesce in the exhaustion. I therefore find myself stimulated to believe that there are certain elements of value which I am not prepared to deconstruct – because I think they are being deconstructed for me from outside – which are of course humanistic values. One definition of decadence is that sense of being caught between two worlds which we perceive in most nineteenth-century writing, coupled with the belief that it would not be right to conspire with either one of the two. In a sense the decadent sensibility takes that contradiction to the ultimate, which is almost a kind of neurasthenia, and then says that something is about to be born: a new *saeculum* is about to come, all I can see is the trembling of the veil, but I don't know what lies beyond it.

You've written very interestingly about the pain to be found in the writings of Evelyn Waugh and Kingsley Amis. Amis's Stanley and the Women, *you've pointed out, is like forceful tragedy which 'takes us, quarrelling, into the pain it feels', and* Jake's Thing *presents a 'late-middle-aged sense of the falsehood of sexual relations' (*The Times, *17 May 1984). Your criticism has taken trouble to highlight the ways in which both of those writers employ comedy as a façade over their pain, and of course the same comic strategy figures in many forms – subversive, parodic, farcical – in your own fictions. Yet your own* Rates of Exchange, *in which the verbal apparatus is comically diverting to a degree, seems to be a less distressing novel than* The History Man.

There's probably not as much 'naked' pain in *Rates of Exchange*, that's true. Well, it doesn't take much psychological cunning – now that we have Waugh's diaries – to perceive the nature of Waugh's depressive personality, and to see that part of his response is comic masking. I think the same is true of Amis: knowing the man and reading his texts, it is not hard to reach the nature of the comic source.

Can you possibly rehearse for me some of the tensions that lay behind The History Man? *Was it chiefly a deep spiritual and moral aversion to the Marxisant radicalism of a figure like Howard Kirk which moved you to write that novel?*

Let me say I was pretty sympathetic to the early stages of the radical movement; as I've said, there was something frighteningly conservative and rigid about the way the moral argument went in the 1950s. But my rising sympathy with sixties radicalism became more and more qualified. One great irony of human behaviour is the way people authenticate themselves through fashion: they think that because they're wearing new clothes they're new people, originals. Every generation thinks it doesn't conform – and its refusal to conform is usually manifested, among other ways, by people dressing exactly like their peers, and thinking just the same thoughts. The revolt against history just *becomes* history as a phase or a fashion. Another irony is that most young people believe themselves incapable of opportunism: they really think that what they are doing is for the best of motives, without self-seeking or personal profit. Of course, if they are successful, this allows them to gain reputation and money from their 'authenticity', to the point where it appears – to others, or to themselves – it is no longer authentic.

'Revolt' and 'authenticity' are today aspects of fashion. The biggest liars claim what they have is truth.

The History Man was largely about that ironic process. The radicals did believe in a kind of millennarian virtue: they had come to cleanse the world, truth would be spoken for the first time. An authentic individual would emerge, as Charles Reich's *The Greening of America* explicitly claimed, a new self, pure, unalloyed, transcendental: it's a version of Emersonianism. I thought that historical over-sell, if not self-deceit of the largest kind, based on a failure of understanding which came to be more and more apparent. The long hair served the season, and the American radicals of the 1960s very quickly turned up as executives of law firms and insurance companies. Utopia and Standard Oil are closer than you think.

But there was a way in which Howard Kirk represented for me positives as well as negatives. The question was whether you could make that sense of millennial novelty – the sense of being reborn into history – a reality, and my ironic judgement was that you could not do so.

As the novel turned out, you did sluice away sympathy from Howard Kirk; the type-portrait you produced does seem to be almost entirely inimical.

That's true, but it should also be said that I had it in for everybody else as well . . . including myself as novelist.

Whether the reader takes the book as satire or as black comedy, I understand that you think of it as in some sense a tragedy. Did you mean that the whole novel speaks for a cultural tragedy?

I suppose I thought of it as a comi-tragedy. There is no one in the book with whom you could keep up any identification, no one whom you could say was nice, philosophically correct, or did all right. In a sense Howard Kirk's victory is a defeat for all those somewhat more sympathetic characters in the novel. Annie Callendar is likeable in the way Victorian fictional heroines are likeable, exactly like that, because that's where she comes from. But her values are hard to sustain in the late-twentieth-century world as Howard Kirk defines it. For me, in some sense, Howard Kirk *was* history, marrying himself to the flavour of the age far more powerfully than any of the other characters. And I think he would still be so. His nature is a mixture of radicalism and utilitarianism: in the crudest sense, he's the user of every occasion, and his philosophical vision takes him beyond that.

Valentine Cunningham, in the New Statesman *(7 November 1975) saw the book as 'a defence . . . of the traditionally liberal fiction, where life's contingency is welcomed and the otherness of other people is lovingly insisted on'. Of course the trouble with that interpretation is that although characters such as Henry Beamish enunciate a view of life which prefers people before systems – he is 'trying to define an intelligent, liveable, unharming culture', he says – his view is not finally vindicated by the narrative. Henry's unwitting buffoonery and unreality is both laughable and piteous, which of course frustrates any reader who would have wished the author to see that his views are victorious. According to the* Sunday Telegraph *(2 November 1975), 'Real humour departs in the face of catalogues of irritable distaste' – the distaste you seem to feel for the character of Howard Kirk. That criticism implies that you were trying to make comic something that was essentially unavailable for comic treatment.*

I think it is available for comic treatment. I was using comedy for the purposes of what one might grandly call a vision. And comedy doesn't in the end accommodate all the things that I want to get into that vision. The result is that there is a kind of offence against the comic laws going on in the book, and in that sense it's a mixture of ways of writing. In an article called 'Putting in the Person' I describe the way that art is simultaneously abstract and humanistic. The illustration on the jacket of *The History Man* was a picture by Goya called 'A dog engulfed by sand', which appears to be an abstract painting until you realize that a living figure is planted in the middle of the canvas: it transforms your perception of this artistic unity. I persuaded myself that in the novel I was trying for complicated effects of that kind: realism intruded into abstraction and tragedy intruded into absurdity.

A somewhat similar question persists in *Rates of Exchange*, where I am extremely interested in the idea of writing a book which doesn't have a central character. Howard Kirk *is* central to *The History Man*, but he is not as sympathetic as a tragic hero must be. He's a kind of anti-character. In *Rates of Exchange*, the central character is described by someone else in the book as 'not a character in the world historical sense'. This is rather against the British habit. On the whole the tradition of the British novel is to assume that there is a significant relationship between a substantial ego and a working society, that you can relate central characters such as Dorothea Brooke to a social world in which they might find opportunity and fulfilment. But isn't it very, very hard to write that kind of fiction about a society like ours today, where our sense of social and historical purpose is actually very thin?

Your narrative strategy in The History Man *was to be uninvolved and basically unsympathetic, to see the characters less as purposive subjects than as motiveless agents. All except for Kirk, of course, whose plot gives a plot to your novel, although even he seems somehow as disingenuous in his plotting as Petworth is pointless in* Rates of Exchange.

Yes, it is very convenient to have a plotter at the centre of one's attempt to make a plot. In *Rates of Exchange* there is in that sense apparently no clear plot to the book, precisely because I want to portray Petworth as a receiver of language and experience from outside. He hears plots and stories, he realizes that in one way or another he is in them, but he never quite understands what plot he's in. Nor does the reader understand it. You have to read back into the book to find out what went wrong to Petworth to make him 'Stupid'.

But does your policy of rigorous detachment in these books point to either one of two things: a suspension of interest in the psychology of character, or a surrender of the authorial power of judgement and valuation?

I think this is an extremely powerful problem for any contemporary writer. The traditional English novel was very slow to take on psychology in its Freudian sense: that is to say, there is such a strong psychological tradition in the English novel, in the pre-Freudian sense, that it didn't open very capaciously to the psychology of Freud and the unconscious, which actually changed a great deal of fiction elsewhere. Faulkner, Proust, even Lawrence, despite Leavis, have a perception of the unconscious which relates to Freud. But the question now is, what has become of psychology? In so far as a writer's insights about psychology may not escape being affected by contemporary psychological ideas, Freudianism is in a total mess, and the most interesting Freudianism is the extraordinary linguistic Freudianism of a Lacan. So the whole question of how you treat psychological perceptions in a novel seems to be somewhat changed. If I had written a novel between *Stepping Westward* and *The History Man*, it would probably have been a rather Freudian-influenced novel, since I was reading a lot of Freud at that time, when I had become more interested in Freud than when I wrote my first two books.

I think that in various ways both *The History Man* and *Rates of Exchange* are psychological novels. But I didn't present psychology in fiction by entering the skull of Howard Kirk, that's technically what I refused to do. On the other hand, I was trying to make the drama of the novel a psychodrama which has to do with the psychological state of living in an aimless, utilitarian world which will be rescued, one hopes, by history. Similarly, in *Rates of Exchange* I am trying to create a sense of a world which is divided in certain fashions between perception – things seen through the eye – and language – things heard and received, expressed through the mouth and received through the ear. Again there is a psychodrama, which is intended to have the flavour of a particular kind of personality opposite to Howard's, the kind that is passive and narcissistic in the face of an over-powering, external sense of history. But I am not writing the kind of fiction which would concentrate on the psychology of one central character. In so far as a novel might be psychological without performing an inward gesture in relation to one character – like much Gothic fiction, for example – I think I am writing *that* kind of fiction.

Is the second part of my question – about withholding authorial judgement – answered by the very fact that you are detached: you withhold sympathy, and therefore implicitly place a low valuation on your characters? And does the novel – The History Man *in particular – then function as a kind of phenomenological study, as a stern document of social interaction rather than as a means of inward and persuasive evaluation?*

I think that's true. But in the end I think it's very hard for art to remain purely phenomenological, since the desire of the reader to enter the work by some form of identification – a desire which is contracted with the writer – is not to be escaped. The flat page that never yields real entrance is finally not to be had. I don't quite want to have it, but I do want to put a lot of pressure on the reader to read the book like that – as a sort of flat surface – which is one reason why the paragraphs are so long, and why the dialogue is incorporated within them.

Various characters in The History Man *speak up for more humane values than Kirk supplies. Carmody, Kirk's student and victim, states, 'I hate this cost-accountancy, Marxist view of man as a unit. . . . I think culture's a value, not an inert descriptive term.' Myra Beamish thinks that Kirk's book, 'The Defeat of Privacy', sounds like 'intellectual imperialism'; and even a minor character like Zachery argues for 'contingency or pluralism or liberalism. . . . That means a chaos of opinion and ideology'. But what I suppose accentuates the bleakness of the novel is that no moral virtue is dramatized or positively claimed. It's as if the proponents of liberal humanism do not even realize that they can function as active antagonists to Kirk. I suppose the most damaging case is Annie Callendar, who disbelieves in 'group virtue' and talks with a wry and self-protective irony that is all too beguiling. So many readers, I think, feel almost betrayed by the novelist who can allow her to capitulate and sleep with Kirk.*

Yes, if it were possible for Annie Callendar to reconceive herself – to stop being the nineteenth-century liberal and become a twentieth-century something else – then there might be an argument.

The accusation against the book, I suppose, about Annie's capitulation to Howard, is that what is performed at the level of the symbol is not performed at the level of the book's actuality: somehow the novelist needs a symbolic capitulation, but the book doesn't prove the necessity of its occurring. In the end that's a reader's question, which the writer can answer only with 'I tried'. All the way through the book Annie is presented as somebody who is systematically attempting to preserve a way of life which she knows must be smashed. She holds a glass egg at the party, for example, and she cocoons herself in her room: it's a systematic process of fragile self-protection of which

Howard Kirk's sexual possession of her is a logical outcome. But I actually wanted to turn this on a sort of teaser in the book; I wanted to suggest the possibility that if the novelist could just intervene a bit more she wouldn't capitulate. So there is a small scene where I try to stop the story, which worked on a delicate fulcrum in the writing. I had to suggest the other version of the story – what the novelist might have done if he had felt a little more confident about the character of Annie or about his own values – and yet at the same time I had to prepare the alternative. I did want to open the reader to that other story.

It's not unlike what John Fowles attempts in The French Lieutenant's Woman.

Exactly. Fowles presents it as if it were a reader's choice, which of course it isn't. Nonetheless, he does present two endings which betoken not a choice for the reader, but his own conception that a novel is generated by the author's desire to grant choice to his *characters*: he's illustrating his own position as novelist. In *The History Man* I am trying to indicate not just that I feel that one choice is more inevitable than another, for some reasons that are in the story, but also how that reflects my own state of mind as I write the book – my own sense of personal incapacity: my own depression, if you like.

Other readers feel taken aback by the end of the story, when Barbara Kirk attempts suicide, but it seems to me that we should not feel affronted or unprepared for that conclusion. The fraught relationship between Howard and Barbara may have been a disguised issue, but she is clearly his implicit antagonist all the way through the story. Even in the second chapter the narrative voice declares that she has 'more gift for feeling than he had', and we see numerous instances of her exacerbated efforts to cope with her life and a household damaged by Kirk. In most ways she is to Howard what Myra is to Henry: 'the optimum point of suffering'.

Yes, Barbara *is* in a sense the hidden central character of the whole novel. If it's a tragedy, the tragic heroine is Barbara. But the point is that her story is not fully represented until you think about it when you've put the book down – and then it's possible to discern what it might have been. I think she's very important indeed. But although she is deliberately not foregrounded, that doesn't mean that the book isn't substantially her story.

The use of narrative detachment or ironic indifference in The History
Man *does of course accord with Bergson's theory of the comic as
depersonalizing. In* Possibilities: Essays on the State of the Novel,
*you explain Evelyn Waugh's comedy as following that principle of 'the
momentary elimination of humanity, the reification of the human object'
– the 'depersonalization and victimization of human figures . . . the
dissolution of the person' – and you go on to point out that it all serves 'to
mock a larger delusion: that we are capable of living in a humane or
proportioned world. . . . Waugh's comedy is a rescinding of significant
plot.' It seems to me that your analysis of Waugh's mode of comedy goes
a long way towards explaining what you are about in* The History
Man *and in* Rates of Exchange.

Yes, I remain fascinated by the argument that went on among
the early modernists: Wyndham Lewis, who was obviously
talking Bergsonism, speaks of the method of the 'great without'. He attacks the novelists who go for inward psychology,
including – interestingly enough – Hemingway, who actually
manages to conduct a very interesting equation between the 'in'
and the 'out' by the peculiar register of his style, which I admire
greatly because it has a considerable content of simultaneous
inward perception and external referent. Bergson obviously
gave very many important clues to modern writers. I've always
been obsessed by comedy, both in theory and in practice. I do
think that most of the great twentieth-century novels are comic,
and in an essential tradition of comedy which has tended towards the method of the 'great without'. As far as the Berg-
sonian position is concerned, I do think the argument returns us
to the classic questions about the relation between abstraction
and humanization in art. Ortega y Gasset defines humanization
in art as the great aberration: there is an extraordinary season of
humanization in nineteenth-century art, but we shouldn't think
of that as the *nature* of art. I have some sympathy with that view,
since my own artistic views have to some degree changed in this
matter.

You see, I teach a course in creative writing, and watch many
people who are near the beginning of their writing. The first
thing they do is to try to engage the reader in an inordinate
sympathy with themselves. The basic literary act is, 'Reader,

please identify with me, and like me', and the real first stage of writing is to get past that approach. So the exteriorization and distancing that we're talking about *could* be defined as self-protection, but from my point of view it's a necessary process for making one's writing more complex, more serious, and more willing to let issues live for their own reasons rather than to suborn them to oneself. All creativity is autobiographical in some absolutely fundamental sense – whatever modern criticism may say about the text, there is no gainsaying the personal source of a book – but there is a process of struggle for the writer not to suborn the world to himself. We all want our books to be signed by ourselves, but a signature can be a very curious and angled thing.

But in using a method of detachment in your stories, with displaced or dissolved characters, there is surely a danger that you might appear to collude with the mechanization and determinism that you would otherwise deplore in our culture?

I agree, that's a profound problem of much modern art, and it is one of the reasons why an awful lot of it is misunderstood. Kurt Vonnegut's *Slaughterhouse 5* fascinatingly faces up to this problem: it displays its own rationale for fantasy, dehumanization and displacement, by telling the most powerful of autobiographical stories, the story of the author in Dresden during the fire-bombing.

And in the case of Slaughterhouse 5 *the story doesn't just release itself into fantasy, it somehow requires it.*

Yes. It seems to me that in a great many of the books critics love to read as purely textual, that kind of intervention is persistent and disturbing. Even Pynchon's *V.* or *Gravity's Rainbow*, which have been read as pure ciphered texts, keep returning to the Second World War in Europe – this comes back to what we were talking about at the beginning – and persistently research that historical crisis of fundamental dissolution as if it is the *cause* of the dehumanization. I would apply that by parable to what I think I'm doing. What I hope that people will do when they put down a book of mine is actually to seek the cause of the dehumanization I'm representing, and that therefore the elements of humanism – which are very much in the books as presences but not as solutions – will matter.

Although you've talked elsewhere about the blindness of the narrator in The History Man, *and about your interest in the 'staging, camera eye', Christopher Hampton's TV adaptation of the book raises a question, I think, in so far as it moved away from strict externalization towards a more psychological account of Howard Kirk's ideological posturing. On TV Kirk becomes a man who needs to be reassured about his potency in every department, as it were. And of course much of the verbal play of the narrative – such as your description of how 'cathexis takes place' at the Kirks' party – has to be forsaken. Were you pleased with the adaptation, or would you have preferred a more cardboard or cartoon-like representation?*

I would have liked it to be more posed, but that would only have been possible if it had been a rigorously directed filmscript rather than a version made on videotape. It would have been possible to achieve far more mannerism on film. I did want it to have a kind of Wim Wenders flavour, but that was not technically possible under the conditions of production. That would have been my substitute for what has to be lost, which is the dominant language of the book. As you say, it's a very written book, and its tone is what manages it: the text dominates the characters within the text.

Christopher Hampton very wisely went for the plot-type behind the book, *Don Giovanni*, which is constantly being alluded to musically in the TV production. He had to make decisions of that kind, since it is very hard to have an ironic camera with video, and I was very pleased with the result. The script was very good, and Anthony Sher was an extraordinarily convincing piece of casting. Like most writers, I had a very strong physical image of Howard Kirk when I was writing – although that image isn't expressed in the book – and Anthony Sher seemed a long way from it; but by the time I'd watched the series he had converted me to his physique and style as a genuine version of the character.

I think of TV adaptation as a form of rewriting, and Christopher Hampton provided a serious rewriting. But I did feel that the story was dreadfully foreshortened by the decision to produce it in four episodes rather than five. Five episodes would have stopped that rapid sexual dance from running at such a speed. Christopher had an interesting problem you've already mentioned: Barbara is the central character, but her scenes are 'absent' in the book. He had to write additional scenes to try to establish her centrality – and the part was played by a very strong actress, Geraldine James – but I feel that more time could have been taken over that aspect of the story.

I would also think that the narrator in the novel is far less 'blind' than you've suggested. It is the narrative voice, after all, that explains about the Kirks that 'each in his or her own way distrusts the other' as early as chapter 2, and there are many other occasions where the authorial voice departs from its apparent impersonality.

I think that's true. One of the things that fascinated me in this respect was whether or not I could write the whole book in the present tense, and of course I don't: there's a section in the past tense. Using the present tense was an attempt to decausalize the telling and therefore to make the narrator far less explanatory. Yet there comes a point when the narrator takes up the role of telling an earlier story which can only be there to explain the present story. So I do have recourse to another narrator in that section.

I think Michael Ratcliffe put it very well when he described the present-tense narration as 'a perfect ironic device for a history of existentially humourless professionals for whom no other element of time is conceivable since they have murdered the Past to bring in the Future now' (The Times, 6 November 1975).

Yes, that's very good.

But do you think that your use of the present tense may also have served in a rather cunning way to put out of question, or at least to diminish, authorial responsibility or accountability?

At the time when I was writing *The History Man* I was very taken by Muriel Spark as a writer: there are devices in her work which struck me as extremely interesting. She uses tenses in a most interesting way, including of course the future tense, and the way she does it has of course to do with the classic analogy of the novelist and God. Although I can't draw on that analogy with *her* Catholic identification, I did struggle for the present tense – I was fighting all the way to get it – to develop that element of moral displacement we've talked about. It diminishes the moral reference as it diminishes the causal reference, precisely because it suggests the dominance of action – it's the tense of film scripts, after all – over interpretation of action. *The History Man* was my first attempt at writing in the present tense, and since then I've done a number of other things in that tense – including *Rates of Exchange* and short stories – and in a way it's become almost an habitual tense for me, so that I actually find it almost harder to go back to the classic preterite. I thought that the present-tense narrative would facilitate adaptation to the screen, but now I'm experiencing exactly the same problems with *Rates of Exchange* as Christopher Hampton experienced with *The History Man*.

During the writing of Rates of Exchange, *and indeed when it was published, you often spoke of it as your 'monetarist' book, as if it were your comment on the Thatcherite epoch. Do you think it failed to become that 'monetarist' novel in any strict sense because your anger about economics was controlled by the concept of a 'disinterested' imagination, which I think you very much respect?*

Yes, I think that may be true. It was the reverse of the problem I had with *The History Man*. I didn't think of *The History Man* as primarily a political novel, but it started to get used like that. One newspaper kept encouraging me to say it was an accurate description of what went on in the sociology departments of universities, which was embarrassing and of course misleading. Fictions are fictions. I think both books are disinterested – in the sense in which you've just used the term – but with *Rates of Exchange* I really did start from the title. The idea of rates of exchange came very early in my thinking, partly because economics had got itself into much the same sort of mess as sociology got itself into in the early 1970s: it seemed to be becoming a supposed total explanation rather than an academic subject. As we know in academic life, all subjects are riven with dissension and have a sense of their own illusoriness. The great danger to them is when people think they're true rather than speculative. In the end that point, that perception, became more important than trying to catch the atmosphere of the Thatcherite world, although that was undoubtedly part of the original intention. I wrote much more illustrative material about London in 1981 than I eventually used, but the year the book was set in became less important and it didn't seem necessary to hold on to it in any detail. When I said earlier that there is a kind of communal bankruptcy that applies to both capitalism and communism, that became the important theme in the end. The dominant image of exchange became much more important than the monetarist theme.

*You've spoken elsewhere about your concept of exchange as meaning discourse on every possible level, how all systems of exchange are attempts 'to turn the word into the world, sign into value, script into currency, code into reality' (*The Times, *26 March 1983). You've also said, in* Books and Bookmen *(April 1983), 'I tried to experience it in a more immediate way by emotional identification with the characters.' I think your sense of that pain may surprise many readers . . .*

I think it's a book about the experience of being in a world where all the safe references disappear, where the sense of foreignness and estrangement is persistent, where there is no clear and stable language. I don't think you need identification with the central character in order to feel that psychic state of having one's linguistic props taken away, the noise of a kind of mild dislocation. Almost everything said in the book is said not by Petworth but by other people, nearly all of whom are using English as a second language, so that they are not pronouncing things in the usual and available discourse. There is a trouble and estrangement – and perhaps a greater emotional depth – to the fact that things are spoken in that way.

Petworth, your lost hero, is most assuredly dispossessed of his identity, and he hardly assimilates the 'message' that he doesn't exist as a person until he is manipulated and determined by political expediency. That in itself must stand as a fundamental check to the aspirations of liberal humanism, the idea that in some sense we have no real existence – we don't have a free identity – except in so far as we are defined by cultural systems?

That's true, yes, except that there is also the hint of an alternative argument which is left ambiguous but which is none the less important. Katya Princip makes the case that although we are all in prison there is nevertheless something about the nature of language or the imagination or the fantastic that lets us out again. In so far as there is a promise of something else in the novel, I think it does come through the idea of story itself, and why we need to tell stories.

When you've spoken about the 'psychic risks' you took in the book, however, did you mean to indicate a lack of faith in fiction's ability to give meaning and form to experience?

Partly that, perhaps, but also that *Rates of Exchange* presents something of a neurotic landscape – the sort of emotional world one can be caught in without actually going abroad, the entering of a state of extreme, self-nullifying passivity in order to see what happens. As I understand it, a lot of people who have schizophrenic or hysterical conditions feel the world to be something like the world I'm exploring in this novel: people speak to you strangely from outside, you can't really connect with what they're saying to you, and you're in the state of inordinate passivity which is characteristic of Petworth. That's not to say that this is what the book is 'really about', but – in order to get the feeling I intended – I did feel that I was entering that semi-hysterical state as I lived with my central character. Just as living with Howard Kirk produced a sense of ironic depression, living with Petworth produced this sense of hysterical passivity. What I'm doing here is explaining the feelings and motivations that go into the process of writing a book. But once one gets in front of the typewriter and remembers that this is a communication, a reaching out to the reader, the ideas that have formed in the way I'm describing take on a different shape. In that sense comedy is a very interesting instrument, and you do start to delight in it. Also, my writing goes through elaborate stages of revision in which some of the initial cause is perhaps worked away through the process of rewriting.

Can you give me some sense of what that process of rewriting means in practice? Do you mean structural revisions or the refining of texture and rhythm?

It's both of those things, but texture above all. I go over the same material many, many times, until I feel that it is fully *written*. Often it's a matter of the rhythm and organization within a paragraph, the way you might finish a poem: you feel that the elegant rules you've somehow invented for yourself have been satisfied.

I know that you absolutely relish farce, but have you ever suspected that in your novels you are sophisticating what is basically a talent for farce?
I certainly feel that it's the other way round, that what makes me write is not so much the pursuit of the farce as the problem of mediating things that are profoundly important and serious through the customary practices of fiction. I do love farce, as you say, and at the moment I'm adapting Tom Sharpe's *Blott on the Landscape*, but that's a very different kind of writing from my own novels. I've written pieces for television, with Chris Bigsby, where the pleasure of farce takes over. In a sense I need an excuse to move from rather serious conceptions into a world where somebody else has conceived the thing in the first place, and then I can straightforwardly exercise that talent for farce.

But you do use farce or burlesque as the means, if you like, of conveying some of the serious concerns of your novels. Do you feel that such a method can have the curious effect of finally appeasing rather than of confronting or challenging the reader? It is clear that you do wish to disconcert the reader of Rates of Exchange.
Yes, that's right. But the belief that comedy is an essential part of writing is absolutely ingrained in me. In a general way it seems fundamental to the genre I use, and I have long managed to persuade myself that every novel I really admire is a comic novel – from *Tristram Shandy* to Dickens to Henry James – so that it seems to me a generic necessity: not just a softening but something fundamental to the form of the novel. There is clearly a strong disposition on my part to get my own pleasure, as it were, as I sit at the typewriter – partly from the delight in some comic move I may make, but just as much from my belief in Meredith's observation that the cause of comedy and the cause of truth are the same.

You have made a direct analogy between economic exchanges and verbal exchanges – the idea that language participates in the process of deception and self-deception, and that what we choose to figure as reality is in all too many ways a fiction. Isn't the logic of that position for you to end up feeling cynical about all human transactions?
Yes, I think I am cynical about all human transactions on one

level, while being desperately anxious to have them on another level. I do have a sort of double vision. I've just been in Japan, for example, which is probably the most 'other' culture I've ever been in, and I watched the extraordinary dance of human behaviour there with enormous fascination and detachment. Japanese marriages are among the most obviously economic forms of marriage in the world. They are arranged in many cases, and they are commercial transactions in which that element is extremely frank . . . but one can still see love and intimacy and warmth in them. We all contrast money and love, but everyone trades, and the trading rituals themselves – and Japan is full of them – are fascinating. Is the self finally a commodity? Or is there a central human self? It's that double vision that conducts me through my life as I go.

I wasn't always this way: I was very romantic as a young man, and some basic piece of information that is vouchsafed to a very large number of people was never quite vouchsafed to me: that is to say, that people do get married for reasons other than love, that a lot of people use other people, and that there is an awful lot of consciously or unconsciously cynical behaviour in the human race. I was a slow learner in that respect, so it may have come as a little bit more of a shock than it does to – shall we say? – young girls who are told to emphasize their marriageable characteristics and to see themselves to some degree as commodities.

Is this the point, do you think, where your vision diverges from that of David Lodge – with whom you are so closely associated – in so far as his novels seem essentially open-hearted and humane, whereas you tend to be more rigorous in your fiction?

I think so. David is of course a Catholic, and a lot of his writing has a very strong – expressed or submerged – religious content, which is absent from mine. As far as his tone is concerned, he is a writer who, in almost all his books, seems to be seeking to encourage readerly identification. Even in *How Far Can you Go?*, which seems to be a flat and chilly book, you are drawn fairly warmly in towards identification with a number of the characters and their problems – to a degree that is far greater, I think, than in my novels. I also think David has ideas of moral salvation which are stronger than mine. In a way he is a novelist of people who come through – they get out of the shelter – whereas I'm not.

And yet, as Claire Tomalin keenly observed in The Sunday Times *(3 April 1983) about* Rates of Exchange, *the character Petworth perceives everything but flies safely out at the end – like Peter Pan.*

The sensation I'm after at the end is that he hasn't really escaped – the witching hasn't ceased, as it were – and that he has actually entered a different world as he comes back home: a world which is much more grotesque.

In utilizing what you've called an 'absent hero', though, could it not be said that Rates of Exchange *is a book which – by premise and as achieved product – finally refuses confrontation with the forces that disable humanism? Angela Carter has defined the 'liberal lie' as a good heart with an inadequate methodology, and indeed those characters in your novels who speak for liberal humanism are shown to be ineffectual rather than on the offensive. Do you feel compelled to write fiction that might in some ways appear to be compromised? You obviously do have a belief in independence of thought and action, a belief you might wish to vindicate in fiction.*

That's true, I believe in that. But I also find myself perpetually challenging it, to the extent of challenging the model of the self in what you've just described. On the whole, liberal humanism supposes a competent and efficient rational ego to live with, and in various ways I feel pressed to question that supposition. I read with great interest a book called *Irrational Man*, by William Barrett, and a new book on the philosophy of irrationalism has taken my eye these last few weeks. Irrationality fascinated the existentialists, of course, and I am extremely preoccupied by those images which are not consistent with liberal humanism. In a sense my liberal humanism might be said to be a capacious envelope which I am prepared to put around many different things, to the point where they become totally inconsistent with each other.

Terry Eagleton has called liberalism the 'impotent conscience of a bourgeois society' . . .

That may be. But to be frank I don't think Marxism has anything better to offer, either in philosophy or moral conscience. His comment puts the *Angst* I'm talking about in its most political form; I would accept it to some degree, but I don't think it's the only form of *Angst*. There is a philosophical form which has to do with the depressing but necessary realization that human beings function not only according to laws of reason, good will, and self-realization, but according to laws of total irrationality, and are in some sense conditioned, externally, through some sort of naturalism, or by the nature of the mind and the body themselves. How does one explain one's emotional or auto-destructive acts in terms of liberal humanism?

The fact seems to remain that liberal humanism can be anguished but cannot act, as your novels show.

Yes, I suppose that in the end I've written a fundamentally pessimistic portrait of a period. At the beginning of my writing I felt that liberalism was finding it hard to act, and it has grown increasingly more difficult as my writing has become more extended. The basic intuition is, I suppose, still there. Forster and Orwell, who were very much central figures when I started writing (as well as Waugh), were very positive and strong starting-points for me. I've not been able to sustain the argument, as it were, in the context in which my growing up has occurred. I'm very interested in those writers who appear to assert the opposite of liberal humanism, especially those American postmodernists who were then attacked by John Gardner in *On Moral Fiction*. One positive, to me, account of liberalism might be to say that it is persistently fascinated by its own opposite; and the pursuit of opposites or adversaries has been very important to me. But in the end, although liberalism may appear to be defeated, it would also appear – to me and I gather to you – that there are a lot of latter-day liberal secrets imprinted in what I write. The liberal imprint is most certainly there . . . but it can only be expressed obliquely, which may be the one thing that I've come to understand.

One of the most substantial reviews of Rates of Exchange *was Blake Morrison's in* The Times Literary Supplement *(8 April 1983). 'Bradbury the novelist', he wrote, 'sabotages Bradbury the critic, cancelling out in comic fiction the causes solemnly espoused in academic prose: among them liberalism, American culture, sociology and linguis-*

tic criticism'. As far as he was concerned, what he called the perfunctory and picaresque plot of the novel succeeded quite happily as an evocation of travel: 'most of its energy is of a traditional, almost conservative temper.' Would you accept the justice of Morrison's remarks?

I would put it somewhat differently. There has always been a quarrel in me between the writer and the critic, as well as an intimacy. I find it harder and harder to write literary criticism, to pursue ideas which because they *are* abstract never quite engage me at a sufficient depth. I do feel that I'm performing important and interesting argumentative functions, saying things that are considered and even true, but the ultimate result of this as a mode of expression is a sense that – however invigorated I am by the practice of criticism – I am not really touching base. I can't drive away the critic when I write fiction, but nonetheless I find it pretty necessary to try to do so in order to begin as a novelist. I find it almost impossible, for example, to write fiction when I'm teaching. Most of my critical books have been a sort of quarrel with the last one, and usually the reason for the quarrel is something that is happening in the fiction. The critical books that come between the novels explain to myself at least something of the argumentative oscillation, and therefore the critic is somehow very important to the writer, as, I hope, the other way round too. I could very easily become a full-time writer, but I feel that I would lose something very important to the writing process itself. I've not felt very easy with many developments in recent literary criticism, not so much because I theoretically disagree with them but because I think they have so much to do with the attempt to make criticism into a science. The one thing that writing fiction can never be is a science, so you end up with a split between the changing practice of criticism – the direction it's going in, and the kind of writing that it's asking you to do – and the practice of writing novels. I've written a piece called 'Writer and Critic', which is about different forms of this marriage.

I would quibble with Blake Morrison's statement that the result is a kind of conservative form, which is the last thing I'm trying to produce. It dissatisfies my own image of myself – it would give me a sense of failure – since my sense of myself as a writer depends on the belief that every novel is a new enquiry. If I were to think that I were using the genre in a simply traditional way, I would have no good reason for writing. All I can say, therefore, is that the pressure that drives me to write is the antithesis of the result Blake Morrison is perceiving.

You have written a number of articles and a critical book on Saul Bellow, saluting him as a 'modern metaphysical comedian' – a status I imagine you'd like to earn with your fiction?

I would like to think that's what I'm pressing towards, yes. I deeply admire Bellow. He is Jewish–American and I'm not, his vision is shaped by intellectual funds and cultural conflict that are not mine. But I have a strong sense of oblique intimacy with him. I've always felt a terrific radiation from his books. The book that first turned me on to him was *The Victim*, which is very much about moral responsibility. Bellow assumes that the world has been dehumanized, and his question is how thereafter to construct an alliance or allegiance. My basic trouble with Bellow is the trouble I have with much American fiction, that he is able to achieve transcendent release at the end of his novels. I am more sceptical, and I think that an awful lot of such transcendence is unearned euphoria. There is of course a distinction to be made between the general tendency of American literature and Bellow's treatment of it in this respect, because the form of his transcendence is much more conditioned than many of his American critics say. American critics celebrate Bellow's Emersonianism, but it's more interesting to see how painfully he achieves the transcendence, even in a rather chilly book like *The Dean's December*. If one bought the Transcendentalist Bellow of recent critics, I can't see any good reason for reading him: he would be a buffoonish optimist, which he isn't. He's a pessimist with hopes.

Your volume in the Contemporary Writers series makes a striking point about the comic or fantastic spirit in Bellow, that it preserves 'the sense of our potency and our distinctiveness, our sense that against the "It" there is indeed a "We"'. And you go on to talk about just how serious comedy can be, suggesting, I think, not just that it's a symptom of disordered values but that the comic manifests a kind of redemptive assertion, 'lying in our gift to know. History, environment, concept and

*the reality-instructors tell us much, and much of it makes despair; but
against that there is a self-presence, vivid and curious.'*

Yes, and the other writer who carries this same spirit and is very
important to me at the moment is Milan Kundera, particularly
in *The Book of Laughter and Forgetting.* The way in which he
conceives comedy as a fundamental mode of escape from ideological imprisonment is very attractive and powerful. In a sense
– although I wrote Katya Princip's passages in *Rates of Exchange*
before I read Kundera – it is what Katya Princip is trying to say in
that novel. I do think that comedy is fundamentally important
because it is an aperture or space between systems, through
which some sense of human possibility can finally escape. But I
don't think that it can escape easily, which is in a sense what I've
been trying to say all the way through this interview: it is only
by living in the adversary world that one can achieve it.

*As you say in your critical book, Bellow has been able to earn a vision
which makes self and imagination transcendent: 'there must be a higher
rate of exchange,' you rather pointedly and perhaps wistfully write. But
do you fear that contemporary culture actually limits such possibilities
for British fiction?*

I think the British novel is now extraordinarily lively, but that
may be because so many of the novelists I'm calling British are
not British – including Salman Rushdie, Anita Desai, Timothy
Mo – and then in addition I'm thinking of Márquez, Calvino,
Handke, all of whom are far more exciting than, let's say, most
Americans are now. One of the things that mattered to me in
Rates of Exchange was the business of writing a novel of which a
considerable part was in English as a foreign language, which
has to do with de-domesticating the novel. The fantastic, the
foreign, the linguistically distorted, are all ways of defamiliariz-
ing and de-domesticating the novel. Habitual domesticity is the
great crime of English fiction. But there are many writers
of estrangement, like Angela Carter, Martin Amis, Salman
Rushdie, who will not use nostalgic and habitual themes and
languages; so there is something very important going on, and I
would want to feel that I was more on that side than the side of,
say, those writers who suppose that it's possible to recover the
spirit, as it were, of *Brideshead Revisited* in fiction. Of course

Waugh is an interesting example of a writer who quite often uses some of the tropes of nostalgia, and from time to time indulges them – as he does in *Brideshead Revisited* – very heavily. But most of the nostalgia in Waugh's work is often misread: it's seen as reassuring and safe. One only has to read *A Handful of Dust* to see that the recapitulation of the past is there in order that it may be taken away again.

Given all that you've said so far, I suppose you would now heavily qualify an observation you made in Possibilities *(1973): 'the primary centre of literature . . . lies in the creative play of individuals responding not to "history" but to life, a response capable of generating forms, orders'? That assertion begins to sound like a rearguard profession of faith.*

Yes, I think so. Narrative theory and the arguments surrounding it have become much more sophisticated since I wrote that book. But some of the impassioned perorations in *Possibilities* do have to do with the fact that I was writing *The History Man* at the same time.

Do you now see the moral function of literature as estrangement, in the sense of making us see just how strange and threatening the world is?

I think the moral function of literature is indeed to estrange, but then to reacquaint. Domestication and easy pathos are the enemies of truth. The really good novel struggles with its nature – the nature of the novel as such – and with its own times. It manifests in some real sense a struggle within the author, so that you feel that it's a form of scepticism – an attempt at discovery rather than an utterance of the discovery. The interest of writing fiction is that it is more than you predict it will be when you start. Although I do build up mental scaffoldings in order to try to help me write a book, I don't devise – and don't believe in devising – an outcome for the enquiry before I undertake it. And the books that give me pleasure by other writers are the books that are created in that way.

· ANITA BROOKNER ·

Internationally eminent as an art historian and critic, Anita Brookner is author of *Watteau* (1971), *The Genius of the Future* (1971) *Greuze* (1972) and *Jacques-Louis David* (1980). In 1968 she was the first woman ever to be Slade Professor at Cambridge. She is now Reader at the Courtauld Institute of Art. *A Start in Life* marked her debut as a novelist in 1981, followed the next year by *Providence* – both books being applauded for their sad and authentic knowledge, and for high wit and style. Although *Look at Me* (1983) drew from some reviewers the opinion that it seemed too dreary in its exact truth-telling, David Lodge wrote in *The Sunday Times*, 'I cannot praise too highly this novel's poise, perceptiveness and purity of style'.

In awarding the 1984 Booker McConnell Prize to her latest novel, *Hotel du Lac*, the panel of judges compared the work to a Vermeer – an observation which some critics chose to turn against the author in a way that was undeniably patronizing. But Anita Brookner's talent is deceptive: her 'little bit (two inches wide) of ivory' gives form to important and substantial matters – including art and reality, aspiration and actuality – with rigorous perception and wit. There is a protest at the heart of her fiction, a shock recorded precisely and unsentimentally: to be gifted but without cunning is to be out of step with modern manners. Brookner's heroines nurse the idealistic and romantic illusions encouraged by art, and they are nonplussed when their sincerity and virtuous intent come face-to-face with the ways of the worldly. Naive expectations, self-deception, dishonesty and flagrant disingenuousness: such are her subjects, and the small scale of her novels should not mislead us into thinking that her themes are narrow. Brookner's unflinchingly clear-eyed inspection of personal conduct and motive, and her exceptional stylistic gifts, make an adroit and painful combination.

Born of Polish parents, uncompromisingly honest, crisply spoken, Dr Brookner lives in a trim modern flat in South Kensington, where I talked to her in July 1984. Insisting to herself that her stories should be 'earthed' in reality, she has now established a pattern of working out 'dreadful summers' by producing a novel each year ('I literally want to see if I can do it again') in her office at the Courtauld Institute of Art.

Anita Brookner believes in the supreme value of reason and accountability; her fiction is the counterpart, the imaginative expression, of the tragic irony incurred by that belief – high standards are not open to negotiation – as she has eloquently written elsewhere:

> Quite obstinately, I prefer the stately dance of reason to any conclusion more rapidly arrived at, however persuasive the display. There are solutions, strategies, stratagems, perceived more easily, and more gracefully, than I shall ever manage. . . . And so difficult is this prejudice to shake off that I now look upon myself as one of those unfortunates who have lost their faith but are still unable to recant, having learnt one lesson, and with that lesson become unable to learn any others. (*The Times Literary Supplment*, 5 October 1984)

Antony Beevor has perceptively written of her fictions, 'The similarity of plot and dénouement has not detracted from the fascination of these novels. . . . With its subtle, dark humour Anita Brookner's prose is like a graceful trireme with an underwater ram. There can be little doubt that she is one of the great writers of contemporary English fiction' (*Literary Review*, September 1984).

★ ★ ★

The heroine of your third novel, Look at Me, *is striving to write a novel, and she regards it as a penitential activity. Is that your own view?*

Yes, it gives me a headache. The reason why I've written novels is penitential and possibly useful. I started writing because of a terrible feeling of powerlessness: I felt I was drifting and obscure, and I rebelled against that. I didn't see what I could do to change my condition. I wanted to control rather than be controlled, to ordain rather than be ordained, and to relegate rather than be relegated.

Look at Me *is the most serious – or perhaps the most unrelievedly sober – of your novels. I've wondered if it was actually the first you wrote?*

No, they were published in the order they were written. *Look at Me* is a very depressed and debilitated novel, and it's one I regret. When I published it, a very old friend of my mother's summoned me and said, 'You are getting yourself a bad reputation as a lonely woman. Stop it at once.' She was right: it sticks.

But would it be true to say that your novels speak of your own condition?

The particulars are all invented, but they speak of states of mind which forced me to do something about those states of mind. In that sense they are very impure novels, and that gives me a lingering feeling of unpleasantness. The most recent, *Hotel du Lac*, is the least impure; it's invention pure and simple.

Hotel du Lac *offers a little parable about being a novelist, I think, in so far as Edith Hope seeks to investigate the lives of other people – testing her percipience – and to make sense of them.*

She never does, of course. She never gets it right, and that's why she has to fall back on her own resources of invention.

You make your novels sound like a sort of self-therapy.

Well, if it were therapy I wish it had worked. It doesn't work that way, which is why I have to keep on doing it. I felt impelled by irritation with circumstances and life, which seemed to me so badly plotted. The morality of novels – in which judgements are meted out – very much recommends itself to me. I am always reading novelists like Trollope whose moral standards are clear within the framework of the novel: the bad are seen through, which is not the case in real life and everyday intercourse. It affects me bitterly – I despair of it – that hypocrisies can be entertained and impudent behaviour preferred, betrayals laughed off and promises broken: I can't bear that.

In Providence *Kitty Maule wishes she had told her students that, so far as the conduct of life is concerned, being attractive and engaging works better than moral fortitude.*

Yes, I see it every day. If you don't practise to deceive, as you shouldn't, it is particularly hard when deception is practised on you, and you write novels out of that sense of injustice . . . or you go under. I think this sense goes for everyone who is perhaps a little timid and never quite successful and ever hopeful.

You have been extraordinarily successful in your professional career at least.

I dispute that. Success is what other people say you are, and I don't feel it.

Does your own background reflect that of your heroines? Do you have eccentric parents or ancestry?

Yes, they were Polish Jews. My mother was born here, my father in Poland. I loved them painfully, but they were fairly irascible and unreliable people. They should never have had children; they didn't understand children and couldn't be bothered. There was a fairly thriving family business, transplanted from Europe, which went under and came up again. As a matter of fact I'm trying to write a novel about that, but I very much doubt that I shall finish it – it seems so heartless at the moment. My parents are dead now, so one can't go home again. They were mismatched, strong-willed, hot-tempered, with a very great residual sadness which I've certainly inherited. We never had much fun. I am now alone, which takes a bit of getting used to; one has to nerve oneself every day. It really is existential living.

One issue that comes up in Providence *is the idea that existentialism is perhaps a late manifestation of Romanticism.*

I would now say that it is anti-Romanticism: it gets rid of all the hopes and the belief that things are worth pursuing. I think my parents' lives were blighted – and in some sense mine is too – largely by this fact of being outside the natural order, being strangers in England, not quite understanding what was happening and being done to them.

You were entirely brought up in England, with a regular schooling?

Yes, but I've never been at home here. I took on protective colouring at a very early age, but it didn't stick. I went to King's College and then to the Courtauld, and I nursed my parents until they died: it's a dreary, Victorian story, with this added complication of not being English. People always say I'm so serious and depressing, but it seems to me that the English are *never* serious – they are flippant, complacent, ineffable, but never serious – and this is maddening. The English think they're ineffable, so they are: it's self-referential, all the time. So I don't know what to do and I don't know what to be: I think it may be insoluble.

You wrote what I think is an interesting review of Anthony Clare's book In the Psychiatrist's Chair, *where you talk about the transactional nature of such dialogues . . .*

Yes, I'm obsessed by that. I get told a lot of things, and I do a lot of listening. Other people's stories always seem so much more urgent than one's own, with more reality somehow.

Do you not identify yourself as a real person?

No, I'm absolutely passive, like blotting paper. I really feel invisible.

Have you been through psychoanalysis?

No, and I wouldn't do it now: it would take too long.

You clearly committed yourself to an enormous emotional investment in writing Look at Me.

It didn't pay off. I saw it through, and predictably I was ill afterwards.

It's a very desolating story in which nothing really happens, other than Frances Hinton's yearning to be admitted to the ranks of the glamorous and charismatic people – people who are in fact careless, like the Buchanans in The Great Gatsby.

It is indeed. I'm very envious of careless people. It's about not being able to be like them, and how the rewards of being that sort of person are infinitely greater. Their moral status ceases to be relevant, which is the desolating aspect.

The surprising thing in your novels is that the heroines never show a trace of cynicism, despite what they discover about relationships.

I wish there were. I am constantly flattened by surprise.

And you don't portray any outrage at the egotism of others.

No, I don't see how you can. Basically I want to know how other people are.

In a little piece in The Author *(Summer 1984) you have written, 'since I believe that writers of fiction . . . are in some curious way the only people telling the truth, I would expect them to feel pretty unlucky anyway'. Is the truth always such bad news?*

It's the Cassandra complex. I learned sad truths quite early, and I never really got out of those coils – that life is a serious and ultimately saddening business. There are moments when you feel free, moments when you have energy, moments when you have hope, but you can't rely on any of these things to see you through. Circumstances do that.

I think all your heroines act in a very deterministic way, and Kitty Maule in Providence *actually announces herself as a determinist. Do you believe that no force of decision or positive moves can change fate?*

I think one's character or predisposition determines one's fate, I'm afraid.

At what stage did you come to that conclusion?

Within the last five years. Before that I was quite buoyant and much more energetic. It's a very perverse energy which has gone into the novels – conversion hysteria, I would say. If I could *say* it, I would; as I can't say it, I have to write it. And I can't say it because there is no one to listen: people don't want to hear it. I wish I could cry, scream, stamp, make myself felt, but I can't. Other people don't want to hear: they find it embarrassing, out of bounds.

Presumably many people wouldn't quite recognize what it is that you want to cry out against in life. You are successful on two counts: as an academic and as a novelist whose books have received a favourable press.

But the centre cannot hold. Those two activities that you've mentioned are outside the natural order. I only ever wanted children, six sons.

Not as extensions of yourself?

Not at all. I wanted characters quite different from myself. I wanted to get away from my own family and to be absorbed in another, more regular set-up, instead of being this grown-up orphan with what you call success. That's the sort of rank statement which I wish I hadn't made, but it is true. My grandfather on my mother's side saw England as the most liberal country in the world: he adored it and adopted every English mode that he could find. But European habits of thought – melancholy, introspection – persisted, and it's a bad mix: it was thicker than the English air.

In terms of your professional life, what particularly attracted you towards the eighteenth century?

The Enlightenment, and the fact that it might just have come out right. The Romantic movement came along and bowled it all over. I do like a rational world, rational explanations and good humour and fearlessness. I'm talking about the eighteenth century in France, painters and writers who by today's standards were extraordinarily uninhibited . . . and guiltless . . .

And always affirmative.

Always. And unashamed.

I felt in reading The Genius of the Future *that you were actually plotting this sorry decline of responses from the eighteenth into the nineteenth century.*

Yes, I think that's true. It's a course I still teach, and the students automatically respond more to the later end of the period: they can more easily identify with complexes than with the guilt-free energy and enthusiasm there was at the beginning. They have no regrets for what has been lost or foregone.

When you published that book, in 1971, you wrote that art criticism today had become a 'rigid toadying exercise'. Did you feel you'd become mired in a false profession at that time?

Yes, I saw a lot of unwise and prudent decisions. Now there's too much Gettyism, the idea that if a thing can be financed it must be right and desirable.

Did you ever formulate for yourself what you thought art criticism should achieve, what it should vindicate or validate? Was it the importance of being a philosophe, *a concern with the morality of art?*

Exactly that. As I teach, it seems to me that it doesn't really matter what your subject is as long as you are teaching method. The material is there for anyone to use if they care to, but getting it in the right perspective is very important. A moral and an historical perspective. What attracted me to art history is the power of images, which act differently from words. Images recur in a way that words don't. Dreams are usually wordless, but they're full of images, and an image can carry over in some mysterious way and generate things. Images are more powerful and primitive than words.

I think I have the impression that you would discriminate between the 'message' of a work of art and its style.

Probably. Subject/object is one thing, presentation is another: presentation is the artist's own slant on what he sees, and in that sense style and moral style are compatible. The artists of the eighteenth century were obsessed with pulling order out of the surrounding chaos, whereas in the nineteenth century it seemed more powerful and more valid to dissolve order . . . more true to the human condition. But order always has to be wrestled out of chaos. Nowadays we have no communal enterprise. It's odd how even in my profession there are frequent attempts to revive the idea of the great *Encyclopaedia*, the thing that's going to process all the information and produce a *summum*, a canonical monument not only of erudition but also of meaning. The desire is there, a desire for permanence, and I see it as quite innocent. But what we lack is the philosophical momentum which values these things, and its absence is desolating, tragic.

Are you going to continue to write books of art criticism?

I doubt it. It takes too long: *Jacques-Louis David* took ten years. I think I've lost what I had originally, perhaps the energy and perhaps the belief that I can do it. The book was not popular; it's quite a good book, but it could have been better.

What is your criterion for judging what is most valuable in a work of art?

That's very difficult to answer. I think it would be radiance, a power beyond the image: vision. The National Gallery has just bought a portrait by David called *M. Blauw*, and I think I'll find it there: it's only a portrait of a man with a quill pen, but it is so articulate and has such integrity.

Do you see any connection between your work as an art historian and the act of writing novels? Is there any natural engagement between one and the other?

The awful thing is that I see no connection at all. It's a sort of schizophrenic activity as far as I'm concerned. The only connection is that I do it in the same place, in my office. I need noise and interruptions and irritation: irritation and discomfort are a great starter. The loneliness of doing it any other way would kill me.

What strikes me about all your heroines is that none of them are dishonest, not even with themselves. Even Kitty Maule would like to assume a posture of carelessness and gracious ease, but she is fully aware that it is not in her.

Dishonesty means betrayal of somebody or something, and you can't do it.

You seem to set such terrifying high standards for yourself.

I'm not aware of this, since I don't know what other people's standards are.

You insist upon moral rectitude in your characters.

That comes from a grounding in nineteenth-century novels and nineteenth-century behaviour. My family was very rigorous in that respect; I've never unlearned these lessons, and I promise you I regret it. I would love to be extremely plausible and flattering and dishonest: there are useful dishonesties. I think it's pleased the critics to see me as a moral success and a personal failure. Since it's now taboo to confess to a certain form of loneliness, it has been stuck to me like a *banderilla*, and I've found it very tedious to be labelled. Even my friends have thought it an impropriety for me to put myself forward in this way, but I don't understand the opprobrium. It's got to the stage where I can't even say it's invented, because nobody would believe me, so I'm in a fix.

But anyone must find it impressive that you can be so sincere.

No, unpopular. My friends now assume that I will use them as characters, even though I don't.

I imagine that you've actually used only your parents in A Start in Life *and perhaps your grandparents in* Providence?

No, they were nothing like; I couldn't do that to them. You have to believe me. My parents were just as bizarre but not quite so fetching. They were very rigorous and complicated people: I think it baffled and saddened them that they couldn't take life easily. I feel I've cut loose and gone out into the storm, but basically I'm still one of them.

I have used certain situations; not characters but situations, situations out of time, taken from twenty years ago, and nothing that could possibly have reverberations today.

Two of your novels are critiques of other fictions, A Start in Life *utilizes* Eugénie Grandet, *and* Providence *a novel by Constant,* Adolphe, *both making the point that literature can damage life and at the same time saying that fiction does provide role models.*

Yes, I believe that. I believe it's the virtue and value of fiction. But I think the lessons taught in great books are misleading. The commerce in life is rarely so simple and never so just. The appreciations are more short-term in life; there isn't the same impetus to see it through. There is in fact no selection in life – one takes opportunities and amusement where one can – it's accumulative, if you like, piecemeal.

I think the analogies and correspondences you draw between Adolphe *and* Providence *are particularly striking and illuminating.*

It's a little bit mechanical, I think, or forced: I wouldn't do that again.

What is extraordinary about Adolphe *is the relentless and cold logic of the hero's career. Adolphe makes conquest of the devoted Ellénore and immediately regrets it, so that we witness every shift and turn of his efforts to be done with the relationship.*

Yes, and he is quite unapologetic about the whole thing. He is serious and in fact extremely grave. It is a moral catastrophe. But he doesn't enjoy it. Ellénore is unsuitable, and it kills her; it ruins him, but of course we don't know for how long.

In your novel Kitty Maule quotes that key phrase about 'the painful astonishment of the deceived soul' which she can't remember later on; and yet that concept is exactly what Providence *is about.*

How clever of you to pick that up.

The men in your novels seem in some curious way to be opaque, perhaps partly because we see them through the prepossessing eyes of the women. They have the common denominator of being staunch Christians, they wear their hearts or hurts on their sleeves, and they are egotistical and uninvolved while apparently being disinterested.

They are conservative, establishment creations, aren't they? And as such impervious to these dark imaginings, these brooding midnight fantasies.

Do you have a particular grouse against Christianity?

Yes, I have many grounds for complaint. I wish I could accept the whole thing – it would make one terribly cheerful, and give one a stake in the country, as it were – but I can't. I am a lapsed Jew – if such a thing were conceivable, but it isn't. Jewishness is a terrible religion, for its relentlessness, its bad-tempered god, its inability to learn anything at all, its self-obsessed quality . . .

Its sense of election as well?

That is not apparent among Jews; it's the fear that exists in the mind of Christians or other religions. This is the hardest thing to bear: we're supposed to be rich, exclusive and devious! How do you dispel that? I know people who have conviction in their Jewishness, and they are genial in ways that are incomprehensible to me. You can never betray the people who are dead, so you go on being a public Jew; the dead can't answer slurs, but I'm here. I would love to think that Jesus wants me for a sunbeam, but he doesn't.

The other women with whom your heroines are associated or friendly provide models of behaviour, but again they are all transparently unsuitable. I am thinking, for instance, of Caroline in Providence, *who is waiting for a man to materialize and pluck her off the unhappy tree.*

I hope these portrayals are affectionate; they are meant to be. I have many women friends, and I'm intrigued by their ways of going on.

Do you find it easier to be friends with women than with men?

No, I prefer men, because they're different. I know about women. I think what I say in *Hotel du Lac* is true, that women turn to each other in their sadness. But all of a sudden there comes that point where fortunes change, and they've gone over to some other side where relations are different. There is a certain inborn competitiveness among women which is a little bit murky, and it has to do with success with men; it's an area in which friendships can become strained. A man can go from being a lover to being a stranger in three moves flat – there is no subtlety about it, you know exactly where you are – but a woman under the guise of friendship will engage in acts of duplicity which come to light very much later. There are different species of self-justification, if you like.

The character of Caroline is perhaps hopeless or harmless, but her passive posture – just waiting for the right man to come along – is terribly enfeebling.

All women think that, and this is why women are trying to get rid of it. But of course they never will.

Do you think you could ever postulate a heroine who takes life in her hands?

If I knew one, I would.

You say that you think your novels are unpopular, and yet a huge number of people must feel a strong sense of identification with your characters.

I have yet to have proof. I know people who have no self-doubts, and nothing succeeds like success. That's what I mean about accumulation. Novels are about selection and just deserts; life is about accumulation and opportunities and the winner takes all.

Is the wit and humour in your books a conscious stratagem to make certain truths more palatable?

No, nothing conscious like that. It comes from a lot of reading. Here is the connection between art history – or history, if you like – and fiction: it's the energy of the eighteenth century I admire. If you have a cause, you have to propound it with energy. My 'cause' is to tell a story or perhaps to cast a moral puzzle. I see these novels as extraordinary accidents, and I couldn't account for them more than I already have done. I certainly haven't modelled them on anybody or anything.

Do you none the less look to certain nineteenth-century writers for touchstones of truly great writing?

It has to be Dickens. My Polish father, who remained very Polish, thought that the best thing he could do for me was to unveil the mysteries of English life which could be found in the novels of Charles Dickens: he really believed that. So I was set to read Dickens at the age of 7, and I read all the novels. I think it's Dickens's indignation which is so grand. For moral scruple I would look to Henry James; for decent feelings, Trollope; and for scrutiny, Stendhal and Flaubert . . . and Zola, where you again find the same indignation. I never felt very easy about Jane Austen: I think she made a tremendous, far-reaching decision to leave certain things out. She forfeited passion for wit, and I think that led her to collude with certain little stratagems which are horrifying in real life. She wrote about getting husbands.

She also seemed to fear an access of romantic passion.

Any sentiment is satirized – such as those girls in *Northanger Abbey* – and it's easy to satirize prim romanticism, but there has to be something in it. Romanticism is not just a mode, it literally enters into every life.

In Look at Me *Frances Hinton affirms the moral necessity for 'civilized dissimulation' . . .*

I think if my novels are about anything positive, they're about not playing tricks.

What all your characters are left with is a resignation which is not even stoicism of a classical order; it's merely learning to put up with the way life is inevitably going to turn out.

Yes, and the horror of that situation is profound.

You also seem to assert in your principal characters a correlation between highly talented intelligence and emotional or social disability.

Yes, they're stupid. They're aware of what life should be, but not of what it is. Stendhal said, 'I walk along the street, marvelling at the stars, and all of a sudden I'm hit by a cab.'

You describe heroines who are emotionally ingenuous, and it might be said that you now write novels against your better understanding. You've had more experience than your characters, who are starting out in life or stymied by their initiations into life.

Don't believe it: I know as little as I ever did. I may have had more experience, but I've learned just as little as those characters. My next encounter will have the same high hopes, the same momentary failure of nerve, and everything will go wrong from there.

To that extent your heroines – outwardly sophisticated innocents – are yourself in quite a strict sense?

I think they must be, though I'm not in a position to say it. One has to use one's own life; one has no other material. Kitty Maule says about Romanticism that in certain situations reason doesn't work, and that's the most desolating discovery of all.

Do you think your writing is therefore deeply coloured by determinism?
I hadn't thought of it, but I would think it is legitimate to think of it in those terms. I would just think of the novels as transcripts from a random passage through life, and a rather unsuccessful passage.

One of the great strengths of your books is this integrity . . .
I would make a present of it to you if I could. I don't think I'm doing anybody any favours, least of all myself: I'm now doubly a victim, in life and in fiction.

I think you never go so far as to damn the plausible and attractive men in your novels. They are, after all, selfish and undiscriminating and hurtfully uninterested, but you stop short of explicitly blaming them.
Such men are very engaging, there is no doubt about it. They know how to make themselves trusted and liked: it's their ideology, and that's where the falseness comes in . . . and the opacity, because it's unexamined. They can pretend that a relationship is simply not happening. But the relationships are *mésalliances* from the start, and the fault is lack of perception.

Do feminists find you half-hearted?
You'd have to be crouching in your burrow to see my novels in a feminist way. I do not believe in the all-men-are-swine programme.

Hotel du Lac *nevertheless enters the lists of the contemporary feminist debate to a certain extent.*
Yes, I think so, and I rather enjoyed it. But whatever the banner, you know, the competition goes on.

The people Edith meets at the Hotel du Lac include Mrs Pusey, the sexually voracious and dangerous woman – I think you call her an 'enchantress' . . .
And dainty with it.

And Monica, who has a somewhat more cynical eye but is in danger of just becoming a remittance woman.
She's a more generous character, I think.

One of the central issues of the book is Edith's realization that she can go along neither with the feminists nor with what she calls 'the ultra-feminine . . . the complacent consumers of men'. She stands up for the principle of a straightforward domestic happiness.

Yes, that is the ideal, isn't it? It is the natural order. She would like romance to end in domesticity.

Mr Neville, the 'intellectual voluptuary' she meets, is a suitable but sinister man. He proposes a self-interested arrangement.

Yes, he's the devil's advocate. He has a five-year plan, everything under his control.

You relate much of their intercourse in a humorous way, but it is horrible.

It is extremely humorous – it's the only way to look at it. But one always escapes the Mr Nevilles if one has any sense. What he proposes is one of those loveless associations that become embittered and self-seeking. He's really a very wicked man, I think; he negates so many generous and honest impulses. Edith is desperate.

She wins her freedom from him by accident, but the end – when she changes the wording of her telegram from 'Coming home' to 'Returning' – is ambiguous.

'Coming home' would be coming back to domestic propriety: 'home' implies husband, children, order, regular meals, but 'Returning' is her more honest view of the situation. To that extent she does break through to a clearer vision.

Is she undefeated?

I didn't see it that way. I think people would have liked her much better if she had married Mr Neville, let's put it that way. I think I can take on the feminists.

Did you deliberately take on the feminists in this book?

No, but I found myself involved in these questions. What women want is the clean part of the programme; how they get it is the dirty part. Of course it's fine to want all the right things, but the real question is how you get them, what manipulations you may involve yourself in, and what sacrifices you make too.

You said to me earlier that you like the work of Fay Weldon.

Very much. The women novelists I really admire in the English tradition are Rosamond Lehmann and Elizabeth Taylor. Outside the English tradition there is a marvellous woman called Edith Templeton, a Canadian writer called Mavis Gallant, and Edith be Born: these are women of foreign extraction who write in a totally different tradition, and they interest me very much. I am apostolic about the novels of Edith Templeton, a Czech who writes in impeccable English: they are extremely restrained and tell strong stories about life in old-style central Europe, with recognizable passions and follies. Lovely, lovely novels. Mavis Gallant, a Canadian writer living in Paris, has written some marvellous stories called *From the Fifteenth District*. I think she's now working on the Dreyfus case, which interests me. Edith be Born is a Belgian story-teller. They all show great bravery in encountering horrifying obstacles: they're much more stoical and less sentimental than English writers.

Fay Weldon is quite different from that.

Well, she's sprightly rather than stoical, but she's savage – she deals with it that way.

She has an unmitigated incisiveness.

Also, she cannot be fooled: I love that. You cannot pull the wool over her eyes.

Might the same remark be made about you?

I don't want to apportion blame. I think writing novels preserves you in a state of innocence – a lot passes you by – simply because your attention is otherwise diverted. The moral examination, self-examination, pre-empts every other perception: you don't even notice what's going on under your nose.

Edith Hope in Hotel du Lac *is portrayed as a rather mild and diminished person, and yet she does have alert and witty perceptions. It's wonderfully funny when she expounds her theory of tortoise-and-hare readers.*

That's all too real, I'm sure, and I mean it. She has to have some perception, I think – perception that might save her – otherwise she would be defeated.

Romantic hopefulness is a constant strain in what you write, in spite of the fact that your premise is a sense of defeat.

Romance may win out, who knows? But both are true. The point is that my personages are not combatants. And you need to take on not only the men but also the women, if it's going to come out in the end – I regret that, but I know it to be true. If we are itemizing the faults of the men, women can't just say – rather self-flatteringly – that they have been too submissive. Women

may have been too devious, but that's not the same thing.
Do you study feminist writings?
Only what gets into the popular press; I don't read *Spare Rib* or anything like that. Germaine Greer is a very intelligent writer; I think she's wrong, but she's well worth reading. *The Female Eunuch* is a fine book, and it's written with great sadness that things should be as they were – that's what saved it – but I couldn't swallow the selective moral blindness that's infected the last book, *Sex and Destiny*. I suppose the first position has been won, but the millennium was not to be found at hand.

Hotel du Lac I meant as a love story pure and simple: love triumphed over temptation. The *ideal* of love. Basically I don't like adversarial positions. I see no need for them, since life is too complicated and it's rarely just.
Your heroines are naive, and what you relish in someone like Diderot is that sense of being naïf *which is actually quite different* . . .
Zest and virtue. It's like *Candide*, when you can't be fooled.
But there's a curious element of self-appointed naivety in what you call your 'personages'.
It's suspension of disbelief, as in all fiction, and I can only demonstrate the naivety of these characters by putting them against the more sophisticated ones. It's faults in perception I'm talking about. Whether that's innocence or stupidity I leave to others to judge. I think it's both.
Do you regret Look at Me *in particular because it's a novel which purveys hopelessness, whereas the others allow for possible ameliora-tion?*
Perhaps. I think the fate of the other characters is probably just as sure, but they may not realize it. My characters exasperate me. I find *myself* deeply exasperating, and so do other people: you can't gainsay that.
What is perhaps most striking in your novels is the combination of serious, intent scrutiny and great wit.
The wit I owe to the eighteenth century, where the master of the put-down, of reductive wisdom, is Voltaire; but for energy *plus* naivety you have to read Diderot, who is undefeated. Do you know he had twenty-three gallstones? Try writing like that with twenty-three gallstones! And three of his children died. I mean,

the man is ecstatic, transcendent, in his writings! Great writers are the saints for the godless.

In Look at Me *Frances Hinton cites Dürer's depiction of melancholy as 'her own disease'. What you've said to me suggests that you feel yourself to have been permanently damaged, either by your upbringing or by your nature . . .*

By having unrealistic goals, I think. They've done me a disservice. I wouldn't forego them for the world, but they've been incompatible with the conduct of life.

Did you at some time make a decision to put all your eggs in the basket of professional worthiness and attainment?

No. I thought I was not particularly viable outside a protected environment, and I liked reading and looking. Writing novels was a kind of first-aid when I found myself in a disagreeable state of will, paralysed: it worked momentarily. I felt alone, abandoned, excluded, and it was no good moping. It was a gamble.

Is writing novels a function of maladaptation as far as you're concerned?

No, I'm not going to let you get away with that. It's a form of editing experience – getting it out in terms of form, because it is form that's going to save us all, I think, and the sooner we realize it the better. I would love to possess imagination, but I have none. I can see that one thing can proceed from another. Invention implies deliberation, not flights of fancy. Everyone possesses certain powers of invention, but imagination is very rare. Imagination, if one had it, must give one a much more glorious sense of the world. The world must be more fascinating if you can imagine other lives. Diderot's imagination made him into a scientist: he *imagined* the molecular structure of the universe. It was true, and he had no scientific training at all.

Would you rather be a painter than a novelist?

Yes. I think you love the world more as a painter. Painters have a healthy appetite for life. I think my personages could be reactivated, if the times were right: I hope so.

I think it's Kitty Maule, in Providence, *who remarks that out of the disorder of her life she found order in her work, but then she yearned to escape that sort of order.*

Yes. I love the safety of what I'm doing and I hate the safety of what I'm doing. I loved it first, and I still do – or else I wouldn't be doing it. I didn't hate it enough to begin with, and I probably hate it too much now.

And you've felt a pressing need to change your life, or at least to change your perspective on what you do?

I felt it in 1980, but I doubt that I've succeeded; I haven't changed anything. I feel I'm walking about with the mark of Cain on my forehead. I feel I could get into the Guinness Book of Records as the world's loneliest, most miserable woman! I felt very pleased about the first novel – because I didn't think I could do it – and people were pleased with me; but since then it's been downhill all the way. I hope this latest novel, *Hotel du Lac*, will slightly redeem me in the public eye.

At one moment in Hotel du Lac *Edith Hope wants to sustain herself by reading some fiction, and she chooses a volume by Colette,* Ces plaisirs, qu'on nomme, à la légère, physiques. *Does that book have special significance for you?*

Only the title. Colette's stories seem to be more or less undifferentiated, and they're marvellous. But this has been overlooked: she is very, very cruel. She is fascinated by everybody's infidelity, and she is there to chronicle it. There's a story called 'Le Képi' which is about a rather unlikely spinster who has an affair in middle life, and Colette is in the story as a much *younger* woman on whom her friend looks enviously while telling her this story. That is always Colette's standpoint, I think . . . so there is even female one-upmanship in the writing of those stories. It works marvellously because one would rather be on Colette's side than on that of anybody else – she's a more attractive person, a more succulent personality, more interesting – but that's deliberate self-protection on her part. Motives are never unmixed, are they?

Your own heroines are given to be unmixed.

Poor little things, I feel sorry for them. They're idiots: there's no other word for them. And I don't know any more than they do.

· ANGELA CARTER ·

The term 'magical realist' might well have been invented to describe Angela Carter, novelist, journalist, feminist. Her gift of outrageous fantastication, resourcefully drawing on folklore and fairy tale, enables her to conjure fabulous countries which have close designs upon the ways and means of real men and women, and upon the institutions that condition their responses and contests. Richly imagined and stylistically uninhibited – with dehumanizing villains, exotic landscapes and lush sensuality – her fictions are in many ways parables of power, desire and subjection.

Angela Carter has published eight novels including *The Magic Toyshop* (1967, John Llewellyn Rhys Memorial Prize), *Several Perceptions* (1968, Somerset Maugham Award), *Love* (1971), *The Infernal Desire Machines of Doctor Hoffman* (1972) and *The Passion of New Eve* (1977); two collections of short stories, *Fireworks* (1974) and *The Bloody Chamber* (1979, Cheltenham Festival of Literature Award) – one of the stories in the second volume is 'The Company of Wolves', which she recently scripted for the highly successful film directed by Neil Jordan – and two works of non-fiction, *The Sadeian Woman: An Exercise in Cultural History* (1979) and *Nothing Sacred* (1982), a collection of her journalism. A wry and exact cultural commentator, she is concerned above all else with the 'material truths' of our world.

Born in 1940, she worked as a journalist before taking a degree in English at the University of Bristol. She has been Arts Council Fellow in Creative Writing at Sheffield University, 1976–8, and Visiting Professor of Creative Writing at Brown

University in the USA, 1980–1. She lives in a rumpled terrace house to the north of Clapham in London, where I talked to her in September 1984. In the colourful kitchen-and-sitting room on the ground floor a gaily painted ex-fairground horse stands in for a fire-guard. She has just returned from giving 150 signatures at Mowbrays Bookshop, and settles down by the tape-recorder on the floor. Her baby Alexander consumes the room and threatens the interview with healthy hubbub. 'Shall we put him in his lobster-pot?' (the play-pen), she wonders. His father quietly and effectively takes control of the child. Alexander likes best of all to eat *The Guardian*, but come 'tucker-time' he busies himself with better nourishment; I escape to the street.

Angela Carter's latest novel is the critically acclaimed *Nights at the Circus* (1984) – a picaresque and allegorical story revolving around the career of Fevvers the *aerialiste*, whom Robert Nye has properly described as 'coarse, uproarious, hectic, inventive, preposterous, soaring through the air with the greatest of ease, the daring young woman on the flying trapeze. Fevvers has to be the most outrageous and entertaining revelation of the White Goddess in a blue moon' (*The Guardian*, 27 September 1984). Valentine Cunningham, reviewing the book in *The Observer* (30 September 1984), described it as a 'stunning novel', and soundly noted, 'This big, superlatively imagined novel may be an extravaganza, but it refuses to be as extravagantly hostile to men's doings and tellings as some of the less well-tempered women's books nowadays are.'

* * *

In the first autobiographical essay of Nothing Sacred *you characterize your upbringing – first as an evacuee with your grandmother in Yorkshire, then as a child in Balham – in a family very much governed by the women. You describe your family as having a life-style 'that flourished on its own terms but was increasingly at variance with the changes going on around it'. Your grandmother, who emerges as a wonderful matriarch, reared you as a 'tough, arrogant and pragmatic Yorkshire child', and you go on to say that the family combined rigorous cynicism and rich sentimentality. Is that how you see yourself?*

Well, all attemps at autobiography are fraught with self-deceit and narcissism. I still have some of my own teeth: that's how I see myself as a person. I notice that I'm getting more sentimental as I get older; I feel I owe it to myself somehow. Indulgent towards almost everything . . . except people like Ronald Reagan. My family was unusual to the degree that most people are unusual. I've been fortunate in that its plentiful peculiarities have tended to be picturesque rather than unsavoury. My family have always behaved anecdotally, and I do perceive every event as having the potentiality for being retold.

Is that why – strange as it may seem to some of your reviewers who think you purely inventive – you set store by the idea of the writer having as much experience as possible?

Yes, I do think a writer should get out and about and around. It's something that you can't programme, though. But there is no substitute for life.

You've also written that you were radicalized in the 1960s primarily through your sexual and emotional experience ('Notes from the Front Line'). Something personal, or did you mean that your mature understanding of society changed your habits of thought?

What I meant was that everything seemed to apply to me personally. I'd always followed politics. I don't think I voted until the late 1960s, but that was partly the result of a political decision not to vote. There comes a moment when many of the things of which you have a theoretical knowledge actually start to apply to oneself. You could walk your calf past the butcher's shop for days, but it's only when he sees the abattoir that he realizes that there is a relation between himself and the butcher's shop – a relation which is mediated, shall we say, by the abattoir.

You didn't mean that there was any one event or situation which jogged you into being a radical? It had nothing to do with a bad marriage?

No, no. I got a degree during the time I was married, and I wrote four novels. Four and a half. I wrote half of *Love* while I was still married: that's a formally flawed book, partly because I moved house halfway through it. It wasn't so much my husband or myself that was at fault: it was the institution of marriage that was making us behave in ways we didn't seem able to prevent.

In a piece you wrote for New Society while being a Booker judge last

year you suggested a question about what a novel is supposed to do in the
general scheme of things. What suggestions do you have by way of
answer?

I would like to discuss it, but I'm really not sure. Just as anything
that wants to call itself a novel is a novel, by definition, so fiction
can do anything it wants to do. I think it can do more things than
we tend to think it can. The novel has some role and responsibility in helping to explain experience and making the world
comprehensible, even if it's only to the person who is writing it.

You've written that the source of art is repression, and clearly the
direction of your novels takes the form of subverting received social and
sexual myths. Fay Weldon has said that her fiction forms part of a
campaign, but I wonder how far your work is motivated by a sense of
radical challenge?

I feel myself challenged by the world. I enjoy writing fiction,
and I set myself a number of tasks each time I write a story or
start to plan a long piece of fiction. I also ask myself a number of
questions, but it's like answering questions in an exam: there are
no right answers. There is a selection of answers which could all
be adequate to some degree, there are no answers which are
unequivocally correct.

Yes, you've written that exploring ideas is for you the same thing as
telling stories: 'a narrative is an argument stated in fictional terms.'

Sometimes they are straightforwardly intellectual arguments.
The female penitentiary at the end of *Nights at the Circus* is where
I discuss crime and punishment as ideas. But my fiction is very
often a kind of literary criticism, which is something I've started
to worry about quite a lot. I had spent a long time acquiescing
very happily with the Borges idea that books were about books,
and then I began to think: if all books are about books, what are
the other books about? Where does it all stop? Borges is happy
with the idea of a vast *Ur*-book, which is a ridiculous proposition. I think that fiction in Britain, and in the USA, is going
through a very mannerist period. I think the adjective 'postmodernist' really means 'mannerist'. Books about books is fun
but frivolous.

I imagine that at some time you felt in yourself a strong quarrel with
naturalism as a mode of writing fiction?

Not really, no. Or if I did, it was so long ago that I'm no longer bothered about it. The first novel I wrote, *Shadow Dance*, was about a perfectly real area of the city in which I lived. It didn't give exactly mimetic copies of people I knew, but it was absolutely as real as the milieu I was familiar with: it was set in provincial bohemia. But very few reviewers believed that it was real; they said I'd been reading too much Carson McCullers. I had written my second novel, *The Magic Toyshop*, by the time the first one came out: that *is* a kind of fairy tale, so I suppose I must already have made a decision about the kind of novel I was going to write. I sat down just to tell a certain kind of story, though. The story is always real *as* story.

The Magic Toyshop is a beautifully written, crystalline story of an adolescent girl's subjection to her autocratic uncle, a man who tyrannizes his family and would reduce her to the status of object or toy. I think the story is totally in your control, but the ending leaves the reader in a state of unknowing: the young couple, Melanie and Finn, are expelled by the wrathful patriarch, and one is left with a sense of ambiguity not unlike the ending of Keats's 'Eve of St Agnes'.

They're escaping like Adam and Eve at the end of *Paradise Lost*. Megalomaniac as it might seem, that was the image I wanted to leave – two people alone, about to depart from a garden.

So you were deliberately tackling the myth of Paradise Lost? Philip is God the Father, a ruthless and heartless man?

Yes, that's it: the Fortunate Fall. I got it wrong, of course, because the theory of the Fortunate Fall has it that it was fortunate because it incurred the Crucifixion, an idea which I think only an unpleasant mind could have dreamt up. I took the Fortunate Fall as meaning that it was a good thing to get out of that place. The intention was that the toyshop itself should be a secularized Eden: that's what lay behind the malign fairy tale I wrote. It is to a degree true that, as we used to say in the sixties, you are what you eat, because what I had been reading were people like Isak Dinesen, Cocteau and Firbank – a certain kind of non-naturalistic writing that was very much around but which nobody seemed to be reading. (Earlier this summer, in fact, I did a radio play about Firbank called 'A Self-Made Man'.) Firbank has a beautiful precision of language, and he's also so very funny and melancholy; his evocation of landscape is as economical and beautiful as *haiku*. I've always thought that he was a plucky little bantamweight.

I suppose that Gabriel García Márquez would figure high in your pantheon?

Not till very much later. I was pleased but not particularly surprised to find a novel like *One Hundred Years of Solitude*, but I didn't read it until the mid-seventies. One of the great novels of my youth was *The Lost Steps*, by Alejo Carpentier, which I remember reading in the late 1950s. Britain became very insular in the 1970s. When Günter Grass was first published I didn't read him on principle – because everybody was reading him – and it was only later that I wished I *had* read *The Tin Drum* when it came out.

Reviews of Nights at the Circus *have sometimes seemed to suggest that what is now known as 'magic realism' has been almost a fresh departure for you, whereas in fact you've been using that mode for going on twenty years. Your fictional world has always inhabited and domesticated this kind of inventive extravagance, and equally always been intent on its demythologizing purposes. One journalist praised the 'fiery abandon' of your fiction, as though that was all there had been to it.*

Obviously I think so too. Robert Nye's review in *The Guardian* was very nice . . . but grudging, I think; he seemed rather reluctant to concede that there had ever been anything more than a lot of high-falutin bluster in my earlier work. But this is bound to happen: I haven't had a novel out for a long time. And also everybody is doing it now. I am older than Salman Rushdie and I've been around longer, but memories are short.

Do you mean that readers tend to talk as if you took your cue from somebody like Márquez?

Márquez is a very great writer, but the kinds of social forces which produce a writer like Márquez are in fact very different from those that produced, say, me. He was very much going back to the Colombian countryside and folklore, just as Salman Rushdie is writing about shamans who are actually *real*. In Britain one has to invent much more; we don't have an illiterate and superstitious peasantry with a very rich heritage of abstruse fictional material. But I realize that I tend to use other people's books, European literature, as though it were that kind of folklore. Our literary heritage is a kind of folklore. In *Nights at the Circus*, for example, the character Mignon is the daughter of Wozzeck – I'm more familiar with the opera by Berg than with the play – who is left playing at the end: she doesn't know what is going to happen. That is a reference to a common body of knowledge, a folklore of the intelligentsia.

I think your use of the heightening devices of folklore does give some readers the impression that you are offering them alternative mental landscapes – at best dream-realities, or perhaps escapist fantasies or just spell-binding excursions – whereas they should be seen as angled challenges or critiques of real social constructs and attitudes.

I don't mind being called a spell-binder. Telling stories is a perfectly honourable thing to do. One is in the entertainment business. But there is certainly a confusion about the nature of dreams, which are in fact perfectly real: they are real *as* dreams, and they're full of *real* meaning as dreams. Dreams are real, but the contents of dreams are not real.

They are just not phenomenally real.

Yes, exactly. I don't on the whole remember my own dreams, but I quite often use the formal structures of dreams – formal structures which I tend to get from Freud rather than from my own experience.

Bruno Bettelheim, I think, takes the view that fairy tales use fantasy materials to reflect inner experiences and processes; they are ways of coping with unconscious processes. Fairy tales are unreal, he says, but not untrue. Do you subscribe to the arguments and interpretations he puts forward in The Uses of Enchantment?

Not really, no. When I wrote my book of fairy tales, *The Bloody Chamber*, I had read Bettelheim, and I was interested in the psychoanalytic content of the stories. Everyone knows that Bettelheim is terrific with children, but I think he is sometimes wrong. I'm not sure that fairy tales are as consoling as he suggests. An historian named Robert Darnton, in a very nice book called *The Great Cat Massacre*, has a long essay about the oral tradition in seventeenth-century France which really lams into the psychoanalytic school of interpretation of fairy tales. He says you can hardly talk about the latent content of stories which are explicitly about cannibalism, incest, bestiality and infanticide, and of course he's right. I do find the imagery of fairy tales very seductive and capable of innumerable interpretations, however. But some of the stories in *The Bloody Chamber* are the result of quarrelling furiously with Bettelheim. It seems to me important that 'Beauty and the Beast' does not come out of oral tradition: it's an art story, written for children – just as my stories are art stories – and it was intended as a perfectly tuned moral tale. Actually it's an advertisement for moral blackmail: when the Beast says that he is dying because of Beauty, the only morally correct thing for her to have said at that point would be, 'Die, then'.

'Little Red Riding Hood' is the starting point for your story 'The Company of Wolves', which has now been made into a film that has rather muddled the critics. Bettelheim dislikes Charles Perrault's version of the story, in which the wolf gobbles up the girl, because it points a specific moral lesson – you get what you deserve if you stray from the path and give in to seduction. He prefers the later Grimm version in which a hunter finally rescues the girl and her grandmother from the belly of the wolf – 'the wolf it was that died.' Your version in The Bloody Chamber *has it that the girl is not scared and lies down with the wolf: it does offer a sort of Blakean solace.*

She eats the wolf, in effect. When my grandmother read 'Little Red Riding Hood' to me, she had no truck with that sentimental nonsense about a friendly woodcutter carefully slitting open the wolf's belly and letting out the grandmother; when she came to the part about the wolf jumping on Little Red Riding Hood and eating her up, she used to jump on me and pretend to eat me. Like all small children, I loved being tickled and nuzzled: I found it bliss, and I'd beg her to relate the story to me just for the sake of this ecstatic moment when she jumped on me. When I was researching the story I looked at a facsimile of Perrault's manuscript, and I found that when he comes to the bit about the wolf jumping on Little Red Riding Hood, it says in the margin 'The story-teller should do likewise' – so that acting out the story has always been part of the story, traditionally. It turns it into something completely different – a rough kind of game – which is obviously something that Bettelheim didn't know; he's only had it as a text, not from the oral tradition. As Darnton points out, you could very easily get eaten by wild animals in the forests of seventeenth-century France. You can of course read the story of its symbolism as it appears to us now, but three or four hundred years ago it would have been a rough nursery game with a real moral: you shouldn't lurk around in the forest, and not because of seducers.

In rewriting these fairy tales for The Bloody Chamber *was it a deliberate part of your task to bring them out of the area of the unconscious?*

Yes. My intention was not to do 'versions' or, as the American edition of the book said, horribly, 'adult' fairy tales, but to extract the latent content from the traditional stories and to use it as the beginnings of new stories. The stories could not have existed the way they are without Isak Dinesen, Djuna Barnes and Jane Bowles – especially Isak Dinesen, because in a way they are imitation nineteenth-century stories, like hers. I wrote them in Sheffield, as you know, which is probably why they are all such cold, wintry stories.

As a film The Company of Wolves *seems to compound possible interpretations. Did you keep a clear idea in mind?*

The wolves represent lots of things, though basically they are still libido in the movie. But they change in meaning throughout the movie. It's not my movie, after all, it's filtered through another sensibility which has a good deal in common with mine but is quite different in many respects. For one thing, Neil Jordan was brought up in Catholic Ireland. I wasn't.

I am always happy to recommend that people should see the movie. The whole werewolf–bridegroom sequence, for example, is quite magical, and I hope there are many other pleasurable things in it. The reason why the girl is pounced on by the wolves at the end is pure contingency, since the original ending that Neil wanted turned out to be impossible, literally not possible. He said that it must end on an 'extraordinary image' – an image of repression being liberated by libido – in which the girl would wake up and do the most beautiful dive into the floor-boards.

It sounds as though your script was dictated by cinematic possibilities, and not the other way around? Was that the case?

We wrote the script together at the kitchen table, and there didn't seem to be any point in writing things he didn't want to film. In the final analysis any film is the director's movie. But the impossible remains impossible.

Even though it can result in a confusion about the point of the narrative or fable?

On the whole I am very happy with it. Its purpose and meaning are not intended to be clear. I'm not sure of its meaning; it is supposed to be an open-ended film, with a plentiful amount of material for interpretation.

You've said that you did not consciously move away from naturalism. How conscious was your move towards folklore?

Folklore was a late addition, and came about as such with *The Bloody Chamber*, although there is a good deal of authentic Irish folklore in *The Magic Toyshop*. But I think I must have started very early on to regard the whole of western European culture as a kind of folklore. I had a perfectly regular education, and indeed I'm a rather booksy person, but I do tend to regard all aspects of culture as coming in on the same level. If fairy tales are the fiction of the poor, then perhaps *Paradise Lost* is the folklore of the educated.

I know that you find it fundamentally important to have an intelligent awareness of society, and yet the highly stylized and decorative apparatus of your novels might appear to be disengaged from the social and historical realities you want to illuminate.

Yes, this is a very real risk, really tricky. Obviously the idea that my stories are all dreams or hallucinations out of Jung-land, or the notion that the world would be altogether a better place if we threw away our rationality and went laughing down the street, or even the one that schizophrenia is an enriching experience, that's all nonsense. I *can* see how it must look to some readers, but the point is that if dreams are real as dreams, then there is a materiality to symbols; there's a materiality to imaginative life and imaginative experience which should be taken quite seriously.

In *The Passion of New Eve* the central character is a transvestite movie star, and I created this person in order to say some quite specific things about the cultural production of femininity. The promotion slogan for the film *Gilda*, starring Rita Hayworth, was 'There was never a woman like Gilda', and that may have been one of the reasons why I made my Hollywood star a transvestite, a man, because only a man could think of femininity in terms of that slogan. Quite a number of people read *The Passion of New Eve* as a feminist tract and recoiled with suitable horror and dread, but in fact there is quite a careful and elaborate discussion of femininity as a commodity, of Hollywood producing illusions as tangible commodities – yet most of that was completely by-passed. I don't mind that, because you can't dictate how a book should be read. But I spent a long time on that novel, which meant so much to me for various reasons, and obviously I was disappointed that it should be treated as just another riotous extravaganza. It's a bitter and probably quite uncomfortable book to read.

Well, yes, especially if you read it from the point of view of the narrator. Evelyn is captured by the figure of Mother, the 'castratrix of the Phallocentric Universe', a self-manufactured chthonic deity who rapes and emasculates him in order that he can enjoy the horrible privilege of embodying the 'parthenogenesis archetype'. Mother has given herself two tiers of breasts so that she becomes a sort of Artemis, and even in the midst of his ordeal Evelyn says that being suckled by Mother was 'like being seated at the console of a gigantic cinema organ' – a simile which discomfitingly burlesques what might otherwise be taken as really woeful.

It was intended as a piece of black comedy. One reviewer, a great gay spokesperson and writer, said he found Mother 'such a cosy person' because of all those tits. But of course castration doesn't hold quite the same terrors for me as it does for you, John! One of the snags is that I do put everything in a novel to be *read* – read the way allegory was intended to be read, the way you are supposed to read *Sir Gawayne and the Grene Knight* – on as many levels as you can comfortably cope with at the time. In *The Passion of New Eve* the transvestite character Tristessa has a glass house – the kind of place in which you shouldn't live if you throw stones – which is an image of a certain kind of psychic vulnerability. Tristessa has set up in the house a waxworks called The Hall of the Immortals, which contains the dead martyrs of Hollywood including Jean Harlow and Judy Garland, and that was supposed to be indicating something quite specific about the nature of illusion and of personality, which Hollywood did and does invent. That Hall is where we first discover the hero–heroine, pretending to be dead. It was intended to say something about representations, but readers seemed to think that it was all just part of the fantastic décor of the house. However, this is bound to happen, sometimes.

As a medievalist, I was trained to read books as having many layers. Using the word 'allegory' may make it all too concrete. Certainly I was using straightforward allegorical ideas in parts of *Nights at the Circus*. Mignon, for example, is supposed to be Europe, the unfortunate, bedgraggled orphan – Europe after the war – which is why she carries such a weight of literary and musical references on her frail shoulders. But it does seem a bit of an imposition to say to readers that if you read this book you have got to be thinking all the time; so it's there only if you want it. From *The Magic Toyshop* onwards I've tried to keep an entertaining surface to the novels, so that you don't have to read them as a system of signification if you don't want to. You could read them as science fiction if you wished – though a lot of the heaviest analysis has come from the SF critics. The idea behind *Nights at the Circus* was very much to entertain and instruct, and I purposely used a certain eighteenth-century fictional device – the picaresque, where people have adventures in order to find themselves in places where they can discuss philosophical concepts without distractions. That mingling of adventure and the discussion of what one might loosely call philosophical concepts occurs, for example, when the characters reach Siberia: they can discuss Life and Art as they stride off through the snow.

The question that is posed about Fevvers, your 'Cockney Venus' heroine – whether she is finally to be seen as a prodigy, a freak, a 'singularity', or just as a person – did that finally matter to you? She is a wonderfully exuberant and vulgar heroine, and even though she encounters dangerous men like the Grand Duke who would treat her as

an erotic object she is the one who takes command and exploits every
situation to her advantage.

Yes, the only way she can earn a living, as her mother keeps
reminding her, is by making a show of herself! But as Gillian
Greenwood pointed out in the *Literary Review*, Fevvers does
become herself – 'whatever that is'. An American friend of mine
congratulated me for at last writing some three-dimensional
characterization – 'especially people like the pig'. Everyone
changes throughout the novel, he wrote, except for Fevvers –
'who doesn't so much change as expand' – which I liked very
much: she does seem to get more pneumatic. Fevvers is basically
Mae West with wings. I'm a great admirer of Mae West. The
way Mae West controls the audience-response towards herself
in her movies is quite extraordinary. Fevvers is supposed to have
something of Mae West's baboon or gunslinger's walk,
although Mae West is a little more graceful. Mae West's walk is
one of the most extraordinary things about her – as though she is
saddle-sore, which makes the mind reel if you think of it in that
way: what *has* she been up to?! Goodness me!

Fevvers has encounters with three different varieties of the
mad scientist, a figure which – as mad scientist/shaman/toy-
maker/male-authority figure – has remained remarkably
consistent, if I may say so, in the particular schema of my novels
for the last twenty years. Each time she encounters a mad
scientist Fevvers gets away, and each time she loses a little more
of herself – until finally she turns the tables on the last one, the
Shaman, who is in any event the most sympathetic. When I was
writing that part of the novel I attended a conference where a
lady anthropologist described to me some shamanic jiggery-
pokery in the High Andes, where she'd encountered a 'vivid
sense of evil' in a *cabana*. She'd really been fooled. Shamans are
actually very good at what they do, because they themselves
believe in it, but that doesn't make it true. So the question of
illusion – what is real and what is not real – comes up again there,
in a tribal group which has a different epistemology. Of course
every social system tends to denaturize people, it's one of the
things about living in groups; since you can't live on your own
and retain your social identity, it's just one more bit of the

difficulty of being! I used that tribal society in *Nights at the Circus* just because there is now so much sentimentality about primitives, and sometimes I feel it too; but, Jesus, it can't be any fun having toothache in a tribal society – they would press a pregnant bat to the cavity.

The plot of Nights at the Circus *ramifies in the second and third sections of the book, when we reach St Petersburg and Siberia, introducing numerous other characters including Mignon, Samson, Colonel Kearney, Sybil the Mystic Pig, and the shaman.*

The last half of *Nights at the Circus* gets very picaresque indeed; the middle section is very elaborately plotted, like a huge circus with the ring in the middle, and it took me ages tinkering with it to get it right. A circus is always a microcosm.

Although we move forward from Fevvers's own narrative of her life so far, it seems to me that you do keep the book focused on her and on Jack Walser, the obsessed and sceptical journalist. Walser has to go through various degrading hoops, and finally to be reduced to someone who can experience things directly.

Yes. The phrase on the blurb about his 'male certainties' is really a mistake, because that's not the point. The whole point about him is that he's *not* certain; he's a sceptical person.

And he wants to sustain that illusion.

Yes, he wants to sustain the illusion of his own scepticism. But, as you've correctly said, his rather two-dimensional idea of himself – as the foreign correspondent, the person in control, the permanent bystander, with the privileged marginality of the journalist – has to be broken down before he can become . . . not a fit mate for Fevvers at all, but a serious person.

So you put him through all sorts of hell?

Not hell at all. After all, he's already been through a lot. Paul Bailey was particularly tickled by the throwaway line, 'a sharp dose of buggery in a tent adjacent to the Damascus road', and said he loved fiction in which an entire novel was thrown away in an aside like that.

He is none the less made into an object.

Yes, he does become an object, and it's amazing how many people find it offensive when you do that to a chap. What happens to him is exactly what happens to another, though a much nastier person who runs away with a music-hall artiste and is forced to personate a rooster – do you remember? – in *The Blue Angel*. But nobody forces Jack Walser to behave as a human chicken. It is a systematic humiliation, but it's not Fevvers who does it to him – it's life. When he's recruited for the circus, the colonel asks him, 'Can you stand humiliation?', which is about the only time the colonel is permitted to say anything of existential interest. It all has a happy-ish ending; it is a comedy, and has to end happily.

When Fevvers declares at the end, 'I fooled you,' are we meant to take that remark at face value? I read it that she does in fact have wings, but has she played a vast confidence-trick all the while?

It's actually a statement about the nature of fiction, about the nature of her narrative. It's shameful to have to admit it, but a lot of my writing comes out of being what my mother calls 'Bolshy'. The first serious short story I ever wrote, 'The Executioner's Beautiful Daughter' (in *Fireworks*), was the result of a bet I made with someone I met in a café who said that fiction has to be kinetic, it has to move. I thought it was nonsense to say anything so categorical about art, and so I went home and wrote a story which is absolutely static – nothing happens in it at all.

People babble a lot nowadays about the 'unreliable narrator' – as in Salman Rushdie's *Midnight's Children* – so I thought: I'll show you a *really* unreliable narrator in *Nights at the Circus*! It's not so much a question of Fevvers's wings, which have now established themselves as part of her physiology – she does have wings, obviously, *and* no navel – as a question about fiction.

Do you mean that Fevvers's hilarious boast at the end – 'I fooled you then' – is a kind of gesture towards postmodernism?

I think people do know what is real and what isn't. Her boast is partly a celebration of the confidence trick, among other things, as well as a description of her way of being: she's had the confidence to pull it all off, after all. She's also fooled him about her sexual intactness, of course.

It's actually doing something utterly illegitimate – in a way I like – because ending on that line doesn't make you realize the fictionality of what has gone before, it makes you start inventing other fictions, things that might have happened – as though the people were really real, with real lives. Things might have happened to them other than the things I have said have happened to them. So that really is an illusion. It's inviting the reader to write lots of other novels for themselves, to continue taking these people as if they were real. It is not like saying that you should put away the puppets and close the box. I didn't realize I was doing that at the time, but it is inviting the reader to take one further step into the fictionality of the narrative, instead of coming out of it and looking at it as though it were an artefact. So that's not postmodernist at all, I suppose: it's the single most nineteenth-century gesture in the novel!

In a review of your essays, Nothing Sacred, *Tom Paulin remarked (*London Review of Books, *3–17 March 1983) that 'the easy fluency and soft stylishness of Angela Carter's fictions is won at the expense of form and mimesis . . . her fictions suffer from the absence of what Keats termed "disagreeables". It could be that her cerulean imagination would benefit from the constraints of the documentary novel.' I suppose he thinks that you could do with a dose of social-realism, which seems to me a radical misapprehension of your methods. But I think it's true that you do embrace opportunities for overwriting . . .*

Embrace them? I would say that I half-suffocate them with the enthusiasm with which I wrap my arms and legs around them. It's mannerist, you see: closing time in the Gardens of the West, as I think Cyril Connolly said. I started off being an expressionist, but as I grew older I started treating it more frivolously and so I became a mannerist. It's the only way I can write. I'm not sure what beautiful writing is. There's a certain kind of flat, pedestrian writing which I know I don't like, but I am cursed a bit by fluency, I think. I *do* like plain, transparent prose. I wish I could do it.

It is understandable, I suppose, that someone could approach the fantastic and exotic surface of your fictions and not be able to bridge the gap to the central point that your theatricality is meant to heighten real social attitudes and myths of femininity.

I should make the point that men live by the myths you've mentioned as much as women, because there has been the idea that fiction that demythologizes them is only of interest to women – as though the dichotomy in our culture is so vast that only women are interested in certain kinds of social fiction, whereas they affect us all very profoundly. Indeed, they affect men much more than women, because women know in their hearts that they're not true.

Nights at the Circus is using the whole of western European culture as though it were an oral tradition, in the same casual way that writers in the sixteenth and seventeenth centuries made reference to the classics. Folklore is the fiction of the poor, and therefore should be taken just as seriously as we take 'straight' literature. The imaginative life is conducted in response to all manner of stimuli – including the movies, advertising, all the magical things that the surrealists would see in any city street. Surrealism didn't involve inventing extraordinary things to look at, it involved looking at the world as though it were strange. I have always used a very wide number of references because of tending to regard all of western Europe as a great scrap-yard from which you can assemble all sorts of new vehicles . . . *bricolage*. Basically, all the elements which are available are to do with the margin of the imaginative life, which is in fact what gives reality to our own experience, and in which we measure our own reality.

You are a committed materialist, I know, and yet your writing unleashes what you've elsewhere called all sorts of 'imaginative gaiety'. So we're left with the paradox – since we can't explain it – that you choose to accentuate the real by writing tall stories in lush locales.

I do like to reduce everything to its material base. It is an odd paradox, I know. A Mexican friend of mine once recognized Gabriel García Márquez in a bookshop, and he was so pleased to be recognized – he said it had never happened before – that he bought her a cup of coffee. She asked him how he came to write the scene in *One Hundred Years of Solitude* where the bald girl levitates; and he explained that he'd been looking out of the window at his wife hanging out the sheets on the patio, and the sheets blew in such a way that it seemed that they were carrying her right up to heaven: up she goes! It was that image – a really concrete image – that stuck in his mind.

Another way of magicking or making everything strange is to take metaphor literally, and in some respects Fevvers in *Nights at the Circus* starts off as a metaphor come to life – a winged spirit. And she's the Winged Victory . . . except that she does have a head!

The Sadeian Woman, *which you called an interpretation of some of the problems the Marquis de Sade 'raises about the culturally determined nature of women and of the relations between men and women that result from it', ends with a postscript quoting a wonderful passage from Emma Goldman: 'A true conception of the relation between the sexes will not admit of conqueror and conquered; it knows of but one great thing: to give of one's self boundlessly, in order to find one's self richer, deeper, better.' You presumably very much assent to Emma Goldman's idea of emancipation?*

Yes, I think Emma Goldman was right about most things . . . except abortion. I think it's the only sane attitude. I'm interested in justice, not vengeance. Olive Schreiner was also right about a lot.

Have you ever felt inclined to put fiction to the service of an idea of feminism?

No. I write about the conditions of my life, as everyone does. You write from your own history. Being female or being black means that once you become conscious, your position – however many there are of you – isn't the standard one: you have to bear that in mind when you are writing, you have to keep on defining the ground on which you're standing, because you are in fact setting yourself up in opposition to the generality.

In your essay 'Notes from the Front Line' you talk about the 'process of decolonialising our language and our basic habits of thought . . . transforming actual fictional forms to both reflect and to precipitate changes in the way people feel about themselves.'

I think that's true.

But it sounds more prescriptive and combative than what you've said to me so far. You don't mean that your fiction is programmed?

No, I write the way I write because that's the way I write. In *Nights at the Circus* I did make space for certain kinds of discussion, however frivolously they're conducted. It's not possible for me to write agit-prop. I just don't know, for example, what Marilyn French meant *The Women's Room* to do: I thought

Norm, the ex-husband in that novel, was such a wonderful man. I finished the book with every sympathy for the men: they seemed to have awful lives surrounded by such dreadful women. I came out of it with an immensely enhanced admiration for American men, which surprised me very much indeed. I wouldn't see the point of writing that novel; I thought the premises of her idea of emancipation were pretty ropey. I don't think it's good art, good fiction or good propaganda – if propaganda is what you want. I do what I do, but I have to stay aware of the area from which I'm coming, as they say.

Chinua Achebe has a very nice essay on *Heart of Darkness*. Conrad wasn't a bad man by any means, and he wasn't a racist, but one of the things Achebe says is that Conrad couldn't have imagined that a black African would some day be in a position to analyse *Heart of Darkness* as a black African. All the suppositions in Conrad are in the text, they are never spelt out – he's quite sympathetic to the blacks – but assumptions of white superiority are implicit: the idea that you go to Africa in order to discover something awful about yourself instead of going there to do wrong to people of equal humanity.

In my work I keep on saying, in what I think is the nicest way, that women are people too, and that everything is relative – you see the world differently from different places. You cannot make any statements which are universally true, especially perhaps in the context of Britain. Everything is determined by different circumstances, and the circumstances of women are different from those of men. Somehow women writers really do keep on making this point, and sometimes they don't even know that they do it – Beryl Bainbridge is not aware that she's doing it. It's a point which men don't make when they write – unless they're loopy like Dostoievsky, or gay – because they really do believe that the world is made in their image. I'm not blaming or castigating men for it. A sense of superiority is all some of them have. One of my favourite books, which is James Agee's *Let Us Now Praise Famous Men*, describes Tennessee share-croppers whose lives are awful, utterly appalling – they're terribly poor and culturally deprived to a degree – and who have only one consolation, which is that at least they're not black: so their lives are still based on that unconscious assumption of superiority. British society is one in which most values are determined by a specific sex and a specific class, and I think that's unjust: that's all. And in order to think about these things you've got to have the language to do it in.

You've used the term 'picaresque' about your work, and from Heroes and Villains *to* Nights at the Circus *your novels do take the form of encounters with various social and metaphysical groups, organizations and dangerous organizers. Do you see fiction as a kind of anthropology?*

Yes, it's a very eighteenth-century pursuit to make imaginary societies which teach one about our own society. I do see it as akin to anthropology, and to sociology as well. *The Infernal Desire Machines of Doctor Hoffman* began as an inventory of imaginary cities. My villains are usually mad scientists, but I really don't know why, since I've got nothing against science as such. The toy-maker, the puppet master, is the ideal villain . . . and the vicar in *Heroes and Villains*, where tribal life if found to be irretrievable: that was the first attempt to get characters out into the wilderness where they could discuss things – just as at the end of *Nights at the Circus*. I think *Nights at the Circus* deals more economically with the idea of the invention of religion. *Heroes and Villains* is a discussion of the theories of Jean-Jacques Rousseau, and strangely enough it finds them wanting. It's actually done very elegantly, though I say so myself. But I wouldn't dream of writing a novel set after a nuclear catastrophe now; I couldn't bring myself to do it – it would be too much like tempting providence, and making hypotheses which are not on. *Heroes and Villains* is a dystopian novel. In the fifties and sixties there was a real vogue for post-catastrophe novels as a sort of pastoral, but it's just not possible to do that now: we do know too much.

You've written in The Sadeian Woman *that 'rationality without humanism founders on itself.' Do you see the novel as a humane medium, however barbaric or satiric the systems and situations constructed in your fiction may be? Are you in fact a moralist?*

The novel as we have it is very intimately linked with certain ideas of the personality: reading is very private and silent work, and it makes a lot of suppositions about the kind of life you lead.

'Moralist' is a newly fashionable word, isn't it? I read English in the Leavis school, and therefore I tend to be a bit mistrustful of the word, moral. I'm never sure where it might lead me: it might lead me into areas of private morality which seem to me no concern of mine. If morals are to do with the way people behave, then I do think the novel has a moral function. But the moral function should not be hortatory in any way – telling people how to behave. I would see it as a moral compunction to explicate and to find out about things. I suppose I would regard curiosity as a moral function.

· WILLIAM GOLDING ·

William Golding gained world-wide fame with his first published novel, *Lord of the Flies* (1954), which has sold millions of copies and – along with J. D. Salinger's *The Catcher in the Rye* – became one of the key texts for campus study during the 1950s and 1960s.

Lord of the Flies, Golding wrote later,

came out of:

1 five years war service.
2 finding out, afterwards, what the Nazis did.
3 ten years teaching small boys.

That anyone can think more – or less – than that necessary as a genesis, makes me despair of the intelligentsia. (Letter to Henri A. Talon, quoted in *Le Mal dans l'oeuvre de William Golding*, 1966)

'Evil enters the world through humanity, and through no other creature', he told Owen Webster (*Books and Art*, March 1958), and his later fictions have sustained an enquiry into that dark premise or conviction, the equation of intelligence with evil. *The Inheritors* (1955), *Pincher Martin* (1956), *Free Fall* (1959), *The Spire* (1964), *Darkness Visible* (1979) and *Rites of Passage* (1980): as fables which are charged with symbolic power and sometimes gain access to the character of myth, exploiting and subverting a number of models or analogues (including R. M. Ballantyne, H. G. Wells, Dante and Greek tragedy), the novels take a radical view of the human condition and emphasize its evil, egotism and guilt. Among Golding's excellences as a novelist is the gift of graphic imagination, which enables him not just to allege but to characterize the dire limitations of optimism, scientific rationalism and any facile concept of 'progress'.

Although his books register and examine disorder, Golding's artistic vision is essentially spiritual. 'I am, in fact, an Ancient Egyptian, with all their unreason, spiritual pragmatism and capacity for ambiguous belief' (*The Hot Gates*, 1965). His fictions are less didactic declarations than painfully imagined demonstrations of the chaos human nature has brought upon itself; less solutions than felt responses. As Golding observed to Peter Bloxam, 'The point is that the writer lives now in a world which has ceased to be explicit because it has ceased to be explicable' (*Evening Herald*, 11 February 1963). Golding credits the sanctions of civilized society, and he intimates the reality of saintliness or sanctity, the possibility of grace and redemption. 'I don't like to be thought of as a person who says man is beastly', he has said. 'I'm really an optimist. Simon is the whole point of *Lord of the Flies* and Simon is love.' In answer to readers who may believe that he insists upon one negative 'moral' – that mankind exhibits nothing but self-engendered corruption – Golding has responded, 'the only kind of real progress is the progress of the individual towards some kind of – I would describe it as *ethical* – integration and his consequent effect upon people who are near him' (Jack Biles, *Talk: Conversations with William Golding*, New York: Harcourt Brace Jovanovich, 1970). The novelist's business is 'either understanding what men are or, if he can't, trying to put before other men a recognizable picture of the mystery', he explained to Owen Webster. It is a task which requires the novelist to retain independence of view and vision: 'a writer must have intransigence in the face of accepted belief – political, religious, moral – any accepted belief' (*Books and Art*, March 1958).

Born in Cornwall in 1911, Golding was educated at Marlborough Grammar School and at Brasenose College, Oxford, where – after first taking examinations in botany, zoology, chemistry and physics – he revolted against science and switched to English literature (he became devoted to Anglo-Saxon, and some years later he also taught himself classical Greek). After five years at Oxford he published his first book, *Poems* (1934), an elusive volume which he now disowns. The next five years he spent working – as actor, writer and director – with small theatre companies. He married in 1939, and has a son and a daughter. During the war he served in the Royal Navy. Except for some months' work at a secret research establishment under Lord Cherwell – 'trying to invent things that would sink submarines' – and another period of six months which he passed in waiting for a minesweeper to be built on Long Island, he spent five years afloat – in cruisers, destroyers and minesweepers, ending up in command of 'one of those damned rocket craft'. He saw action against the *Bismarck*, in the D-day landings on the French coast, and in the invasion of the island of Walcheren. From 1945 to 1961 he was a schoolmaster, teaching English and philosophy at Bishop Wordsworth's School, Salisbury, a career he intensely disliked.

Photographs of Golding often image him with austere and prophetic mien, but that is partly because he hates being photographed and invariably assumes a self-consciously severe expression. To meet him is to discover more of his affable and impishly witty side. Characteristically, he once teased his publishers with the suggestion that *The Spire* should be called *An Erection at Barchester*. He is generously hospitable and a fine raconteur, though he maintains a certain guardedness when submitting to a formal interview.

The one book he will not discuss is *Darkness Visible*, of which William Boyd has written, 'There is no doubt that the writing of the novel was something of a purgative experience – Golding has stated that he refused to read a single review of the book' (*London Magazine*, February/March 1981); Tom Paulin, reviewing *Darkness Visible*, observed very perceptively:

> although his novel is sometimes victimized by the cultural chaos it dissects, its uncompromising vision of spiritual love triumphing over evil and stupidity is so powerful and so intensely wise that it must force us to accept a theology and a theophany . . . those who believe that we are simply conditioned by our environment and that the civil power is the

sole guarantor of our freedom will find no comfort in this brooding and magnificent parable. (*Encounter*, 54, January 1980)

Golding inscribed in my copy of *Darkness Visible* the telling legend 'Sentio et excrucior' – a simple but terrifying motto which surely speaks for the *corpus* of his fiction.

I talked to him at his Wiltshire home in October 1980, just two weeks before he won the 1980 Booker McConnell Prize, and began by asking him about *Rites of Passage*, the book that took the prize. In 1983 Golding received the ultimate accolade, the Nobel Prize for Literature.

* * *

Can you tell me something about the genesis of Rites of Passage?
When you read nineteenth-century life and literature, it seems quite remarkable how many people suddenly died: Arthur Hallam, for instance, lay down on a couch and just died. I don't understand it, but it is something that deeply interested me, and it seems to have occurred more often in the nineteenth century than at any other time.
But the character in your novel, Colley, becomes cataleptic and seems to embrace death . . .
That's how it seems, yes. But though it looks to some extent a hard, even merciless book, in point of fact it's an attempt to explain something that actually happened – it's an attempt to invent circumstances (which may be artificial or theatrical) where one can see that this kind of thing can happen: that someone can be reduced to the point at which he would die of shame.
What is the example you had in mind?
I think a reference in Wilfred Scawen Blunt's diaries. There was a convoy travelling from the east coast of India across to Malaysia, I believe, and the Duke of Wellington went aboard from one of the other ships in order to cheer this chap up, but his efforts were no good and the man just died. That's the provenance of my story.

I imagine that when the literary critics come to work on the book, they'll find analogies with Melville, Conrad, Hawthorne. . . . Does that kind of critical procedure trouble you?

There may be a degree of truth in source-hunting, since in literary terms I'm highly educated; but equally I've spent my life as a human being living among other human beings. One of the defects of the scholastic literary critic who doesn't know his arse from his elbow is that he invariably deduces the making of one book from the making of another, without ever considering who, in that case, made The Original Book. In other words, that sort of critic – either through ignorance or jealousy – tries to explain away the act of creativity. I think it's possible that my books sometimes have a kick-off in other books, but only because my *human* experience has made me feel that, in those circumstances, I know better. *Lord of the Flies* had a sort of genesis in seeing how ridiculous a picture of human nature *Coral Island* is. But I have to say that as a child I took refuge in books like *Coral Island*.

The reader of Rites of Passage *is compelled for a long time to empathize with Talbot, whose journal provides the frame of the story, and yet the final effect is that the reader himself is shamed by this complacent, fastidious, snobbish character – more shamed, in fact, than the character himself. Did you originally plan that sort of consequence?*

That brings up the question of drafts. The point is, after completing a draft, the writer can sometimes be seduced, in a sense, by the brilliance and the tickling. In this case, Talbot – the ego of the book – does grow up to some extent and becomes more aware, but I took heed of the fact that a man doesn't grow up overnight. Talbot doesn't undergo a conversion on the way to Damascus; his change has to be partial; he becomes more aware of himself and of other people, but not totally aware. How much of it I actually believe word by word, I don't know. When I re-read the book the other day, it did seem to be a valid picture of the way a person develops. Talbot's learned certain things, but not other things the onlooker feels he should have learned – just as we haven't in our lives.

In fact, Talbot suppresses the responsibility for someone else's tragedy. Ultimately, he won't take it to heart.

That's right: he'll be aware of the tragedy and be sorry for it, but it's not going to alter him root and branch. It will add a little bit – a sentence, no more – to his knowledge of human nature.

Can you recall at what point you introduced the character of Summers, who figures as a spokesman for humane values and right thinking?

There are, in fact, three mysterious characters in *Rites of Passage* who are not explained. Summers comes the nearest to being explained, but in a sense I think he needs another book to be explained . . . He started by being much more saintly in the first version, but I came to think that was ridiculous: I therefore reduced him to someone who could be insulted and who could find that his social standing was a thing of great personal moment to him.

In the case of Captain Anderson, the cruel anti-cleric, you do eventually provide a rationale for his resentment of the clergy, and I wonder if the novel really needs that explanation? It may be that he could have remained as enigmatic and incomprehensible as, say, Ahab in Moby Dick.

The only answer I can suggest is that in *Moby Dick* the one monumental figure is Ahab; Moby Dick, the great white whale itself, is a force, not a character. In my book, Anderson is not the hero, not even a *deus ex machina*: he's a thing from which other characters bounce. So, in my view, there was no harm in giving a relatively small explanation of why he is like he is. At the same time, I confused it by making him really a rather lovable character in terms of his attitude towards plants. If it feels like a defect, then it is a defect. It's how you feel which is the genuine criticism.

Was the whole shape of the book apparent to you before you started writing it? I'm thinking, for example, of the way we're given, as it were, two distorted mirror images – Talbot's journal and Colley's letter – which the reader has to adjust. In a curious way, Talbot's experience and Colley's run parallel, but while Talbot can priggishly pull rank, Colley is socially and temperamentally infirm, and comes to grief.

What you've said may be true, but it's one of those things of which I was entirely unaware when writing. Time and time again people bring to my notice parallels, oppositions, appositions, levels, of which I was unaware. The writing of a novel is at once simpler and more complicated than what people say about it after it's written. I would say that until this moment I never noticed any parallelism between the two characters. The root of the differences between them, I would say, is not so much innate character as their different social positions – Talbot is a gentleman, Colley a promoted peasant, if you like. I would reduce their differences to the question of their respective positions on what I've come to think of as the social pyramid. But obviously they are different in character – that, however, brings up the unanswerable question of how far character stems from social surroundings and how far it is innate.

Did you begin the book in terms of your involvement with the position of Colley, a man who chose to die?

I wonder whether he chose death, though? I don't know how or why he died. All I know is that he did die. But yes, the impulse of the book came from Colley. Talbot came along later as the person who would see what happened to Colley, and it seemed natural that, in a subtle way, Colley should be killed by Talbot. That, of course, is a subtlety beyond a subtlety, since it's a series of levers from Talbot that kills Colley. That's the constructional way in which I thought: once I had that in mind, the book wrote itself.

I imagine, then, that you wrote Colley's letter first?

Colley's letter was written by itself, yes, before anything else (I wanted to keep that quiet, but that's what happened), and the rest was wrapped around it. I could take Colley through one trauma, but not through the trauma that killed him, which has to be alluded to. The more you look at the characters, the more you'll find that none of them are entirely explicable. If a novelist makes an entirely explicable character, then his story drops dead; he's done away with the possible human attribute of free will. One thing I worried about is that, when you start to read Colley's letter to his sister, there's a sort of points–change and the feeling that you've been over it all before. I took a little comfort from the *Odyssey*, where, after a number of books telling the story of Odysseus, you suddenly find Odysseus telling his own story in Phaeacia. He goes back over the ground, and I thought that if Homer can do it, so can I . . . but I'm left with an uneasy feeling. I've really come to the conclusion that what is OK is what you can get away with.

Your strategy in the book involves totally disarming the reader, disabling his evaluation of what he thinks he's learned. Are you in fact very conscious of having such designs on the reader, to the extent of abusing him?

I would accept abusing the reader to some extent. I don't think that anybody, except Pepys, has ever written without an audience in view. Pepys is inexplicable, and I'm glad of that.

I mean, when you employ an ironic structure in the book, the irony can rather harshly betray the values the character embodies.

In a way, I suppose I do pre-empt the privilege of God by seeing the situation from the point of view of two people, and therefore – since no two people can ever see the same universe – undercut both of them. Once you start to see the universe from more than one point of view, all hell breaks loose: characters start turning over in a great wind – like one of Dante's circles – and I think, to some extent, that's the way I feel about life. Also, in the second half of the twentieth century, one has no surety, no safe, solid plank on which to stand: one has to drag out of one's own entrails some kind of validity. In a curious way, one has to look for personal validity without even knowing what validates personality.

That leads me to the question of the modern novelist's relationship to his audience. It seems to us now, for instance, that Trollope and his audience understood one another very well; he raises no question in his books which isn't finally answered. Our modern world obviously lacks a mutually agreed dispensation and common grounds of discourse.

You've really got to be a skull-cracker today. It's a brutal situation in which to write; it's nearly impossible even to try to know what one begins to think. Everything's shifted. I believe in looking out from behind a couple of eyes and seeing what goes on.

Do you ever feel that you can be made too self-conscious about the act of writing – especially when you consider that the critics are in hot pursuit of you, defining and evaluating mythic patterns, ideas and levels of meaning, which they're avid to see realized or modified in each next book?

When I'm writing, I'm not thinking of anything else, that's one thing. Second, I've never read a criticism of my work which is half complicated enough. It's far more complicated than it looks. The third point I should make here is that I find many things much more interesting than writing: I find music, for example, more immediate and emotionally engaging than literature; playing the piano I find much more fascinating than writing, and I've anguished for years because I'm so incompetent at it. I shall die incompetent, but I'm a dedicated amateur pianist.

What actually went on in your life in the gap between the publication of The Pyramid *in 1967 and the publication of* Darkness Visible *in 1979?*

Well, I'm a man of many interests. By 1967, I'd not only made a comfortable living, but had every prospect of being kept in the state to which the world had brought me, so there was no reason why I should write anything if I didn't want to. In that period I wrote at least two long short stories, a film script and a novel from the film script which I've never published because I didn't think it was good enough, as well as half of two other novels which I abandoned. I kept an ample journal, I travelled a lot, I indulged my love of, or obsession with, the piano.

I did a lot of sailing, and I got sunk in a boat – a traumatic experience which stopped me doing anything for two or three years – not because I was frightened but because my wife and daughter had accompanied me. Afterwards, I gradually realized that but for very fragile circumstances I could have drowned them both. I had to come to terms with the fact that I was never again going to be responsible for anybody else's life at sea.

So an awful lot went on in that time. It certainly wasn't any question of having a writer's block, I've never had a writer's block. If I have an idea I can write about it, even if it goes uncompleted. Those years were simply very full of things which have never reached the public.

When you wrote your first published novel, Lord of the Flies, *would it be true to say that you were concerned above all else with telling a good peppy story? Or were you all the time conscious of the full meaning and wider implications of the book? Perhaps it was a coalescence?*

There was a great deal of coalescence, but also a great deal of opening up which at the time I was naive enough to control, whereas perhaps I should have let it rip. I think the book was a kind of escape out of a drab England into the South Seas – followed by a sad realization that, even if you make your surroundings beautiful, you will take yourself with you. I deliberately put in all the elaborations and implications the critics have noted, and a few that haven't been noticed. I felt a tremendous visional force behind the whole book . . . At the end, for example, there's a scene where Ralph is fleeing from the fire on the island, and the point is not just that the boy is being hunted down, but that the whole natural world is being destroyed. That idea was almost as important to me as Ralph himself: the picture of destruction was an atomic one; the island had expanded to be the whole great globe.

You always had it in mind that the boys' drama should be the commentary on a larger text?

Yes, completely. The book concerned what human beings were doing to each other and to the world in which they lived.

When you look back on any particular book do you find that it has reduced in your mind to one predominant idea or motif, or does the complete texture remain with you?

The idea mainly – the generalized idea in *Pincher Martin*, for instance, of what happens to a man when he's dead.

If you begin a book with an idea or theme, do you find that the process of writing about it leaves you feeling more commanding or more helpless?

What generally happens is terribly English. One feels like Sir Roger de Coverley: there's much to be said on both sides – *tout comprendre, c'est tout pardonner* – and that may be awful. One starts in *Rites of Passage* with the idea of this gentleman, Talbot, who completely concurs in the death of this ludicrous little man . . .

Concurs?

Yes – but, instead of that, I find myself having to bring Talbot more and more round to the point at which he recognizes his responsibility, understands it, and then shies away from it. One is always – unwillingly, I think – engaged in the process of being human, or else you're writing articles about chess.

In one of your essays you compliment Stevenson, I think it was, for having complete control over the effects he wanted to achieve. And yet surely no writer is entirely in control of his material?

That is true. Yet I have an innate respect for the idea of genius, in the sense that there are great flaming things that burst out of a great writer, things that a genius may try to control but cannot. *Hamlet*, and bits of Dickens. Below that level, there's the kind of workaday writer who is really a carpenter and makes literary furniture. The chair you make must have four legs of an equal length, so that you can sit on it and forget you're sitting on a construct. The novelist is in control, and yet at the same time he's not in control. That's how I think of the novel. I think Jane Austen was almost as completely in control as anybody has ever been, but was George Eliot? *Middlemarch* runs into the sands in the middle, then emerges from the sands. Casaubon, the scholar, has to run into the sands, and I'm sure George Eliot felt it and had to run into the sands with him – that gives the book its shape. Perhaps the best critic is the ordinary reader, who is interested solely in the degree to which he can allow himself to be absorbed by the deed of the writer: that is the reader's instinctive complicity, which is not the same thing as the willing suspension of disbelief. The writer is, in a sense, split between writing for the desirable naivety of that type of reader and for the equally desirable sophisticated awareness of the literary critic.

Do you think the writer has no business to complain when his book is treated as a sort of joint-stock company?

Provided he is being bought by people, he has no right to complain at all. If he is not being bought, there is a strong argument for saying that he ought not to be writing. It's not a complete argument, because it could put James Joyce out of business . . . which would not be as bad a thing as people think . . .

I'd like to ask you about the issues of moral choice and responsibility in your novels. To take the example of Sophy in Darkness Visible . . .

We're not going to talk about *Darkness Visible* . . . But in general terms, the question of moral choice and circumstances is so complex and vast that I think we're all like Diogenes' man with the lamp, walking through the dark and looking not just for a good man but – more than Diogenes – for a situation in which we can say to ourselves, I am good.

Do you believe that the final reckoning is to find atonement with ourselves and with our own actions, for good or ill, and not with what society has done to us?

I think that in a sense there is nothing but the nowness of how a man feels. One side of me thinks that, and the other side of me – with thousands of years behind it – thinks that you are the sum of your good or your evil. If you have sufficient nonconformist or pagan background, you're stuck with what you are, and there's no easy get-out, no way of ridding yourself of it, for example, in confession.

Robert Frost said that a poem ends in a clarification of life. To what extent do you as a novelist feel that you have to make sense of life?

It's a very interesting question. One could say that to people like you and me life is a series of novels: our assumptions about life are, to a large extent, founded on what we've read rather than on what we've experienced. Surely one of the aims of education for the last 500 years has been to substitute what people have read for what they've experienced, and one could therefore say that the novelist is shaping life. I do think it happens, although the capacity for the novelist to shape life has shrunk as the reading public has shrunk.

If a reader suspects that in Darkness Visible *William Golding hasn't made his mind up, what would your answer be?*

I would pass it off as I pass off any other question about *Darkness Visible*, as one that I'm not willing to answer.

But would you concede the point that the novelist can have his cake and eat it?

Yes, absolutely. Sometimes, but not always.

There are several levels of meaning – or perhaps I should say available interpretation – in respect to the character of Jocelin in The Spire. *The reader is enabled to interpret his* idée fixe *in psychopathological terms, for example, or as sexual sublimation, or as complete vaingloriousness. Equally, he might be a true mystic or a false mystic, or his obsession might be the product of a psychological illness. To put it crudely, do you feel that it's not the novelist's place to come clean about it?*

The point of a novel like *The Spire* is founded, I suppose, in a writer's hubris – in the sense that he thinks or believes that his book will outlast his own life. In that case, what the hell does it matter what the writer thought of his book? The book is on its own. But I am well aware of all those choices you mention. Whether the character is a psychopath or a dedicated mystic who is chosen – like Ezekiel, if you like – to construct a spire which will stand as a sign to the faithful . . . The writer is aware of that whole spectrum, but he doesn't choose between them. What does the right choice matter, so long as the spectrum is there?

And you don't think it necessary to answer the question even to yourself?

I don't think it's necessary at all. One possible way of being a writer is to be what Huxley called a foetalized ape – that is to say, someone for whom nothing is differentiated to the ultimate point; who always leaves his options open, because that's what life is like. The writer probably knows what he meant when he wrote a book, but he should immediately forget what he meant when he's written it.

And you have forgotten what you believed of Jocelin?

Entirely forgotten.

You're asking me to believe that?

I'm telling you to believe it, but whether you're capable of that great act of faith is up to you . . . But of course my own personal belief is that Jocelin was used to make the spire, and that his original vision was absolutely right. That's *my* view.

And yet the means he uses to that end immediately complicate the issue?

But the point is, could he have used any other means? That's what I was interested in. I accepted the fact, the postulate, that Jocelin had a valid spiritual vision of completing this bible in stone, or whatever you like to call it – then the human problem is, how does he do it? I could see no difference between that and any other problem except taking refuge in a kind of quietism. If you're going to do anything like that, you have to use what means there are to hand. Therefore you're going to affect people: that to me was a basic thesis, and I still see no way round it. Equally, the whole spectrum is there, and you *can* call him a bastard; I can't, but you can if you want to.

At the end, you give him a vision of the kingfisher and the apple-tree, and so you remain committed to him?

I remain committed to him, yes, for better or worse.

The genesis of the book presumably lay not in the character of Jocelin but in the very fact of the spire at Salisbury?

Yes, I spent about twenty years teaching in a room with the spire outside the window . . . looking over all these bowed heads and wondering how they built it. It became necessary to explain it and the chance they took in building it where they did, in a swamp. In fact, there was originally a preface to the book which explained that, but I never published it.

I'd like to believe that Bishop Poore had a vision of the Virgin Mary who told him to shoot an arrow and build a church where it landed – because that makes human sense to me. It had to be an act of faith, I could understand that completely. If the faith aspect of the book disappears, that's just my bad luck.

In general, I suppose, readers would like to regard the poet or novelist as a seer, in the old-fashioned sense, perhaps a prophet. Do you have any sense of yourself like that . . . as someone with a message?

Intellectually, I would think that the novelist takes note of more than most people do; emotionally, I don't feel that. Emotionally, I feel that I notice less about people I meet than other people do; I think of myself as being much more preoccupied with what I can only call a nameless mode, in which some *form* of the people we know operates and to which the novelist engages himself. But here I'm saying something which doesn't mean anything about something of which nothing can be said.

Is it the case that, in your own terms, you have a much less ambiguous and uncategorical view of life than you would actually dare put into a novel? Do your own opinions matter to the act of writing a novel?

I have a much more aspirant, hopeful view of human life in the cosmos that I would dare put in my novels. If I can go on talking in terms of paradoxes: I have a categoric view of the cosmos in terms which cannot be categorized. It's surely a fact of human experience to say that in every direction you go you have what cosmologists or astronomers call an event horizon. Theologically speaking, for example, if you examine the doctrine of the Trinity, you come to a point at which you have a black hole . . .

or a white hole, if you like. At that point, there is nothing more to be said, because you go beyond the capacity of the human totality, beyond the capacity of the human intellect to have ideas in it. The same thing is true in every direction. Ultimately, you come to an event-horizon. There is a bound, inside and outside, beyond which we cannot go. That there is a bound is the mystery to end all mysteries – that is all we can say and that it's in place of the light that Newton shed. The Newtonian universe which went on forever is the ultimate damnation. And we now know that's not true. We know that, in every direction, we come to the end of what our human nature can discover, describe or even feel, and this seems to me to be a kind of boundless mercy. We understand that we are not only mysterious in ourselves but in a situation of bounded mystery. It's a controlling factor in my life and in what I write.

Is it important to you to believe that there is a God, and perhaps an afterlife, and that, in some sense, we're answerable to an ultimate destiny?

I cannot *not* believe in God. I hope there is no afterlife. I don't think it matters whether there is an afterlife or not, if God exists . . . and I've never been able not to believe in God. I don't believe in myself, I believe in God, and the problem is much more whether God believes in me. The real point is that, if you believe in God, it is not necessary to believe in yourself, and you can envisage your complete extinction with great cheerfulness, because it is enough for God to exist. Cosmos and universe mean the same thing, but I've decided to make them mean different things. I make the universe mean the thing astronomers see and which Einstein guessed at or defined – and I feel that there must be more than the universe. My guess is that there are infinite cosmoses, infinite universes, and beyond that there is a thing that I call the Good. It seems to me that there could be infinite modes of life, and that they would all be sustained by the beings that inhabit them. In other words, we have invented our own universe. We have discovered that there are black holes out there because we have Hiroshima and Belsen in here: we have made black holes in here and then discovered them out there. I think that we have invented our universe; it is a figment of awareness. I don't think a tree has an awareness, but I think maybe a forest has some kind of glimmering, dreamlike awareness. Maybe there are universes of awful suffering, maybe there are universes of awful pleasure, but I guess that beyond them there must be a Good which is Absolute. I don't see any reason why partial flickers of awareness like us should want to have any further life. It might be that each partial awareness returns to its source. If I have a *scintillans Dei* in me, it's so little like me that you might just as well say that, when I die, I disappear. I'm indifferent to that, and I suppose that the being of God is enough. I'm being quite practical and even impious in talking like this, but the terrible thing is that you are always taken as being goody-goody if you even begin to think in these terms. It is not so. All our grossness, our bestiality, our murderousness, our sexual contrivances and antics, our meanness, criminality, dishonourableness, viciousness: all that is there, in me, and I have *no* wish for that creature to be infinitely extended. So when you ask me if I believe in God, it's not a matter of what I believe, it's what I suspect.

And if there's any question of accounting for ourselves, it's purely a question of answering for our actions here and now?

I'm not even sure whether we can do that.

In novels such as Pincher Martin *and* Free Fall *you postulate a character who is undergoing a kind of purgatory, but you wouldn't project beyond that?*

To project beyond that would imply that one had some kind of knowledge of what it is like to perfect a man, and who knows that? The most a novelist can do is to suggest that this process will go on, and my guess is that, if it were carried far enough, you would disappear. I find it very difficult even to think in terms of freeing the *scintilla* from the perhaps necessary imperfections that have amassed themselves round it.

Do you accept the critical view that in your earlier novels at least you placed most emphasis on aspects of human malignancy?

I would, yes. Before the war I paid lip-service to a progressive view of humanity, and I got desolated by what I discovered during and after the war. I recognized the folly of the naive, liberal, almost Rousseauesque view of man as being capable of perfection if left to himself. I really have to say I found out things which made me feel that human beings do have a strand – or element, if you like – of real malignancy. I think we ignore it at our absolute peril. I also believe that we have a great capacity for love and self-sacrifice, but we can't refuse to recognize that there is active human evil. You only have to examine the Nazis closely: there was deliberate, specific human evil at work in the middle of it. But it is true that as one gets older and more objective, one loses some of the passionate, concentrated earnestness about the problem of a particular generation – my own generation.

One of your critics, I think, has pinpointed your chief concern as being 'moral diagnosis'. Well?

Well, I would be very happy to meet someone who could tell me one single, incontestable truth. I've never found one, and if I start putting one in my books you'll know I'm suffering from hardening of the arteries. The twentieth century is the ambiguous century and I'm a child of my century. I don't feel any enormous, ultimate certainties, except perhaps these tenuous ones I've been talking about – this cosmic view, the multiple universe I guessed at. I think I'm right to present my books in this ambiguous way, because any given universe is partial.

If you're not a truth-seeker, would you say – without hanging yourself – that you're more of a dialectician?

I would put myself very much more on the side of the rhetors than the dialecticians. Nobody would even bother to think of me as a dialectician if they hadn't met me and been seduced by me as a rhetor. Is that not so? I'm neither a philosopher nor a psychologist, I'm a story-teller. I really am a rhapsodist.

How would you describe your own temperament? Are you an obsessional man? An extrovert?

I think I'm obsessed by almost everything. I'm both extrovert and introvert. An optimist, but in my own terms – a cosmic optimist and a universal pessimist.

And not an idealist?

I've never understood that term. I don't know what it means. I don't think we evolve or work towards anything. The real joke on twentieth-century man is that he's taken over evolution from Darwin and applied it everywhere else. The best novelist writing today cannot be better than Jane Austen, he can be different; there's no question of evolution.

Which of your books do you set most store by?

My favourite is *The Inheritors*, which nobody reads. I suppose I sank myself into that book in a way I've never sunk myself into any other, though that's not quite true. Arthur Koestler said that my wife and I were the two Neanderthals, which can be taken as a kind of backhanded compliment with most of the emphasis on the backhandedness. But it's perfectly true that I felt more in sympathy with the Neanderthal people than with *homo sapiens* who destroyed them. The interesting thing about that novel is that at the same time as I was writing it – as I found out later – some archaeologists were excavating a cave in Persia called Shanidar, and they discovered two things about the Neanderthals: (a) that instead of being the man-eating, tooth-gnashing wild animals they were supposed to be, these people had carefully looked after one of their own kind who was a cripple; (b) that they buried their dead in flowers. It's all in a book called *Shanidar* and in a later article in *Scientific American*.

Are there any of your books or indeed parts of books which you regret and might have written differently?

Oh yes, I would probably write them all differently now, though I wouldn't have the strength to do so. I think I would certainly have rewritten *Free Fall*, which is about a young man's adolescent traumata. But I don't know how I would have rewritten it. I do think it's unsatisfactory, although a lot of young people have said how much it meant to them.

Did you feel it reached the wrong conclusion?

I can't even remember what conclusion it reached. I just had the feeling that something was wrong.

Do you share the critics' sense of a co-ordination and development running through your novels, or do you regard them all as different ventures in different modes?

I would have thought they were as different as chalk and cheese. I would agree with the submission that there's an obsessional idea in each book, but any suggestion that it's the same obsessional idea would be new to me and I'd disagree with it.

The act of writing is obsessional. In the last ten years, however, I've cunningly evolved a way round that by writing a journal, which solaces and anoints my need to write. Not that it's stood between me and writing a book. Since *Lord of the Flies* I've had no need to earn my living because people have gone on buying it and buying it – sales in America, for instance, have just hit seven million – so I've got no reason to write a book other than the inside impulse, when it becomes so unbearable inside me that I have to produce one.

To what extent would you countenance D. H. Lawrence's remark about shedding one's sickness in books?

I think he's probably right . . . to some extent but not entirely. There is an objectivizing factor in writing a book which is not based on this self-cure idea, but there is certainly self-help, self-heal, perhaps even self-forgiveness. Equally, there is the coldness of finding a way to approach the big issues of humanity. A book is produced by the whole man, who is more complicated than any other single object in the universe, and its motivation is therefore just as mysterious and ineluctable. Ineluctable – that word makes both of us feel good, doesn't it? We're talking high stuff. Like so many clever one-sentence statements, though, Lawrence's remark is probably susceptible to every conceivable qualification. I think it's broadly true to say that in *Lord of the Flies* I was saying, 'Had I been in Germany I would have been at most a member of the SS, because I would have liked the uniform and so on.' I think that maybe in *Lord of the Flies* I was purging myself of that knowledge . . . I don't think one can go into more detail than that.

Why are you reluctant to talk about Darkness Visible?

I'm not reluctant, I'm just not going to. I decided not to talk about it when I began writing it.

Can you at least tell me how it began?

No, I can't tell you. I don't even know.

I want to ask a question about the way eroticism figures in your novels. With the exception of the Neanderthal people, it seems to be depicted not as a creative force but invariably as an unhappy – even rapacious – symptom . . .

The Neanderthals are human beings.

Yes, but in a sense their love-making is almost impersonal.

It could be that making love to a person is too private to be described, too peaceful . . . and too healthy, too natural an activity to have a part in stories, which must be based on some kind of conflict. I believe and know that love-making can be enhancing, but I also know that it can be a destructive exploitation of another person. Where you have fulfilment and enhancement, you don't get a story, you get the end of a story. There is no *story* about a happy life, there is a happy life. Happy is the country that has no history, happy is the life that has no careful record of the passing of time and of who owes what to whom – but no novel can be made out of that. I think happiness is attainable. It's like Johnson's remark about freedom: every argument is against it, and all experience is for it. We all know what happiness is, we've all experienced it. If happiness is extended into contentment, then it is the end of the story, not the beginning.

Would you have liked to include in your other books the sort of humour and urbanity you put into The Brass Butterfly *and parts of* The Pyramid?

I like to laugh. I like wit and humour, funny stories – clean ones and dirty ones . . . I suppose my outlook is ultimately tragic, but I think it can still be funny. After all, we have great exemplars – people who wrote tragedies with humour in them. I would like to put more humour in my books, but it cannot be spooned in. It's so easy to design the books one would like to write, but in point of fact one writes the books one can write. If someone would present me with a great social comedy, I think I would go very near to selling myself.

Though it might mean changing your nature.

That I probably wouldn't be prepared to do. Hell is probably being in a place where your nature doesn't fit your surroundings.

Have you looked on Greek tragedy as a model in your work?

Enormously, yes. I've taken Greek drama very much as the model for writing. If you examine most of my novels you'll find they fulfil the Aristotelian canons of tragedy – except for *The Pyramid* which is in sonata form.

Do you believe, though, that a tragic vision has 'relevance' in the modern world? As far as the classical definition goes, tragedy invariably has effects on the society in which the hero lives, if only to the extent that his death is seen as a sort of relief, a life-giving and a blessing. The deaths in your novels tend to be more like closed circuits, significant only to the individual destiny.

I suppose I could answer in Dr Johnson's words, 'Ignorance, ma'am, pure ignorance', meaning that I haven't paid sufficient attention to the post-mortem effects of the hero's fall. I do agree that in some curious way there is life-enhancement in the body of classical tragedy. One does feel uplifted by Lear's death. I don't think – and this shows what a critical ignoramus I am – that it's ever occurred to me to think in terms of the hero's death being enhancing to the next generation . . . and the more I think of it, the less I believe in it. When Ralph weeps at the end of *Lord of the Flies*, something is being healed; I think it's an enhancement of life that, in his grief, Ralph understands about the nature of man. I think that is what students feel and why they've gone for the book; in a sense they grow up a bit through the book, because Ralph grows up. Equally, in *Pincher Martin*, this temporal construct called Pincher is destroyed by the merciless cruelty of God which is going to release whatever there is, whatever this wordless, nameless, indescribable thing is. You have to have a basically religious nature to see that.

In Free Fall, *on the other hand, Sammy Mountjoy has run a course of moral dereliction, and there seems to be little suggestion that his death could in any way propitiate what he's left behind.*

That may be what I feel is unsatisfactory about the book: we go down and down, and we don't come up. Mind you, this coming-up business is not as easy as it looks. I don't think *Othello* comes up; I think it's the wrong kind of tragedy, and I'm never going to see it again. It's the wrong shape for tragedy.

There is an ambiguous hopefulness at the end of Free Fall, *isn't there? What happens?*

He's released from his prison in two senses.

Yes, but it is arbitrary, isn't it? It's such a hell of a long time since I last read it, but as I remember it, it was the slight awkwardness of saying something which I was not capable of saying . . . this arbitrariness . . . though I still think people are let out of gaol for no reason. In other words, I still believe in the grace of God. Equally, I think the way I handled it wasn't the valid way.

You mean that a moment of caprice operated as you wrote it?

Yes, caprice rather than grace. It was meant to be grace. I was very likely trying to be too bloody clever.

Is there any particular play you take as a paradigm, or one dramatist you take as a model – Euripides, perhaps?

Euripides was the one I was going to mention. I feel that Euripides was the greatest of the Greek dramatists and the most imperfect. Both Aeschylus and Sophocles could write more coherent dramas, but Euripides completely out-tops them by his very deficiencies. In a kind of rage he produces these incredible pictures with marvellous poetry, and he has to end with a *deus ex machina*. In point of fact, he's producing these great human dilemmas to which we don't know any solution. I've always felt a great kinship with Euripides, and sometimes toyed with the idea of writing about him. I remember now that his example was the justification in my own mind for the *deus ex machina* at the end of *Free Fall*. But it's misfired because people very seldom read Euripides. You write your novel and take the consequences, and the consequences might be that nobody reads your book – a book to which there is no key unless you happen to have read certain other books. Homer had to write his rhapsodies in the awareness of who would understand that particular poetic language.

Is there one particular play by Euripides which stands as a touchstone for you?

I think the *Ion* is one such. A girl has been raped by Apollo, and there are two ways of looking at it: you can take it either that she's been raped by a completely irresponsible force or that Apollo must have a priest for his temple, a priest who must be born of a woman. Euripides chose to turn it into a human drama, and he goes so far that at the end Apollo is ashamed to explain, and Athena comes and does it for him. Similarly, in *Iphigenia*, Artemis steps in, snatches the girl and leaves a stag to be sacrificed; but that's a very complicated play because it was written twice. I am full of admiration for Greek literature. It was always fettered to the basic questions of human behaviour and human life, and therefore it is always relevant. How Shakespeare did as much without having an altar on the stage, I don't know. As far as I'm concerned, when I came to write naturally for myself, rather than for the novel public, what I wrote was fettered to these fundamental human questions . . . how to make society work, what happens to the good man in society, can the good man rule . . .

Would you then acquiesce in the view that you are much less concerned with social questions than with moral, ethical and spiritual questions?

It makes me sound like a po-faced monster. I don't feel like that, but I do feel that questions of good and evil, or how to live in society without exploiting anybody else, are more immediate than anything else.

I think it would be true to say that you haven't given a licence in written form to a large part of your personality, wouldn't it?

This is absolutely true. My friends keep telling me that there's a great deal of me that doesn't get into my books, and I would *like* it to get in. A little bit of it comes in *Rites of Passage*.

Which of your contemporaries do you enjoy reading?

I enjoy Graham Greene, Iris Murdoch, Lawrence Durrell, Angus Wilson, Anthony Burgess . . . I read and enjoy whatever books come near me, but I don't rush out and buy the latest novel. Ann, my wife, is in a way my sieve, and she's a far more acute critic than I am; she's read everything.

You don't find it necessary to disembarrass yourself, as it were, of what other people are writing, in order to get on with your own work?

No, not at all. I'm slightly envious of people who are so firmly rooted in a given area of the twentieth century that they can write about it in great detail . . .

In social terms?

Yes. I'm thinking of Iris Murdoch: *The Black Prince* is a very fine piece of work indeed. I can't locate myself in the twentieth century. It is literally a place in which a man cannot locate himself. When I'm feeling cowardly I rush off and write a novel which has its provenance in some age with which I'm more familiar. Or else I pull up my socks and write about life as it is at the moment.

And of course you put a lot of that in Darkness Visible, *the novel you won't talk about?*

That's absolutely right.

What role does Ann play in your writing?

In a curious way she's my audience.

What in your view is the real reason for writing a novel? Is it to vex people, delight them, to explore a philosophy of life?

Yes, perhaps all those things. And one other: the desire of the novelist to cry for help and hope for somebody who'll provide an answer. Can you understand that one? There is this problem posed with no solution . . . the novelist is saying, look how clever and masterful I am, but he is equally saying, I am one of these poor God-awful creatures caught in this trap – will nobody save us?

There's a paradox involved here in the sense that the reader usually places himself in a passive position and looks to the novelist for his answers.

Of course it is a paradox, and there is nothing that can be said about human life which is not paradoxical. Nobody has ever been able to prove or disprove the solipsistic claim, for instance, if you want to make that claim. So you begin at the lowest level with something that cannot be proved or disproved, and you go on from there into positions which become increasingly ludicrous. That is how we live.

I don't think people should regard writing too much as a sacred office. I would like to feel that the mystique is being taken out of me, because there's an awful lot of mystique being pumped into me one way and another.

· RUSSELL HOBAN ·

Seemingly endless in the fertility of his imaginative and linguistic resources, Russell Hoban writes magical and bizarre
parables, and has been compared to J. R. R. Tolkien, Kurt
Vonnegut and Herman Hesse. He has published more than
forty children's books (including a modern classic, *The Mouse
and His Child* (1969)), and five acclaimed adult novels, *The Lion
of Boaz-Jachin and Jachin-Boaz* (1973), *Kleinzeit* (1974), *Turtle
Diary* (1975), *Riddley Walker* (1980) and *Pilgermann* (1983). By
turns funny, grotesque and puzzling, he creates and enquires
into the mysteries of time and place and pattern. Like the
eponymous hero of his masterpiece *Riddley Walker*, he is essentially a 'connection man', drawing together metaphysics and
magical fantasy. Riddley Walker's profoundly weird and compelling odyssey – his quest for the meaning of the evil riddle of a
post-apocalyptic world – has been widely acclaimed as one of
the outstanding fictional achievements of recent years.

An American expatriate, Hoban has lived in England since
1969. Born in Pennsylvania in 1925, he served in the American
Army during the Second World War and was awarded the
Bronze Star Medal in 1945. He worked first as a successful
illustrator and magazine-cover artist, and then in American
advertising agencies, before taking up his productive career as a
full-time writer.

He now lives with his second wife Gundula and their three
sons, Jake, Ben and Wieland, in a comfortable terraced house
fronting Eel Brook Common in London. The view takes in a
children's paddling pool encircling a wooden bench which

Hoban sees as 'walking on the water'; beyond that, the silver tubes of the District Line dog down towards Wimbledon, up to Fulham Broadway. A segment of the ground-floor sitting-room, a bright cluttered area thrust up against the front bay window, forms Hoban's study: a bulwark of luminous yellow papers, books, equipment (including a communications receiver and a cassette tape-recorder), a festoon of maps (England, Europe, the World), mementos and props – a geometrical design of tiles in red and white, a Punch puppet, a postcard of Lord Shiva from the V & A, and a photograph of a lion with the reassuring legend, 'the race survives'.

A ruminant, keenly observant and decidedly likeable man, Hoban passes disciplined days in the service of his vocation. After a full morning's work, an afternoon nap is followed by more work, while the evening – with the children put to bed – is applied to yet more work or television. The routine is so well established that he sometimes spends days at a time without stirring out of the house, and neglects to take exercise. He gave up cigarettes after suffering a heart attack some time ago, but encourages conversation with generous gins. I talked to him in 1981, a year after the publication of *Riddley Walker*, when he was still working on *Pilgermann*. He is carefully responsive to being interviewed, with the proper proviso that to ask certain kinds of questions is 'like asking the eggshells to explain the omelette'.

★   ★   ★

You came rather late to writing, didn't you – you were over 30, I think – after working as an illustrator and as a copy writer?
I used to win poetry and story competitions in school, and was always writing fragments. But yes, the first writing I sold was in about 1956, a little essay for *Sports Illustrated*.
Do you feel that your early career nourished you as a writer, or that you took some wrong steps?
I used to regret it, but now I think that – all unknowingly – I organized things quite well, because it's only recently that I've had anything to write about. I fell into children's book writing in 1958, so that now I have enough of a backlist – an economic base

– and can do just what I like in novel-writing. It feels to me as if my thinking is just getting ripe, which doesn't necessarily mean that I'll write more. As my thoughts get more and more interesting to me, the output of books becomes less and less pressing. I *say* that while in the middle of writing a book, and when I've finished writing one I itch around until I get another one going, but it's occurred to me that one needn't always be putting together a book.

Was it necessary for you to formulate a policy about what a children's book should be, or was your procedure far more pragmatic? Based perhaps on the fact that you had children of your own and wanted to find ways of interesting them?

No, there wasn't any purposeful going at it at all. My first book was a picture book that I wrote and illustrated myself about construction machinery. The second one was *Bedtime for Frances*. From then on I wrote many of that kind of book, little domestic conflicts which get resolved in a plausible or humorous way. I have complete conviction about what I'm writing: it's between me and the matter itself, not between me and critics or the public.

My children's stories are not all of the same quality. It can happen that I've been asked to write a Christmas book or something, which I can crank out, and sometimes those books are thinner in texture than others. *Harvey's Hideout* is not in a class with *A Bargain for Frances*. Recently my children's books and my adult novels are coming from the same place more than they used to. Not long after I wrote *Lion*, for example, I wrote *How Tom beat Captain Najork and His Hired Sportsmen*, and they both had to do with a rebellion. Tom rebelled against his aunt's authority by fooling around, and Jachin-Boaz rebelled against the life he had got himself into. *Riddley Walker* is a kind of mythic book, and I've also been getting into that area in recent children's books. A book that will be out soon, *The Serpent Tower*, is about a boy who's looking for things that no one can teach him, words in the rain, the essences of things. He buys a wooden box in which there are hexagonal iron pieces like weights. At midnight he stacks up the iron blocks and finds in them a green serpent which is the world serpent . . . the green and living essence of things. Once he's found it, he feels good, he knows what he didn't know before. *The Dancing Tigers* is about a rajah who has a stereo tape cassette player on the howdah of his elephant. When he goes out in the jungle playing light classics, the tigers are offended by his violation of the silence and they dance him to death.

So you're not in the least bit chary of treating any subject or situation in a children's story?

No, I think children can grasp and have an appetite for almost anything if it's done right. But obviously it hasn't occurred to me to deal with adult sexuality in a children's book.

Would you acknowledge any models or influences on your work?

Dickens and Conrad are two of the writers I admire. I read hardly any novels at all now, no contemporary novels. I had always been a heavy reader, but there was a particularly fruitful period in my 30s when the books I was reading opened up for me more than they had before that. I read *Nostromo* about four times, *Remembrance of Things Past* and critical and biographical material. Although I wasn't planning to be a novelist at the time, I seemed to crave the total structure that included Conrad, the man and the work. I'd be very surprised if anybody could find detectable influences in my work, but Dickens is for me a standard of energy and vigour in language, and Conrad a standard of density and muscle. I learnt a lot of lessons during that ten years or so of reading.

In *Nostromo* or *Lord Jim*, for example, you are simply not allowed to go straight to what you think is the heart of the matter. It's a worthwhile approach to the mystery of things to work in veils and baffles, to keep the action enmazed as the reader proceeds with the writer. *Nostromo* is Conrad's best, I think. Even though the story is a model of lucidity in its expression, you somehow never grasp it, and you feel that Conrad equally could not grasp it. He was able to put before you with great verisimilitude a number of historical models of action – governments are overthrown this way, political activists conduct themselves this way – and yet you still can't grasp what happened. So the thing never stops, it goes on living in you.

What about influences on your children's writing?

There's certainly a strong Hans Christian Andersen influence, notably in *The Mouse and His Child* and other stories about toys. But it's difficult to know, if Hans Christian Andersen had not posited talking toys, whether I would have originated that approach. One uses the past as well as one can.

In The Mouse and His Child, *the figure of Manny Rat could perhaps be seen as the archetypal vengeful exploiter and racketeer. Were you at all conscious of using a Jewish stereotype in calling him Manny – which I take to be short for Emmanuel – Rat?*

No, and I'm Jewish myself. I was simply thinking of 'Ratty Man'.

It's a novel that can be read profitably and seriously by both adults and children . . .

To be honest, I thought I was writing an adult book at the time. I didn't make any concessions. Since then I've thought that it's not an adult book, because no adult would take seriously the idea that victory in the battle for the doll's house would make everything OK. To that extent I hadn't grown up when I wrote it. It seemed to me then that winning a territory could make a resolution, and now I don't think that.

Yes, I think a number of critics have considered it an easy and even perhaps a sentimental conclusion.

At the time I was wary of attempting validation through tragedy, which I think the inexperienced writer too frequently attempts – on the premise that if you make it heavy, maybe it will be good. I don't necessarily believe that an unhappy ending is to be taken more seriously than a happy ending. It also coincided with a time in my life when I was trying hard to put things together. I'd left my wife and stayed away for about three months. We got back together and built a brave new house, and I was on for seeing things being resolved by a determined putting-together of elements that had exploded before and might explode again.

Every now and then a critic has taken issue with the happy endings of my adult novels; one critic said that my writing rings truest when I'm dealing with misery and unhappiness and tends to sound false in the happy ending. But in *Turtle Diary* I didn't have a trumped-up happy ending: the book stopped and the people presumably went on. The ending of *Riddley Walker* is one where Riddley has found what he's good for, and the resources to carry on being himself.

And in Kleinzeit *there's a temporary stay of execution?*

That's right. He's made friends with Death and with life. *Lion* resolves in a happy ending, but up to now [1981] my own son and I haven't resolved our estrangement.

Your novels commonly figure two principal characters . . . presumably as a form of complementarity . . .

Yes, I'm quite obsessed with the twoness and the oneness. As a writer, if you feel something very strongly, you feel it must be the universal condition. I intuit that the twoness interfering with the oneness is universal . . .

Interfering rather than complementing?

No, I mean as it manifests itself in *Riddley Walker*, when Riddley was trying to stay one with Lissener and found he was coming in two. We try to stay one with an ideal or with another person, and we find ourselves coming in two all the time. I think there is an explosion in the centre of us, and that not only is all of evolution in us but also all of cosmogony. The original big bang is still in us. In 1965 Penzias and Wilson found that there was a background radiation temperature of 3° Kelvin permeating the entire universe, the fading warmth from the original big bang in which the universe burst out of space–time singularity. I think *everything* is in us.

Did The Mouse and His Child *come to you episode by episode, or did you prefigure the whole story, including the virtuoso excursions concerning the muskrat and the snapping turtle?*

I didn't think that I *was* starting a novel when I began. The possibilities kept opening up, and then at some point I saw what I thought a good kind of episodic structure: a war episode, a science episode, an art episode, a philosophy episode. It's the only one of my novels that I've ever worked out in that way. Since then I don't really impose any structure.

The issue of 'The Last Visible Dog' – the play which Serpentina devises in The Mouse and His Child – *would appear to have bulked*

*so large as to augur some major thematic interests in your adult novels
. . . questions about the nature of time and infinity?*

I do have an obsessive mind, and 'The Last Visible Dog' goes
back to my childhood, when there was a brand of dogfood called
Marco which had the kind of infinity label I described in *The
Mouse and His Child*. What fascinates me is the way the intent
becomes the actuality: although technically they cannot show
you an infinity of dog food cans, once they have established the
intent, then I take it that the infinity follows. In my current
book, *Pilgermann*, I'm preoccupied with Islamic patterns, repetitive patterns. Once you establish the repetitive pattern, it *is*
going to infinity, and your stoppage is simply arbitrary.

*I'm interested in the way Manny Rat has almost as much prominence as
the mouse-and-child. He's credited, for example, with a 'sheer tenacity'
proportionate to the 'nightmarishly durable' mice, and therefore assumes
a sort of negative equivalent of their heroism.*

Oh yes, it's the negative equivalent without which the father and
child could not be, they could have no victory. In *Pilgermann* I've
written, 'Any sequence of events is interesting because of its
positive and negative shapes. Take a pair of scissors and cut
something out, anything. Why not a devil with horns and a tail
and cloven hooves? So, there is your paper devil in your hand,
and there on the table is the paper with the devil-shaped hole in
it. Two devil shapes, one positive and one negative, and both of
them made at the very same moment.'

Did you intend 'The Last Visible Dog' to be a parody of a Beckett play?
Yes.

And what about Muskrat, the misguided mathematician?
Muskrat is a scientist, and crippled; I think science is crippled in a
way.

*Muskrat and Serpentina are funny cameos, though they're treated
ambivalently. We certainly laugh at them, and yet Serpentina does
introduce a notion which I think you take very seriously elsewhere: I
mean his reference to 'the very ISness of TO BE, cloaked in fun and
farce' . . .*

It's my natural bent to see the ridiculous along with the serious
aspects of things. If a work of art is any good it lends itself to
various uses, a number of thought systems.

The Lion of Boaz-Jachin and Jachin-Boaz is a beautifully constructed story or fable. What I'd like to ask about it is whether you now feel that it was too determined, too polished, too completely self-referential?

No, it just worked itself out. It might be that wishful thinking overtook me in the end, with the father and son reconciled, but I didn't plan it. All of my adult novels since *The Mouse and His Child* have just started from some kind of impulse. The impulse for *Lion* came from seeing a photograph of the lion-hunt relief in King Ashurbanipal's North Palace – a tremendous piece of work – which is in the British Museum. It was in 1968, when I still lived in Connecticut, that I first saw the photograph and started making notes; I thought I might get a little supernatural story out of it. I had many notes accumulated by 1970, when I left my family, and it was in 1971 that my current situation put itself together. The lion became something that was evoked by the rage of my son and my own guilt.

Lion then became a parable of the way you would have liked your life to work out?

Lion, yes. *Kleinzeit* arose from a stay in hospital, where I'd gone for tests having to do with my diabetes. I was in a ward where people were dying from all kinds of things, and it came to me that Hospital, like Madhouse and Prison, were always waiting behind the safe façade, and that at any moment one might crash through and find oneself in Hospital. *Turtle Diary* got started when I went to the aquarium to see an octopus . . . there wasn't one, but I saw the turtles. *Riddley Walker* started when I went to Canterbury and saw a reconstruction of the painting of the Legend of Saint Eustace . . . There's a reservoir of all kinds of things waiting to find a channel to hook up with. With each of my novels some object or picture or experience or thing has provided the channel that hooked up with everything that was waiting to put itself together.

The figure of the lion as it manifests itself in the novel is an enigma, as my colleague Ian MacKillop has called it in an essay [Ian D. MacKillop, 'Russell Hoban: Returning to the Sunlight', in Dennis Butts (ed.), Good Writers for Young Readers, *St Albans: Hart-*

Davis Educational, 1977], and I imagine you'd like it to remain so . . .
you wouldn't wish it to be seen in any categorical terms?
No, one wouldn't want the lion to be reducible to some simple
definition. It is whatever it is.
It does incorporate two central aspects in the novel, though – the aspect
of time and the aspect of the son's rage against the father. Can you say
how and why you came to associate those two elements?
I don't remember being that scientific about it. I say in the book
that the only place is time, and the only time is now. As I worked
on the book, the lion became a less and less definable force; it
became whatever was needed as a vital force.
It would presumably be reductive to take the lion as a metaphor for
consciousness, thought, telepathy?
That would be reductive. There is a very short chapter which
says what the lion was ('Ignorant of non-existence he existed,'
etc., chapter 23).
Jachin-Boaz, the father, eventually comes to participate in the anger
through which his son first resurrected the lion. Can you explain why,
at that moment, an outsider – the police constable – actually sees the
lion?
Well, the lion had actuality, it was not simply a private fantasy or
subjective vision. It was something that, in one way or another,
could manifest itself to other people. When the father got angry
enough, when he had realized sufficient of the lion in himself,
the lion then became visible to somebody else.
I'd like to ask you about Boaz-Jachin's – the son's – encounters with the
woman in the red car. On the first occasion, which is treated very
wittily, they read each other's minds, and she rebukes and dismisses
him. The second time around, she hits him, he beats her and makes love
to her, and he's described as 'one who had arrived with chariots and
spears'. Can you say something about that nexus of events?
He becomes the victor in that situation. I've never analysed it,
but at the second encounter the woman acknowledged her
desire, and he was able to cope with her mode of experiencing
the thing on his own.
It's quite a brutal scene.
Yes, but it felt true to me. I think the brutality of that love-
making scene will stand up to examination. Just as in nature we

can see that if the male and female scorpion don't make the right signals, it's disastrous, and we don't recognize that with people. The urge to tear one another apart is always latent even when the intent is to make love. In this case, Boaz-Jachin had to assimilate the twoness and the oneness. In the oneness of desire there was the twoness of destruction, and he absorbed it. He was victorious, he became the kingly victor of the situation in that he triumphed over the immanent disaster.

The women seem to take a secondary place in this novel. Jachin-Boaz's wife occupies a resentful posture, for example, and his new girl – Gretel – an acquiescent one . . .

Well, I have to write from where I am. In *Lion* I saw the action mostly from the male point of view.

But maybe I can ask you to say something more about Gretel, who does not challenge the man's right to do what he wants. She is unusually accepting . . .

I think that would stand up to clinical analysis. The book is autobiographical to the extent that I met a younger woman. Gundula is eighteen years younger than I am. It could be said that any woman who goes for a man almost twenty years older than herself is to some extent looking for a father-figure, someone she can respect and lean on, and – at least at the beginning – be subordinate to. As wives do, Gundula has become more critical over the years, but the binding element in the start of the relationship is that the man wants someone who is going to be sweet and pretty and not give him a lot of static, and the woman wants someone who is older and more experienced and can look after her. Inevitably the woman gains confidence and recognizes herself as someone to be reckoned with, and the man must perforce recognize her as someone to be reckoned with. Parity is established.

One of the central images in Lion *is the map. Am I correct in believing that, at least in this novel, you ultimately reject the concept of mapping anything – and of knowing anything – in favour of surrendering to experience . . . just as Boaz-Jachin and Jachin-Boaz both reject the knowledge they might have acquired from scientific pursuits?*

I *am* a map freak, I love looking at them, and at the same time I recognize that a map is anti-reality. It's an illusion, it's an apparent ordering of things than cannot be ordered; it's the illusion of prediction and control over what cannot be predicted and controlled.

In the last scene of the book, when father and son come together and fling themselves on the lion, is it intended that – in a sense – they exorcize the lion and acknowledge one another?

Yes, they're absorbed into the lion and they absorb the lion into themselves. It hasn't happened between me and my son.

Do you feel then that the ending was at all dishonest?

No, I think it could just as well happen that way. The way things have happened between my 26-year-old son and me is because of the manipulation that has taken place. He was forced to make a choice, because his mother let it be known that he couldn't have her *and* me. There are three thousand miles between us, and she was his source of everything; he opted for her.

Would it be fair to say that – at least in Lion – *you were less interested in characterization than in story, metaphors, formal relations, and the ontological questions that come up again in* Kleinzeit?

I'll accept that. I think it was weighted in favour of ontology versus character.

But you don't feel that it's a weakness in the book?

No, I don't . . . I have to tell you about a seminal experience in my life which took me years to understand. Shortly after I'd begun to freelance as an illustrator, in about 1957, I had a studio in New York City, and I'd sometimes stay in town and sleep over at the studio, which I shared with another artist. We occasionally went to a jazz club called the Five Spot, and one drizzly November evening Ornette Coleman and his group played what I think of as a kind of Proustian jazz, very elliptical . . . he would get something going, and it would disappear, and he would pick it up at some point farther along in the progress. During the break after one of the sets, I spoke to one of his musicians, a horn player, and said, 'I really like the music you're playing because it takes risks.' He said, 'Man, we're not taking any risks. However we're blowing it, that's how we're blowing it tonight.' It took me years to catch up with that. At first I thought that statement was indicative of the decline in artistic standards. But I revisited that statement and that scene for years afterwards – I still revisit it – and began to understand that it was a recognition that you could only operate from where you were operating from, you couldn't put yourself in another place. There was an absence of risk in the sense that you weren't putting together your art for approval by a certain standard, you were putting it together in response to that present moment. That experience has been a great help to me. I recognize the primal truth in it: the work is an expression of where you are at that time. In everything I do, I work on that principle. The book I'm doing now, *Pilgermann*, for example, could easily be open to a number of critical charges – of being self-indulgent, of material being introduced arbitrarily. But my answer is that as the line of this book developed, as the thread of it unwound, certain thought clusters arose at particular places and so they're introduced at those places. I'm not in the business of making clockwork novels which go from A to B when you wind them up, I'm at the service of the material that enters me. It takes me where it wants to go, and I might not know why I'm going there. That's all right. The material requires of me that I make it manifest as clearly and as beautifully as I can. There my responsibility ends, and whether you or I understand it is secondary.

Yes, it strikes me that Kleinzeit – *where we witness the relationship between the writer and his yellow paper – is a novel which seems to work out the view that the writer is not the maker of what he utters but a receiver and transmitter.*

It hasn't occurred to me that that was so much evident in *Kleinzeit*, but that is how I feel. I don't think of myself as the creator but as the medium through which certain things come. It's difficult for me to see how other people can feel otherwise. I never use the word 'creative' in connection with writing. I feel as if we are all particles of a single consciousness, and that the vital force which moves the universe requires of us to be its organ of perception.

You mean, the writer is gifted in a double sense?

He's gifted in the perception of something that wants to be made manifest, and he has ways of making it manifest.

You're saying that the writer should abandon the rational and the deliberative, and yet it could seem ironic that your own work – with its brilliant organization, inventiveness and ingenuity – provides something of an argument to the contrary.

I'm flattered, but I think what you're finding is a responsiveness to the essence of things. I think that if you take in and offer anything as well as you can, something essential and primal will have happened. There's a combination of humility and arrogance: humility in the sense that I'm not a creator – I can't originate anything, I'm a perceiver – and arrogance in that I have faith in my own perceptions, that if I leave myself completely open it will put itself together in a way that will matter.

Much of your thinking in recent years – as it's appeared in Riddley Walker, *for example – is taken up with aspects of energy and what you've just called the essence of things. Can you give some account of your recent thinking on those matters?*

I don't want to really. My current thinking on these things is in the context of the book I'm working on now, *Pilgermann*, and the language of these thoughts is in the idiom of that book. I don't want to pick the raisins out of the cake before it's served, and I don't want to turn the kinetic into the didactic.

Can you say how the instrumental figure of Redbeard came to be introduced into Kleinzeit? *He's a character who challenges the yellow paper, refuses to be killed off by it, acts as an agent for Kleinzeit by providing him with an unaccommodated environment – a bare room in which he can write – and yet finally cedes his position to Kleinzeit . . .*

There actually *is* a Redbeard. When we lived on Beaufort Street in Chelsea, I used to go jogging along the Embankment in the morning, and used to see a bloke there with a red beard, and a bottle, who was obviously sleeping rough. One morning he said 'Good morning' to me, in the way a certain kind of person can say it who's freed himself from convention by not being a competitor. He said 'Good morning' in the way that showed that, if allowed, he would enter into my life all of a sudden. I took note of it, and noted the truth and plausibility of the fact that – if things had been facilitated for him at all – he *would* have become part of one's life.

Redbeard would have been someone who'd had a go at the

yellow paper, and he'd want to get it off his back and onto Kleinzeit's.

Some of the other voices in the book – I mean, Hospital, God and Death – are differentiated in their effectualness, aren't they? God is not useful, Death turns out to be kindly and indulgent, while Hospital is perhaps less of a burlesque figure and offers cryptic but cumulative suggestions of Orphic harmony. For instance, he does give Kleinzeit hints of a possible access to the 'inside of things, the places under the places'.

Hospital is more pragmatic than the other two entities. He's of necessity accustomed to the nitty-gritty and the crunch situation. God doesn't come into it except as an offstage voice.

The attitude Kleinzeit has to adopt is one of struggle and enquiry, while the goal is acquiescence. How do you account for that paradox?

It's true somehow, and I couldn't exactly explain it. In one book – I think it's *The Midrash*, which is a commentary on the Bible – it explains that Jacob never actually died, he got so tuned in to things that at the end of his life there was no difference between his mortal state and the next state. I must say that there's truth in that, because I used to be very much afraid of death when I was young, and I find now that the idea of fear and the idea of death simply don't enter into it the way they did then; it's simply the kinetic rejoining the potential. These are big heavy things, and for there to be such profound changes in one person's consciousness must mean that there's some validity in the idea. How could one progress from being afraid of death to not being afraid of death unless there were some truth in these developing perceptions? In the novel I'm working on now the protagonist is dead; he's been dead since 1099, and he's speaking from a state of being waves and particles . . .

I wonder if you'd find this comment by Hazlitt appropriate to reading Kleinzeit: 'That wit is the most refined and effectual which is founded on the detection of unexpected likeness or distinction in things, rather than in words'?

I think that the thingness always grabs me . . . There's a little piece in the latest issue of *Time* magazine about slips of the tongue, how words and their opposites form a kind of constant partnership in the mind – and not just the opposites but all kinds of peripheral and secondary meanings. I think that that's so, there's no such thing as a simple meaning for anything: things always move in reflective, refractive and diffractive modes.

Have you given much thought to what actually constitutes a novel by definition?

No, I'm not troubled with any definition or limitation of the novel. It could well be that I'm getting to a point where to classify the book I'm working on now as a novel is an act of charity. Maybe *Pilgermann* isn't a novel, maybe the thought material is more important than the narrative. It could well be a progression of fragmentary essays rather than a novel, and I don't really think it matters. A book is an action – something is moving – and whether it happens pre-eminently as character and event or as thought and elucidation doesn't matter.

Would you agree with Henri Bergson's remark (which might again be most suitably applied to Kleinzeit*) that 'The comic expresses, above all else, a special lack of adaptability to society'?*

Well, society has to do with consensus. Everybody agrees on the lowest common denominator of reality that they can deal with, and the comic or the visionary or the ecstatic may choose not to abide by that consensus. I don't. People often ask me, what is fantasy? What I say is, if there are several people in this room, and if one of us has in his mind a green dragon, then the dragon is part of the reality of this room. By that token, I accept that reality is whatever comes to me, in any mode whatsoever. Wittgenstein said, 'The world is whatever is the case,' and I think that's what reality is.

Did you wish the reader to feel implicated in Kleinzeit's experience, or does the comic aspect have the function of maintaining an ironic distance?

I don't concern myself with the reader's relationship to Kleinzeit. I'm telling it how it was, and that's always the truth for me at the time that I'm telling it. I'm *with* it, I'm there.

In Turtle Diary *you again employ a 'twoness' – in this case, through the characters of William and Neaera, who occupy alternate chapters. The two figures are differentiated in certain respects but are curiously alike in their nature and responses . . .*

It came to me that they would perceive things in a similar way, and yet they wouldn't be able to get together beyond the one action they accomplish.

Do you in fact see them as one character split into two for narrative purposes?

It could be argued that there is only one consciousness and all of us are parts of it . . . and that these two facets of it are only facets of the one thing, they can't do anything with each other.

The adventure William and Neaera undertake together in liberating the turtles turns out to be totally unhindered. It's an exhilarating experience to read, and we have to reckon with the fact that the emotional and psychological undertow of their experience is in the end just as important as what they do. Both protagonists, for example, feel a sense of inertia and disappointment after the event . . .

But they're both better placed to continue after the event. I haven't read much Kierkegaard, but in *Anxiety and Dread* he talks about the dread of the possible, and I think that in *Turtle Diary* both William and Neaera had dread of what *might* happen. We're not afraid of what we *can't* do, we're afraid of what we *can* do.

Neaera eventually begins to find a new life with George Fairbairn . . .

Not so much a new life with George as a new life in which George has been the catalyst, let's say.

. . . while the effect on William seems to be more ambiguous, since he goes through another trial in which he fights with Mr Sandor.

Neaera points out in an early chapter, 'Sometimes I think that the biggest difference between men and women is that more men need to seek out some terrible lurking thing in existence and hurl themselves upon it. . . . Women know where it lives but they can let it alone', and Sandor is William's monstrous challenge.

But weren't the turtles a monstrous challenge?

Not in the same way. The turtles were not antagonists to William, they didn't set themselves up as the enemy that had to be dealt with. There are situations in life to which the only satisfactory response is a physically violent one. If you don't make that response, you continually relive the unresolved situation over and over in your life. William made that response. I haven't always in my life . . . I've rarely made that response, and because of that I'm doomed to relive the unresolved situations over and over again.

What George Fairbairn offers Neaera is an acceptance of life which is paradoxically close to surrender or indifference . . . passive and unstriving. In a sense she seems to resign her struggle by opting to live on George's terms.

Neaera isn't resigning her struggle, she's advancing to the point where she needn't make a false struggle.

Gillian McMahon-Hill has pointed out ['A Narrow Pavement says, "Walk Alone": The Books of Russell Hoban', Children's Literature in Education, *20, Spring 1976] that William is closer to you personally than Neaera is, but I wonder if that's entirely true? It seems to me that Neaera offers perceptions which are crucial to your own thinking – 'anything is whatever it happens to be' . . . 'Nothing to lose, the present moment to gain, the integration with long-delayed Now' . . . 'The things that matter don't necessarily make sense' . . .*

William and Neaera are both me . . . Putting together a book has to do with the use of what we think of as the male and female elements – the male element as active and entering, and the female element as passive and being entered – and it's possible that the strongest elements in *Turtle Diary* have to do with what are thought of as the *passive* elements. Sometimes what we think of as the balls of the thing – its pre-eminent strength – has to do with what could also be called the passive element. I thought of William and Neaera as two aspects of one entity.

To what extent is the book an autobiographical allegory?

All I can say is that I recognize myself as a particle of consciousness, and it's *on* me, it's my responsibility, to offer my perceptions of what was happening. There's no barrier between the mental life and what happens to me in the world. It occurred to me today – and I wonder if this is universal? – that I don't attribute to other people the amount of thought and mental experience that's happening in my own head. It's as if I think that people out on the street have solid heads, while I have a hollow head, I'm thinking about every possible thing since the time when my consciousness became lit up. So I assume that there's a continual falsity going on, because I know that the head of the passer-by is as hollow as mine but I don't know what's going on in it.

In the case of Riddley Walker, *the eponymous hero is striving for an interpretative organization of his experience, but what the book seems to put in question is the very notion of systematic truth.*

What it comes down to in the end is that Riddley recognizes himself as one on whom it is to think about these things that happen that are not easily explicable.

In one sense the book is an exercise in logomachy. It's presented in a degenerate kind of English. Did you decide on an argot when you first started work on the book?

No, the first version began in straight English and went on to page 500. I didn't theorize about it, but as I worked it obstinately insisted on moving out of straight English into a corrupted English. Now that I think of it, I don't see how it could have been conceived otherwise. Language is an archaeological vehicle, full of the remnants of dead and living pasts, lost and buried civilizations and technologies. The language we speak is a whole palimpsest of human effort and history. The language of the debased and degraded future that Riddley lives in is bound to be full of uncomprehended remnants of what we have today; to have written that novel in received English would have been ridiculous. One thing I thought it would do would be to slow the reader down to Riddley's pace and level of intake; the reader would have to plod through word by word and take things in along with Riddley.

The first version also had too much action and too many people; I realized that the thing wanted to be much more concentrated, with fewer people. I think I returned fourteen or fifteen times to page 1 before I finally got a version that would go all the way. The process had to do with distributing a more reduced scope of action among a small cast of people. I had found myself becoming too concerned with physical movement and being pulled away from the central matter of the book. It's a question of getting the material into words that are appropriate for the mode of being for that particular book. Goodparley and Orfing become the complementary parts of the authority that Riddley rebels against, and Lissener and Riddley the complementary parts of the rebellion against this authority. Riddley himself is a particular kind of artistic consciousness.

Can you enlarge on that?

Well, as he says on the last page it's on him to think about certain things: Punch's crookedness and why Punch will always try to kill the baby. And a whole lot of other things that he tells us about in the course of his story: oneness into twoness and wood into stone and the thing that's in us 'afeart of being beartht'. He's a connection man and it's on him to make connections. Years ago I read a science-fiction story (was it by Heinlein, Clarke, Azimov? I'm not sure) in which a member of the crew of the spaceship was a nexialist – it was his function to make connections. That rang a bell with me and stayed in my mind because the word worked so well and gathered to itself so many significances. It seems obvious to me that all things are connected and a function of art is to explore the connections and engage with the action revealed by them. The artist must therefore have a lower threshold of intake than the non-artist. All kinds of flashes and flickers, bleeps and glimmers come into the mind, and it is my belief that the artist must deal with all of them, cannot shut out anything as being without significance. And to me much of what is immensely significant cannot be explained, it can only be told about – such things as the wood into stone in the forest of columns in the crypt at Canterbury or the iron rings at Portknockie flaking into rust that looks like wood bark – there's not much you can say except, 'Look!'

As a sort of mythographer, if that's the right term, Riddley comes up against the barrier of a radical etymological confusion. Can you say any more about why the corruption of language became so central to the book?

I can't give you a rational answer, but why is it that language is always expressing a vulgarization and a debasement of everything and yet is still connected to past nobility and exaltation? Language is always a many-levelled thing, and in *Riddley Walker* the language carries in it the ghost of a lost technology and a lost scheme of organization.

The book does seem to present the view that language cannot communicate any conceptual truths, and that psychical responses should be seen to take precedence over rational deduction.

I suppose it does in the sense that the '1st knowing' that Riddley and Lorna Elswint talk about is not something that comes with language, it's pre-lingual. Certainly the rational knowing of anything only gets us up to a point, and that point is not far enough.

Can you give any account of how and why Dionysus, St Eustace, Punch and Judy, and Orpheus came to be combined in your thinking about the book?

There can't be a simple answer to that . . . Walter F. Otto writes in *Dionysus, Myth and Cult*, 'The elemental depths gape open and out of them a monstrous creature raises its head before which all the limits that the normal day has set must disappear. There man stands on the threshold of madness – in fact, he is already part of it even if his wildness which wishes to pass on into destructiveness still remains mercifully hidden. He has already been thrust out of everything secure, everything settled, out of every haven of thought and feeling, and has been flung into the primeval cosmic turmoil in which life, surrounded and intoxicated with death, undergoes eternal change and renewal' [trans. Robert B. Palmer, Bloomington and London: Indiana University Press, 1965, p. 140].

What did you find so compelling about the Legend of St Eustace that it inevitably formed part of the syncretism of the novel?

Well, after I'd left my first wife, I had the feeling that my children were diverging in all directions from me. I felt an immediate identification with St Eustace – this poor bastard treading water in the middle of the river while his children are carried away from him. I intuited that there was something universal in that situation.

And the 'Eusa Story' that figures in Riddley Walker, *should that be strictly taken to suggest a debased version of the Legend of St Eustace?*

As well as I can remember, when I saw the Eustace painting several things came into my head at once – the idea of the corrupted Eustace legend and the travelling puppeteers telling the story in this desolate landscape long after our civilization and our technology have been destroyed. I also remember seeing Percy Press and his son do a Punch and Judy show. He's dead now, but Percy Press was more or less the foremost practitioner of Punch and Judy in London, and he had a little patter with his son before Punch appeared . . . I had that in mind too.

What about the figure of Lissener in the novel, the deformed child without eyes?

In the earliest version he was a full-grown man and not deformed, but at some point I wanted him to be a child, about the same age as Riddley. I wanted Riddley to be one thing and Lissener another.

The quest that all the principal characters undertake is both sacred and temporal, isn't it? On the one hand, it seems to be a quest for the spiritual and the numinous, and on the other hand it's a quest for knowledge and power . . .

Yes, and there's a constant confusion between the two. Given a debased population, I think they would instinctively reach out for the thing that destroyed the technologically advanced people who came before . . . they'd want the thing that went bang. Riddley lends himself to the production of the '1 little 1'; he can't withhold himself from it. That's why, at the end of the book, when the kid says 'Drop Johns ryding on his back', Riddley is aware that he carries some guilt.

I think *Riddley Walker* is a religious book, and it took me up to a certain point from where I proceed in this new book. It's a religious book because it's a response and an offering to the numinous in everything. I say it's a religious book because of what I feel working in me as I write and because of the action that I feel in the writing.

Does your sense of religion involve a god?

It involves a god, but it isn't a god as He, it's a god as It, a force that has no comforting personification of any kind.

I know that you're interested in Indian music, and in Indian myths. What aspects of Indian myth or teaching most appeal to you, or strike a chord with your own intuitions as to man's being, endeavour and destiny? I wonder, for example, how seriously you actually take Lord Shiva's entrance in Kleinzeit *(despite the jaunty treatment of his brief dialogue with Kleinzeit there)?*

It's an impossibly difficult question. Everything in my being
adds up to where I am now. And my memory is so rotten that I
can't say when it was that this or that idea that seems always to
have been with me arrived. To separate individual ideas from
the mass immediately creates a falsity because then the words
stand there in a vacuum and look like slogans or mottoes. At
some point the idea of reciprocating creation and destruction as
personified by Shiva accorded with my experience of the world.
At some point the Zen idea of the archer, the shot and the target
being one thing became part of me. At some point the Zen
saying, 'A long thing is the long body of Buddha; a short thing is
the short body of Buddha' suddenly leapt into significance. At
some point the words from the *Heart Sutra*, 'Here, O Śāriputra,
form is emptiness and the very emptiness is form; emptiness
does not differ from form, form does not differ from emptiness'
[trans. Edward Conze, London: Allen & Unwin] became very
strong and active for me. Also I take in a lot from pictures, I
always have. I have a big book, *Early Cola Bronzes*, by Douglas
Barret, published in Bombay, full of wonderful photographs of
bronzes of Shiva and Krishna and Parvati and other gods and
goddesses in various aspects and attitudes. I've got a lot out of
that book – not thinking, just taking it in through the eyes. Just
now the Islamic idea of multiplicity arising from unity is much
with me. There are no dead gods, there are no false religious
ideas, they are all part of the continually developing action
between It and us.

Are you a cosmic optimist?

I don't know that I could say that. In *Pilgermann* the character
says that maybe the purpose of life is to manifest death, 'God
being no longer agent has been absorbed into process and
towards unknowing at the wheel with the rest of us. . . . One
assumes that the world simply is and is and is, but it isn't. It is
like music that we hear a moment at a time and put together in
our heads.'

Is your work moving towards a synthesis, a philosophy of life?

No, *Pilgermann* is a bit further on from *Riddley Walker* and a bit
deeper into being. I don't think I could state a philosophy of life
. . . because this book has many different attempts to say what's

what for the narrator from many different angles of approach; some may overlap, some may be contradictory.

The epigraph you chose for Riddley Walker *is a logion from the Gospel of Thomas in the New Testament Apocrypha. Did you deliberately fashion the 'Eusa Story' in the novel by analogy with that Gospel?*

Well, partly. The Littl Shynin Man says, 'Yul fyn me in the wud yul fyn me on the water lyk yu foun me in the stoan,' and in the Gospel of Thomas Christ says, 'Cleave a (piece of) wood: I am there. Raise up the stone, and ye shall find me there.'

Do you find you can assent to all the logia of the Gospel of Thomas – quite apart from their place (albeit uncanonical) in the teaching of the Christian Church – or are there just a few of them which touch you and inform your intuitive sense of 'religion'?

What I need gets absorbed by me, what I don't need doesn't.

Some of the logia seem almost impenetrably gnomic.

Well, if you don't try to penetrate them, they seem acceptable without explication.

What does the Punch story mean to you?

Percy Press, old Punch professor, said to me, 'Punch is so old he can't die', he is immortal, he triumphs over everything. Punch is that force that has no morality, no law; he wants immediate gratification for whatever urge he has at the moment. *Our* task, our burden, our human inheritance, is to try somehow to put together our need for a system of morality and our recognition of the amoral, unlawful urges in us. But as soon as you try to abstract the essence of the thing and spell it out, it sounds very dull.

In terms of novel-writing, then, you much prefer pictures to diagrams?

Yes, indeed. Certain things become absorbed in the writing, but the final synthesis becomes whatever it becomes for the reader. To get the full amount of juice out of my novels, you don't need to systematize and analyse. The novels have to be let live as they manifest themselves.

Do you have strong feelings about the real purpose of literature?

Some years ago I read *The Dynamics of Creation* by Anthony Storr, who says in essence that art is a survival-adaptation. And I agree with him. Art gives us ways to approach actuality, gives us handles to reality, ways of dealing with what is happening. Whether or not there is any point to our survival, I couldn't say. All I can say is that as part of the collective consciousness that seems to be required by the vital force of this universe, my function seems to be to take in the world and to put together my intake in certain ways that afford handles to reality. It's my nature to do it, and it seems to be the nature of the material to offer itself to me that way. Beyond that it doesn't seem to matter. Certainly I'm on the side of the human race, I want us to outlive this planet and to go out into space and colonize other planets, but at the same time I can recognize that we might simply be an effort that will exhaust itself and go no further. The function itself is the answer to the question, why function? It feels like what I'm meant to be doing. I always feel as if the novelist is a shaman who is functioning for his tribe, he's offering his experience for the use of the rest of the tribe.

In conclusion, can you explain a little more what you meant when you said that your children's books and adult books are drawing closer together?

I think that my children's books now are being less didactic and are going deeper to the essences of things. They are looking for ways of dealing with the same things that my adult novels deal with . . . life and death and birth.

· DAVID LODGE ·

Professor of Modern English Literature at the University of Birmingham, where he has taught since 1960, David Lodge is married with two children. After graduating from London University, he spent two years, 1955–7, as a conscript in the Royal Armoured Corps, an experience which gave him the subject for his angrily anti-establishment second novel, *Ginger, You're Barmy* (1962). 'My first two books, *The Picturegoers* and *Ginger, You're Barmy*, had had their moments of humour', he has written, 'but both were essentially serious works of scrupulous realism' ('An Afterword', *The British Museum is Falling Down*, 2nd edn, 1981). With Malcolm Bradbury in 1963 he wrote for Birmingham Rep. a first review entitled *Between These Four Walls*, which galvanized his taste for satirical and parodic writing.

> Comedy, it seemed, offered a way of reconciling a contradiction, of which I had long been aware, between my critical admiration for the great modernist writers, and my creative practice, formed by the neo-realist, anti-modernist writing of the 1950s. (ibid.)

In 1964–5 he won a Harkness Commonwealth Fellowship to the USA, where he completed his first mature comic fiction, *The British Museum is Falling Down* (drawing on his own experience as a postgraduate research student).

The British Museum is Falling Down (1965), whose subject is the effect of the Catholic Church's teaching about birth control on the lives of married Catholics, was 'essentially conservative in its final import', Lodge has explained, 'the conflicts and misunderstandings it deals with being resolved without fundamentally disturbing the system which provoked them'. He again rehearsed the subject, more extensively and far more disturbingly, in the comic chronicle of *How Far Can You Go?* (1980, Whitbread Book of the Year).

Lodge's exuberant satirical gifts found an equally apt subject for *Changing Places* (1975, Hawthornden Prize, *Yorkshire Post* Fiction Prize), in which two academics, Philip Swallow and Morris Zapp – the one an Englishman, the other an American – suffer perfectly observed cultural shocks when they swap countries and campuses.

Blending benevolent comedy and satire, Lodge's most recent novel takes the form of a quest: *Small World* (1984) relates the global romping and plotting of assorted academics, including Zapp and Swallow. As the guileless Persse McGarrigle pursues the 'pure ideal' of Angelica – his Grail – so the gurus of literary theory make their plays for power. Dogging the always elusive satisfactions of romance, Persse's career runs parallel to, and perhaps implicitly comments upon the manoeuvres of the many other characters who intrigue for professional success. In the context of one of his book reviews (*The Sunday Times*, 27 February 1983), David Lodge has pertinently written, 'Narrative and sexual intercourse have in common, as Roland Barthes observed, that the pleasure of each is enhanced by the postponement of climax.'

As an established academic, Lodge himself undertakes global travel on occasional short lecture tours, and in recent years he has delivered papers including 'Mimesis and Diagesis in Modern Fiction' and 'Joyce and Bakhtin: *Ulysses* and the Typology of Literary Discourse' (in Lausanne and Seoul respectively). He has published four books of literary criticism – *Language of Fiction* (1966), *The Novelist at the Crossroads* (1971), *The Modes of Modern Writing* (1977) and *Working with Structuralism* (1981) – in all of which his willingness to attend to the practices of modern literary theory, without subscribing to any one critical camp or doctrinaire ideology, is in accord with the essentially humane cast of his fiction. 'The more the characters are allowed to speak for themselves in the narrative text, and the less they are explained by an authoritative narrator,' he has written elsewhere (*The Times Literary Supplement*, 5 November 1982), 'the stronger will be our sense of their individual freedom of choice – and our own interpretative freedom.'

I talked to him in March 1984 in his large standard office – burdened bookcases, attendant chairs, the bare expanse of a seminar table, all evenly lit by big modern windows providing a view of grass and paths and student processes – at the University of Birmingham, and began by inviting him to describe his career and background.

★   ★   ★

I was born in Dulwich, south London, in 1935, and was brought up in a suburb called Brockley, a somewhat seedy, neglected bit of London. My father was a professional dance musician (now semi-retired), an artistically gifted man from a poor background; he'd left school at 14. He started playing saxophone and clarinet in dance bands, and then went professional and played in nightclubs and BBC bands; he started to sing on the radio just before the war. He is English with a Jewish grandmother. My mother had an Irish father and a Belgian mother: she was a Catholic, and that is why I was brought up as a Catholic. My father is a non-denominational, vague Christian. I was an only child; my mother lost a child after I was born, and my father went into the Air Force as a musician. He was away for most of the war. My mother and I lived in the country, in Cornwall and in Surrey, for long periods of the war. So I had that experience of being torn away from home at about the age of 4½, because of the war, and being separated from my father. It's the experience I drew on in *Out of the Shelter*, which is in some ways the most autobiographical of my novels.

After the war we came back to the same house in London. The middle of the road had been blasted by a flying bomb, and there was a big bomb site which became a kind of adventure play-ground for me and my friends. I then went to a Catholic grammar school in Blackheath. My father had a little group in a nightclub called the Studio Club in London, and his connections in show business provided a sort of avenue out of what was otherwise a rather drab, lower-middle-class, suburban existence. He would meet fairly well-known people and mention that his son wanted to be a writer: he showed my stories to people like Kenneth Tynan.

On the other side of the family, both my mother's siblings ended up in Europe after the war. My aunt worked as a civilian secretary for the American Army of Occupation in Germany, and I had a couple of holidays in Germany at a time when it was very difficult for British people to travel to the continent – certainly for people of my class. My aunt lived in this rather affluent and euphoric American expatriate community, which was really having a ball in post-war Germany. I first went out there at the age of 16, from austerity into an extraordinary world of plenty. My uncle, who had also been in the Air Force, married a Belgian girl after the Liberation and settled in Belgium, so I also went to Belgium quite a lot. That gave me periods of escape from the simple and restricted life of the 1940s; it gave me an appetite for travel and broader horizons which I might otherwise not have had.

I was a classic product of the 1944 Education Act, the first generation who got free secondary schooling. A state-aided Catholic grammar school propelled me out of my class into the professional middle classes, and I went to read English at University College London. My school, I think, had never sent anyone to university before my year, and it couldn't give us much help: I didn't *know* there were universities other than Oxford, Cambridge and London. I didn't presume to apply to Oxford and Cambridge, so I applied to the local place. It was fortunate because UCL was an exceptionally good department in those days, with people then at the lecturer grade who went off shortly afterwards to get Chairs – Terence Spencer, Randolph Quirk, Harold Jenkins, George Kane – and the main literary professor was James Sutherland. I was also taught by Winifred Nowottny, a very charismatic teacher who had a big influence upon me critically: she turned me on to linguistic and stylistic approaches to literature. Without doubt I think it was at that time the best English department in the country, and it was quite by chance that I ended up there.

I went up very young – too young, I think – at about the age of 17½, so I floundered for about a year. I got a first in my degree in 1955, and at the time of taking my finals I had ambitions to be a writer and wasn't really considering research. I felt I wanted broader horizons (I didn't quite know what) and I had to do national service anyway, but because I got a first-class degree they offered me a state studentship, which I had not actually applied for; I thought I would accept it and defer it until after I had been in the Army. After about three weeks of Basic Training – as you will know from reading *Ginger, You're Barmy* – I was quite sure that I wanted to go back to the academic life. The plot of *Ginger* is invented, but the background is a literal transcript of what happened to me in the Army. So in 1957 I went back to UCL to do an MA, which in those days was a two-year research degree. I had started writing *The Picturegoers* while I was in the Army, and finished it shortly afterwards (I had already written one novel during my first long vacation as an undergraduate), and I sent it to Michael Joseph at the suggestion of my school English teacher, who had been a great influence upon me, but it was turned down. I eventually sent it to MacGibbon & Kee, who took it, and my editor there was a man called Timothy O'Keeffe; they gave me a contract for £75 in three instalments. By that time I had become involved in writing this enormous thesis, which turned out to be about 700 pages long, on 'Catholic Fiction Since the Oxford Movement'; they decided to change the rules and put a word limit on MAs after another guy and I submitted theses of that length.

The Picturegoers was published only in 1960, because I had to postpone any revisions of it until after I finished the thesis, although I had started writing the novel in 1956–7. I got married in 1959, and I started to apply for university jobs, but without any success at first, so I took a job with the British Council in London, a one-year-contract post teaching English to foreign students and giving a weekly lecture to French *Assistants* on literature from *Beowulf* to Virginia Woolf: it was fun for one year. Then I came to a temporary assistant lectureship at Birmingham in 1960, and they have kept me on.

You've had a very successful career, both as a university teacher and as a writer. How much, do you think, would you put it down to the fact that you are dedicated and scrupulous in your work?

I think I am fairly diligent and work-oriented, and I'm patient. I have had quite a lot of disappointment – who hasn't? – and I don't think I was particularly privileged or favoured in my early years. In fact I always felt that people slightly underestimated me, and they were surprised when I came up with the goods. But I certainly have no complaints about fortune or the way the academic world has treated me. I have been very fortunate to the extent that such success as I have had didn't all come in a rush when I was young: it is very difficult for young writers who make a big hit with their first novels, living with that success and the strain of expectation which is based upon it. My first novel was only a modest success and did not win prizes, and the second novel, *Ginger, You're Barmy*, was quite well received, but I don't think I really made it as a writer until *Changing Places* in 1975, when I was 40. I went through a crisis of faith in myself after my fourth novel, *Out of the Shelter*, which did seem to flop; from the publishing point of view it was a total flop, and yet I had invested a lot in that book: it was very personal. I was very discouraged when it received very few reviews indeed, after a good reception for *The British Museum is Falling Down*.

Out of the Shelter is perhaps the most sober of your novels. Did you write it as a sort of therapy?

I wasn't conscious of it as a confessional or purgative novel in that sense. I hoped it would have some cultural–historical representativeness, a sort of international novel in the Jamesian sense, and also be a kind of *Bildungsroman*. In the late 1960s I was very conscious of remembering the war, feeling myself on the other side of the wall from everybody who came afterwards. I wanted to recover that sense of growing up through the war and into the period of austerity, being a meritocrat and so on; and that experience of going to Germany at the age of 16 had been a rite of passage. In 1951 England had been turning its back on austerity and socialism, and getting ready for the boom of the

Macmillan years. So I tried to write a really ambitious socio-cultural novel, in the form of a *Bildungsroman*: it didn't quite come off, but that was the motivation.

I think it's a much better novel than readers obviously thought when it came out, in 1970. Although it starts in a very low key, it develops really quite a powerful sense of personal and political discovery when the boy Timothy goes to Heidelberg: the narrative cleaves to his point of view, and we learn with him about the false paradise he witnesses, the desperate and hectic spending of the expatriates, his own initiations and his recognition of why his sister would reject the paucity of life in England.

I am now tempted to rewrite the book and reissue it, though I'm not yet sure whether I would just trim it – because I can see redundancies – or do something more radical. If I were writing it now I would not use that restrained monotone, the conventionally realistic mode; I think I would have more stylistic variety, more differences of perspective.

Both Ginger, You're Barmy *and* Out of the Shelter *seem to offer a 'message' of disillusionment . . .*

No; the epilogue in *Out of the Shelter* was meant, in a way, to reflect what I felt had been my own experience. Timothy had enjoyed a richer, wider experience than his background might otherwise have prepared him for – through visiting Germany in adolescence – and I think the note of disillusionment or sadness attaches itself to the figure of his sister, whose life is seen as somewhat empty: she is in some sense a victim. Timothy is presented as having a temperamental cautiousness which holds him back from having a really adventurous and important kind of life, but he is still satisfied with the feeling that he has been pretty lucky: he is happy with his wife and family, and with his academic job, and he feels a bit guilty about the difference between his fate and that of other people.

That sense of lucky cautiousness, together with a refusal to make judgements about other people, comes through in a large part of your work, I think; it seems to be your nature as a novelist to be tolerant and open, to show a decent acceptance of the way people behave (however meretricious they might be).

This is a level of implication of which the writer himself can hardly be aware; it's something readers seem to infer in almost intangible ways. I certainly don't think of myself as a dogmatic writer, someone who has a message; I would regard myself as a liberal, and in some ways a rather secular kind of liberal in spite of the fact that I'm a Catholic – I'm not the kind who wishes to persuade other people to accept his Catholic beliefs. Catholicism happens to be the ideological milieu I grew up in, that I know and write out of.

I wonder, though, if you sometimes suspect yourself of a kind of failure of nerve – I mean perhaps even in formal, artistic terms – when you draw short of enunciating logical or moral conclusions? It's a question, I suppose, about hesitating over or withholding formal closures to your novels which reflects back on the whole aesthetic and moral shape of books such as Changing Places *or* How Far Can You Go?

Again it's an area where I can't change myself, or make myself into a kind of D. H. Lawrence, for instance, with a passionate, quivering conviction about certain things. I think I am by temperament tentative, sceptical, ironic, and so that reflects itself in the structure and texture of what I write. I am well aware that I tend to play off different ideological or moral attitudes against each other, and I can see that one could say it is evasive: in the abstract it clearly could be, but I would hope that in the concrete it isn't. I hope it comes across in the novels more as honest doubt than as evasiveness. But I quite accept the point that I do sheer away from strong resolutions of the narrative line in my novels which would affirm one position rather than another. I tend to balance things against each other; my novels tend towards binary structures – with, for example, opposite characters – and they very much leave the reader to make up his own mind. *How Far Can You Go?* is an example which deals with very specific controversial issues but has been read in two very different ways: both conservative and progressive Catholics read into it, in a way, what they wanted to see; and the novel really doesn't take up a clear position on the question that the title raises, it explores the question.

The title (and the sub-sections) set up the illusion that it is going to be a moral tale with a lesson for us all, and yet you reject any possibility of authorial dogmatism by way of using a querulous, postmodernist kind of

*narrator. That narrative mode can give out a lot of information in an
essayistic way, and it also conveys the author's comic and ironic doubts
about his characters.*

Yes, I was exploiting the authorial origin of the book – this also
fascinates me from a critical point of view – and yet it seemed to
me that the more prominent the author is, the more he becomes
a rhetorical trope, and the more difficult it is to identify that
voice with me.

*It stresses the whole area of comic play in the novel – the fictive
inventiveness – more than anything like authorial omniscience, and yet
it seems to me that you focus a good deal of conventionally realistic and
moral energy upon what happens to the characters of Dennis and
Angela in their marriage. They have a double grief: they have a mongol
child, and their next child is killed in a road accident; the narrator
specifically remarks that the death is not going to be presented because it
is 'too painful to contemplate', but the narrative later comes back to
deliberate upon how the couple cope with their fate, and its human and
ethical implications. In what is very much a semi-comic novel you
emphasize the nth degree of possible affliction.*

That strand of the plot does have a personal origin, which I don't
mind talking about now that the novel is receding into the past.
My wife and I do have a Downs' Syndrome child, born in 1966 –
a boy, not a girl as in the novel – but we didn't, I'm glad to say,
lose another child as the characters Dennis and Angela do. I
connect it with the whole curious business of Catholic teaching
on birth control: there is a certain amount of evidence that if you
try to use the so-called 'rhythm method' you are possibly –
though it can happen to anybody – more likely to have some
congenital problem. That causal connection is only lightly
touched on in the book; what interested me is the whole
problem of how you cope with what appears to be a tragedy,
and whether or not religion is any use in that eventuality. When I
first thought of writing the novel I knew I would deal with
changes in Catholicism both in their comic aspect and as they
impinged upon the most serious things in life. Whereas my
previous novels had been either serious and rather drab *or* comic
and exuberant, *How Far Can You Go?* would somehow be both.
I was undoubtedly drawing on a certain amount of painful

personal experience, but I tried to do it through a technique which would not be basically confessional or emotional and sentimentally involving.

One of the wonderful things about writing fiction is that I could go beyond my own experience and think of people coping fairly well with the one problem but then being struck by some other unforeseen and apparently unfair tragedy. One does know of cases where it seems that a person or family is doomed to one disaster after another, and that raises profound questions about good and evil and the existence of God. That's why I thought of inflicting another tragedy on the characters Dennis and Angela, and exploring how they might react to it; but I was deliberately avoiding the identification of reader with characters of an emotional kind – I was looking for something vaguely Brechtian, if you like, the occasional breaking of the psychological illusion, so that the reader would be shocked back into thinking about it intellectually as well as emotionally . . . and then again reasserting the circuit of illusion and creating the pleasure of that sort of writing. That is, I think, the most powerful, emotional part of the book; and Dennis and Angela are a more interesting couple than Michael and Miriam, who are more reflectors of the ideological trends of Catholicism over the period. Dennis is a very different kind of person from me, and Michael is much more like me, so that in a way I split myself into those two characters. One of the possible weaknesses of the book, which is an almost inevitable result of dealing with a homogeneous social group, is that the characters are likely to be confused with each other in the reader's mind.

I assume you wanted to have so many characters in order to underline the idea that the historical dilemmas of Catholicism are communal?

Yes, it was an historical project in that way. It was a subject nobody else seemed to have dealt with, what had happened to the Catholic Church over the last twenty-five years. Even the people in the Church haven't realized how it's changed out of all recognition, because it was a gradual change, and I needed a large number of characters in order to illustrate all the varieties of change – priests dropping out, for example, and nuns having to throw off their habits and adjust to the modern world; sexual

problems in marriage, mixed marriages, changes in the liturgy –
I could immediately think of a whole set of incidents and
situations that I wanted to incorporate. It would have been a
huge saga novel if I had treated it in a realistic mode. I also knew I
had to find some way of communicating to a non-Catholic
audience a lot of theological and ecclesiastical information. So
thinking in terms of a short novel with a rather rapid pace, with a
lot of characters and a lot of information to communicate, I was
led inexorably to use a dominant, intrusive authorial voice
which would communicate that information in a way I hoped
was itself amusing. It meant cutting down the characterization
to a fairly summary form, and having many characters of more
or less equal importance.

*The last section of the book – 'How It Is' – takes the form of a transcript
of a videotape of the Paschal Festival all the characters attend. Part of
the game, I think, is to recognize that one voice – which according to the
text is unidentifiable – is actually yours. The voice says quite sanguine-
ly that traditional Catholic metaphysics is fading away, and that we can
look forward to the real possibility of ecumenism. And yet what we see
of the characters is that they are still mired in rather trendy high jinks; I
think the reader can feel uncomfortable about the notion that they are
being abandoned or perhaps patronized.*

The idea is that all the characters are at a religious festival, which
mirrors the first chapter where they all more or less believed the
same thing. In the last chapter they are at this extraordinary
pluralistic happening, where the variety of attitudes is displayed
in the dramatic form of a scenario, the transcript of an imagined
TV documentary. The reader is indeed in a position to identify
the voice-over as the narrative voice, and those speeches do
represent my own view as authorial narrator about the whole
issue that I've raised: that would be a proper way to read the
book.

*But the characters are left in a comically absurd and even piteous
condition, whereas the narrator can be genial and acquiescent about
change.*

I need to qualify that by saying that what the narrator says in
those voice-overs is a kind of serene summary of the position, as
you suggest, but at the very end the same authorial voice

confesses that in some ways his predictions have been upset by the election of the present Pope, so that all bets are off; the narrator takes a very much less secure position then, he's seen as part of the flux, as uncertain as are the characters of what is going to happen next. In fact, what I found quite fun to do in that book was to show the provisional nature of writing. Most texts like to give the impression that they have been effortlessly produced, that what they've said is the only possible way of saying what they meant to say – Yeats has some nice lines about that:

> I said, 'A line will take us hours, maybe;
> Yet if it does not seem a moment's thought,
> Our stitching and unstitching has been naught . . .'
>   ('Adam's Curse')

– and I break this rule. A little example is the way, in *How Far Can You Go?*, in which the writer is revealed to be hesitating over the names he will give his characters: such a device undermines the normal kind of authority which a text claims; and the very last page of the book does it again, saying that things have changed even while I was typing it up. So I wanted to convey that sense of provisionality, and to end on a somewhat modest or self-questioning note; I wasn't claiming any authority or certainty.

You are temporizing both for artistically experimental reasons and because of the nature of the reality you are reflecting; you take on board some of the devices – the artistic self-consciousness – of the postmodernist mode, without fully assenting to it. I think it's true to say that you're teasing or hedging both with the realistic illusions of the traditional novel and with recent lines of critical theory about the novel, exploiting both positions.

A book which very much influenced the form of *How Far Can You Go?* is *Slaughterhouse 5*, which is in my opinion one of the best post-war American novels. Nothing else by Vonnegut has ever satisfied me quite so much. He is groping with a subject to which he finds it impossible to do justice in fictional terms, and he manages to do it by confessing the conventions he's using – not attempting the big, solemn saga, but doing it in a jokey, oblique, digressive way.

I am a bit of a magpie – like most writers perhaps – and I do use critical ideas in my fiction, as you say, ideas I don't necessarily subscribe to as a critic.

You do still subscribe to the idea of the traditional realist novel . . .

I did up to writing *Out of the Shelter*, but I'm not sure that I still do. I still 'believe' that it is worthwhile creating that effect of recognition which the classic realist text can produce, that sense of fidelity to history and to social texture. I like to give that to my readers, but I don't any longer think that it is enough to do just that; it no longer satisfies me to do it throughout a book, so the metafictional apparatus of *How Far Can You Go?* questions the realist convention at the same time as the book is using that convention.

In your essay 'The Novelist at the Crossroads', I think, you gave a big yes to the ideas of persuasion and 'truth-telling' in the novel. I wonder if you now find yourself in a position of compromise towards the various creative and critical theories which have come to prominence in England during the last decade or so?

I don't take up strongly defined positions. I am by nature a kind of compromiser, I suppose, looking to reconcile apparently opposed positions. As a critic I am a domesticator of more extreme types of continental criticism, and as a novelist I use certain experimental devices but in a way that is slightly tamed as compared to the kinds of books from which they are borrowed. I am now prepared to take more risks, I think, and I felt *How Far Can You Go?* was quite a risky book; I was pleased that it seemed to come off. I am not like Joyce or Beckett, who would follow their own sense of artistic logic – indifferent to or defying the literary institution or the public. I'm not sufficiently self-confident or self-assertive to do that, so my books will probably always pull back from extremes.

I think in terms of your novels it gives you a human scepticism before the radical scepticism of extreme theorists: you can gesture towards them.

I think too that it's a reflection of the kind of life I live, which is on the whole orderly, sedate and protected, and I would find it totally inauthentic to pretend to such vision as one finds in Pynchon or Norman Mailer. Part of the formal integrity of what you write must have its roots in what you are and in the life you live. Because I am basically in the English tradition of realistic fiction, working within a version of the world that will be recognizable to those who share it, that makes me a different kind of writer from somebody drawn to fantasy or the surreal. Because my fiction aims to have at least a basis of recognizable representation of the real world, it will reflect the limitations of my own character and experience.

A harsh critic might then say that while your work has every validity it might reflect some kind of insincerity in you.

I obviously wouldn't accept the word 'insincerity' . . . but perhaps equivocation or tentativeness is applicable.

All your books, I think, contain some grand scene of farce, usually having to do with a sexual encounter – even in Out of the Shelter, *where Timothy gets himself locked in a wardrobe while eavesdropping on the beguiling girl next door. That scene leads to what could be an unhappy sexual crisis, but it doesn't happen then, because Timothy is to be saved up for the much more romantic consummation with his dream girl, Gloria.*

As far as Timothy himself is concerned, it's not funny: it's acutely embarrassing and worrying. I think it may have been a way of signalling to the reader an authorial distance between me and that character. The book is written from a naive viewpoint, and obviously the reader and the implied authorial presence are bound to know more about sex than he does, so that there is an irony. That incident is completely invented . . . which may make it even more significant from a psychoanalytic point of view.

It happens again in Small World, *where Persse secludes himself in Angelica's bedroom. That sort of scene seems to me to be both formally available as an artistic strategy – in accord with the idea of arousing and eventually satisfying the reader – and a romantic distraction, since the reader does not know whether you as author are going to fulfil or to thwart the romantic promise.*

Yes, there is an analogy – which Roland Barthes and others have written about – between sexual excitation and narrative interest, and the novel as a form has always given more attention to sexual relations than to any other aspects of life. The question of whether a given couple are going to unite or not is also a leading motif in romance, although it's not generally treated there with the kind of psychological and physical explicitness of the novel form. *Small World* is a novel about desire, and not just sexual desire but also the desire to succeed; I conceived it as an academic comedy of manners which would have a romance plot underneath it, and in some ways the two elements are incompatible. Satire is the antithesis of romance, because romance is ultimately about the achievement of desire; satire is saying that you won't get what you desire, you don't deserve it. In the scene you mention from *Small World* it's essential that the hero is denied the satisfaction of his desire at that stage in the story, or else the story would finish. The fact that Dempsey is also disappointed is part of the satire of the story: the prof. is chasing the action at the same time, and he gets his come-uppance.

Whether there is some deeper psychological reason why I frequently write non-consummated sexual scenes, I don't know. I suppose I do often feel that lyrical scenes of consummated sexual love can compromise the truth-telling element in novels. My novels are sometimes regarded as rather shocking and explicit, but only pornographic novels will move from one ecstatic sex scene to another: that's precisely the difference between a pornographic erotic novel and a literary novel about sexuality. Possibly I overdo the disappointed and absurd side of sexuality out of a wish to avoid falling into a false lyrical sentimentality about sexual love.

And also perhaps to avoid moralizing about it?

That's a more complicated question, which partly involves the moral position of the characters themselves, and also the mode. Adultery can be treated comically within the comic mode – there's a whole tradition of adulterous unions in the comic context – but if it's in a serious context you have to face the real pain and anguish that it causes in reality. There's an enormous difference between Philip Swallow having it off with Désirée in *Changing Places* and Dennis going off with his secretary in *How Far Can You Go?*: they have very different resonances because of their literary contexts.

Small World seems to me quite a different kind of novel from

Changing Places, *although certain of the major characters – such as Swallow and Morris Zapp – are continuous with the earlier book. For one thing, the element of play in* Small World *seems to have tremendous structural importance, since you're playing with ideas out of romance, the picaresque and the quest myth – everything becomes part of a large game within one novel. But I wonder if you fear that you might be criticized for apparently capitalizing on the success of* Changing Places?

I didn't have any intention of writing a sequel to *Changing Places* until I came to write *Small World*, thinking of a novel about the global campus, with a lot of characters. The romance motif came later, and I started with the idea of a satirical novel about academic travel. Since I had to include so many characters, I then thought that it would save work if I used those characters from the earlier book – since I had conveniently left indeterminate the ending of *Changing Places*. Philip Swallow and Morris Zapp had originally represented two academic cultures, and I thought they could now represent two different positions in the controversy about literary theory. I thought they would be minor characters, but as things worked out they assumed more important roles. My main problem was to maintain continuity in a very different kind of novel without it becoming bizarre. But also, as you say, it's a different kind of novel, much more playful, with more literary allusion in it.

You must then be very confident about the audience for whom you write, because you are addressing yourself to like-minded people, in a sense, who will instantly comprehend literary allusiveness.

In that respect it's a bit like *The British Museum Is Falling Down*, which also contained many literary parodies. Yes, I obviously do write for an educated audience, and also for a peer group of academics and novelists, but – like all modern novelists from Henry James onwards – I write layered fiction, so that it will make sense and give satisfaction even on the surface level, while there are other levels of implication and reference that are there to be discovered by those who have the interest or motivation to do so. That is partly what you hope will guarantee the re-readability of the book. I think *Small World* will give pleasure to readers who don't catch allusions to Lévi-Strauss or T. S. Eliot because it has a strong plot, which is the great strength of romance as a genre.

Would it be right to see, behind all the playfulness, a concern to reassure your readers, and not to disturb them in any way?

It's not meant to unsettle at all, it's not that kind of book.

And yet you use the word 'satire' about it. 'Burlesque' might be the more appropriate word. You don't seem to show moral indignation, for example, which we'd normally associate with satire.

There is an element of pointing out affectation and hypocrisy, which I think of as the satirical edge of comedy. It's not a censorious kind of satire, but I don't think that in good faith I could satirize in a destructive way an institution which I belong to. I think I can stand back from the academic profession enough to see its absurd and ridiculous aspects, but I don't think it's really wicked or mischievous. That's probably why the overall impression of *Small World* is genial: fun-poking rather than denunciation. I hope one of the main sources of humour in the book is the perception of incongruities, which are actually there in the social behaviour I'm describing: the juxtaposition at conferences, for example, of serious professional debate and hedonism. It's the sort of delightful incongruity you find in Evelyn Waugh's early comedies, and there's obviously disagreement about whether or not they are satirical. Waugh himself said they weren't satires, because for satire you need a firm basis of agreed values, a standard against which everything else is measured and found wanting. I don't actually think that standard is necessary for the liberating effect of ridicule in comic writing, and I think there is an element of pure play in the early Waugh's discovery of ludicrous contrasts.

It strikes me that there is one small message, as it were, in Small World. *Philip Swallow has his idyll with Joy, and Persse has his pursuit of the eternal feminine ideal in the person of Angelica, and both of them are ultimately denied any continuing fulfilment; so the reader can take away a little moral about the illusoriness of their ambitions, if he can see that they have fake notions of romance.*

Yes, this is where the analogy between realistic comedy and romance can no longer be sustained. Romance is inherently a myth of satisfied desire, with everyone happily united, and that kind of ending is parodied with the minor characters in *Small World*; but for the major characters it doesn't really happen, because I had to think about whether I could follow the romance myth to such a conclusion, and it seemed to me I couldn't. The major plot is about the unattainability of one's desire, which is the message of the realistic novel. Even Morris Zapp doesn't get the Chair, though he gets a woman, and he has to settle for a more modest sort of existence. I also remembered Northrop Frye's observation that in its most primitive form romance doesn't end: a character has one adventure after another until the author dies of exhaustion. So I left Persse still questing; it's not negative, because it leaves the reader with a sense that he is off on another adventure. Endings are fascinating in that they force on the author a view of what the ultimate import of a book is going to be. I usually don't know how I am going to end a book until I get quite near the end.

Tell me more about how you managed to structure Small World, *which has so many cliff-hanging episodes and interweavings of characters. Even an apparently incidental character such as Miss Maiden eventually has an important part to play in the* peripeteia.

I start a notebook on the book I think I'm going to write, with brief synopses of the plot as I see it. Then I begin the novel with a very vague sense of where it's all going, and at various stages when I think I must make a decision about the plot–direction I will write another synopsis. So I accumulate about six or seven synopses which are different, and the book itself is actually different from the last synopsis. As I worked at *Small World* I became more and more interested in the romance idea, weaving in as many romance motifs as I could, and I very deliberately exploited the narrative codes of mystery and suspense. I wanted to have a lot of enigmas and moments of uncertainty, and if you have a good many characters you can naturally create suspense by leaving one character and moving to another.

Did the character of Persse, the innocent abroad, come to you very early on?

I think I originally thought of having an *ingénue*, a girl whom both Philip and Morris would be pursuing, but that idea was dropped. Then I thought of having a young man as the novice,

and a girl who would be rather more knowledgeable about the world . . . so Persse came in, and I could make him improbably uninformed about academic life. Percival in the myth is a knight who has very humble origins, and he's also very pure, a virgin.
You originally had Percival in mind, rather than Perseus and Andromeda?
That myth came in later – with the whole striptease theme – when I read Ariosto, where that scene is repeated again and again: the knight rescuing and gloating over the naked girl. Many of the characters derive from several stereotypes, but I first had Percival rather than Perseus in mind for Persse. I also thought that the characters would have to keep on meeting up with Angelica, but then it seemed more appropriate that she should be a shadow Persse was pursuing. I often had to back-track and rewrite an early passage in order to incorporate some new development. The idea of having twins in the novel provided the solution to the problem of how I wanted Angelica to appear to be sexually degraded and then to turn out to be innocent after all, which Frye says is a common motif in romance. It kept the plot going, with Persse in a state of deception.

In a way I was aiming at something like the tone of *Orlando Furioso*, which is highly literary and yet in a curious way frivolous, rather than something just like *The Faerie Queene*, which has a much more morally loaded use of romance motifs. I made a big structural decision at the beginning of Part Two, which introduces a whole raft of minor characters from different countries, instead of having the main characters meet others in a picaresque fashion. I felt I had to introduce them all, so that the reader should have a sense of simultaneity. That chapter was really very hard work: I had to invent so many new characters from scratch, giving them a language and context. I reckon it took me two or three months to write. It's a very important chapter in that it gives a new impulse to the book, expanding the novel from the fairly familiar form of campus novel it has at the beginning, so that the idea of the global campus is actually being unfolded. I aimed at a gradually increasing tempo through-out the novel, hoping for the effect that all the characters would seem to be going around the world with great speed. *Most of your books display innocents who are suddenly given access to glamorous possibilities, a wider world which is more grasping and mendacious than they could have envisioned, but also a world whose glamour they can suddenly exploit (I'm thinking, for instance, of Philip Swallow's discovery in* Changing Places*). That theme presumably reflects hedonistic discoveries in your own experience?*

I think Lionel Trilling among others argues that the passage from innocence to experience is the plot of all novels. The experience of growing up in the war, a time of great material privation, has had an effect on me. One of my predominant mental images is of a black-and-white film turning coloured, and my own life has often taken that form: a sudden flooding of colour and opportunity and enjoyment into what had been a somewhat restricted and grey existence. Going to America on a Harkness Fellowship in 1964 had that initial effect on me: they gave us a brand new Chevrolet to drive around America in, and that was certainly one of the formative experiences of my life.

What interests me here is that even though you're now worldly-wise there doesn't appear to be any cynicism in your novels. You have an extraordinary generosity towards all your characters, even those who might otherwise be considered shits.

Well, some readers found *How Far Can You Go?* a cold or savage book. But, yes, I do relish a character like Morris Zapp in *Changing Places* and *Small World*, although he has traits which one can imagine being unpleasant in certain people – arrogance, ambition, rudeness – I don't think that he is in the end a negative sort of character. There's a little bit of Morris Zapp in me, I think, and I respond to that witty, abrasive, thrusting Jewish type of American academic: I always feel that life starts to move twice as fast when you're in their company.

In Small World *Philip Swallow is still baffled but he has more dignity than he had in* Changing Places.

I built up his character a little; he's a bit more successful and assertive. I do know one or two men who in middle age put on a dignity they never had before, and they apparently become sexually desirable in an unexpected way . . .

I'm waiting.

. . . whereas Morris is on the opposite escalator.

Apart from your obvious delight in using different idioms and some wisecracks, what you write is principally situation comedy, I think.

Yes, I think I might have ended up writing situation comedy if I hadn't gone into academic life; a former Head of BBC Light Entertainment wanted me to write situation comedy after he read *Changing Places*. Comedy was a fairly late discovery for me, and it was only the experience of writing a revue with Malcolm Bradbury that made me realize I could do it. My first two books were written in a rather sombre realistic mode. I am rather fascinated by the idea of genetic inheritance, and I see that little eighth of Jewish blood in me as one possible source of this delight in comedy and the absurd. I like comedy as a genre, and shrink from heavy emotional drama in other media.

I have to use self-discipline, because I am sometimes tempted to use a wisecrack which isn't right in context, but I feel a glow of satisfaction when I can work in a one-liner which is contextually appropriate.

When Morris Zapp suddenly blacks out while jogging in Part Four of Small World, *I immediately assumed that he had had a heart attack. But you leave the reader in suspense, and we are later reminded of that suspense by the narratologist's remark about the 'narrative retardation' that incident has caused.*

I'm fascinated by what you say, because it never occurred to me that Morris had had a heart attack. It's a very good example in support of the argument for the intentional fallacy, because I felt so clear in my own mind that he had been kidnapped. But it's beautiful if the reader does jump to the other conclusion. It was one of the delightful incongruities that struck me on a trip to Zurich in 1979, that all these great American gurus of deconstruction went off jogging around the hills.

Did you find it difficult to write the passage which asks the reader to believe in the serious sentiment of Philip Swallow's affair with Joy?

Yes, I rewrote it a lot. I had to make the transition from treating him as a farcical victim to making him capable of grand romantic passion. I found it tricky to write the part which begins with him waiting for Joy in the station at Ankara; it could easily have gone wrong.

Was it particularly hard because you felt shy of writing a scene of straightforward romantic passion?

No, it was the difficulty of keeping that balance between the comic and the romantic. That scene had to be romantic: you had to believe that Joy would run off with a guy who is elsewhere shown to be absurd, and that they would have a rapturous reunion. I think I decided at a fairly late stage that Philip Swallow's romantic idyll had to collapse, because his wife Hilary could not be just casually ditched – not within the comic romantic tradition. It's an interesting case where genre and psychological reality in a way conflict. Philip is rather punished when his erotic adventure is punctured, because he has been untruthful and hasn't got the gumption to admit it – he tries to dissociate himself from Joy – although I only decided that at the point of writing the scene. The dissolution of that romantic relationship is a down-beat part of the novel.

Do you figure the comic genre as being essentially subversive?

In my critical capacity I've been reading a lot of Bakhtin, a Russian post-formalist who has become a very fashionable theorist. One of his theories, which he elaborates in a book called *Rabelais*, is that there has always been a tradition of writing which is not one of the canonical forms, like epic or tragedy – a mixed form which is seen in the satyr plays of ancient Greece and carnival in the middle ages. It is writing which is always anti-authoritarian, satirizing and travestying the canonized genres and by implication the hierarchies of power in society those canonized genres tended to reinforce. Basically a folk tradition, it erupted and became absorbed into high literature in Cervantes and Rabelais. I find this grand historical thesis very attractive: the idea that the novel draws on discourses which are not those of high literature, and that it's a mixture of discourses. It provides a rather impressive theoretical case for the comic mode, which I think is not just entertaining but performs a very valuable hygienic cultural function: it makes sure that institutions are always subject to a kind of ridiculing criticism. Bakhtin very much associates this with the assertion of the body, particularly processes of eating, excretion, copulation, all of which religious and governmental institutions try

to deny and suppress in the interests of mind and power. Comedy reasserts the body, and the collectiveness of the body is what really unites us rather than ideologies. I think this rather grandiose idea explains a lot of what I write in my novels – my attitude towards the academy, for instance, which is not meant to destroy the institution but to remind it that its interests are not all-absorbing and all-important, and that those interests to some extent depend on the suppression of certain facts about life of a low, physical, earthy kind. The novels show that people in academic life are subject to the same drives and appetites and physical needs as anyone else. Umberto Eco uses the Bakhtinian theory in *The Name of the Rose*. Bakhtin also provides a kind of rationale for the scatological strain in my novels. I like the scene in *Small World* where Philip unwittingly uses his lecture notes as toilet paper.

You obviously have a very good and supportive relationship with Malcolm Bradbury, but do you like to recognize or insist upon a differentiation between the kinds of novel you write? Or do you read his work and feel that you could have written it?

I think it was essential that we separated when he left Birmingham to go to East Anglia, because we are both rather imitative writers. I sometimes write a line that I realize Malcolm could have written, but I think the ultimate structure and drift of our respective types of fiction are actually very different.

· IAN McEWAN ·

Born in 1948, Ian McEwan started writing short stories in 1970, after studying at the University of Sussex and at the University of East Anglia, where he gained an MA. His first collection, *First Love, Last Rites* (1975), won enormous praise and the Somerset Maugham Award 1976 for its sophisticated depiction of sensuality and depravity. A second collection, *In Between the Sheets* (1978) has been followed by two brilliantly executed novels, menacing and exact in their psychological penetration, *The Cement Garden* (1978) and *The Comfort of Strangers* (1981). His play for television, *The Imitation Game* (directed by Richard Eyre) – which Clive James applauded as 'a "Play for Today" of rare distinction' – earned him a wider audience and even hotter critical attention. So, sadly, did 'Solid Geometry', a television play adapted from one of his short stories, which the BBC aborted just before it went into production. The three television plays he has written to date are available in *The Imitation Game* (1981).

A man for all media, McEwan has also written a deeply felt oratorio about the nuclear threat, *Or Shall We Die?*, set by Michael Berkeley and performed in February 1983 by the London Symphony Orchestra and Chorus, conducted by Richard Hickox, and a feature film about contemporary England and the tragedy of forgotten history, *The Ploughman's Lunch* – also directed by Richard Eyre, and starring Jonathan Pryce, Rosemary Harris and Frank Finlay. Most recently he has been at work on the filmscript of a novel by Alberto Moravia to be produced by Bernardo Bertolucci, and he has started another novel.

I talked to him in 1983 at his home in south London, where he lives with his wife, Penny Allen, and her two children by a former marriage.

★ ★ ★

You established your reputation as a writer of short stories; then you wrote two novels and a television play, and most recently a feature film and an oratorio. I think there is a sense in which you've maintained continuity in so far as much of your earlier work concerns diseased minds and your more recent writing deals with diseased and unsettling societies.

Yes, but it is all after the event. It turns out that what I've written is unsettling, but I don't sit down to think about what will unsettle people next.

You are on record as saying that you were surprised when critics chose to emphasize the shocking and the macabre aspects of your early stories, their concern with degenerate or dislocated behaviour.

I honestly was very surprised. My friends, most of whom had had a literary education, seemed to take for granted the field of play in the stories; they had read Burroughs, Celine, Genet and Kafka, so that lurid physical detail and a sense of cold dissociation did not stun them. I was not aware of any pattern, and each story seemed to me at the time of writing to be a fresh departure, often with very trivial rhetorical ambitions like writing a story in the present tense ('Last Day of Summer'). They often proceeded out of doodles that had a certain kind of automatic quality.

I was quite surprised, for example, when the BBC banned 'Solid Geometry', but then TV is so safe and dull. It doesn't put on anything funny about sex. I've never seen good sexual jokes on TV.

What was the especial significance for you of the bottled penis that figures in 'Solid Geometry'?

On the most basic level it was playful, to show a man working on his great-grandfather's diaries with a preserved penis on his desk. It had to be an erect penis, because that's apparently how they're preserved. By extension, the fact that he won't make love to his wife suggests that his own penis is bottled up, as it were, and it provides her with a splendid opportunity (which would have been great fun to do) to bust it open: it's an appropriation, since she quite reasonably wants his cock. But once the penis is out of the jar he goes and buries it and carries on with his work. There's no stopping him.

Since you've mentioned rhetorical ambitions, have you ever felt tempted to be dishonest in writing, when you recognize a trick you know you can get away with?

Yes, all the time; it's amazing how many bad ideas you get on bad days. But when you finish a piece of work you rapidly forget all the confused alternatives that existed along the way, and you imbue it with intention. Writing *The Comfort of Strangers*, for example, helped me to articulate ideas and notions for myself. But *The Comfort of Strangers* got written in the most lugubrious way possible, because I would finish one chapter and have no idea what to do with the next. I felt that I would never finish, because the novel was giving me so much personal pain. I had a rough idea of what to do in the first half, but no ideas in advance for the second.

Can you tell me how you set about writing The Cement Garden?

It has a definite genesis in one paragraph of my notes, at the doodling stage, where I suddenly had a whole novel unfold about a family living 'like burrowing animals . . . after mother dies the house seems to fall asleep'. Then I saw the four children: 'the initial spread of power . . . the girls steal youngest to babyfy . . . gives narrator more space'. I remember writing that paragraph and then lying on the bed and falling into a deep sleep for an hour in the afternoon. When I came back to work I made a false start, and later I realized that the beginning really belonged with the father. I also wondered for a time whether I shouldn't have each of the children recounting the novel. And then for a long time I thought it would turn out that the second sister would be the true narrator, since she was keeping a notebook. I kept thinking the narrator was going to go completely crazy: 'His imbalance becoming an issue and the household cannot contain him'. I thought for a while that Jack would just go under. [Quotations are from Ian McEwan's notebook drafts.]

I think that one character in The Cement Garden *who really authenticates the fantasy, as it were, is the outsider, Derek, who envies the world of the children: he wants both to enter their world and to break it.*

Yes, I sympathize with Derek, because I was a sort of only child, and when I went to stay with friends who had brothers and sisters I would fantasize that my own parents had dematerialized to enable me to join a large family. *The Cement Garden* has a source in my childhood wish to have sisters. The other incestuous stories have rather similar tenuous roots. Another source of the novel was my wife's childhood.

In 'In Between the Sheets', the title story of your second collection, the reader is tempted to share the erotic fantasies of a father towards his daughter. You place the reader very close to his consciousness, especially when at night he overhears what he takes to be her erotic restlessness, to the point where one is convinced that incest will take place. But then she appears as just an unsettled child. The reader is agog with a sort of shared excitement, but the tact of the story returns both father and reader to decent normality.

I'm glad you see it in terms of his *imagination* of her erotic behaviour, when he hears sounds and has such violent and confused ideas towards his daughter. I was uneasy about the way I had him pursuing his writing in a way that takes him away from any real relationship to a point when he is deeply fearful of women and their pleasure: that's reflected in the rather arid way he sets about his day's work, filing things, writing in a ledger, counting the number of words. Perhaps the connection is too simple. But then, I do think short stories demand simple and incisive sets of oppositions. You make a choice of where your complexity lies, and you must concentrate and pursue it.

'In Between the Sheets' ends with the image of 'a field of dazzling white snow which he, a small boy of eight, had not dared scar with footprints'. It is a marvellous metaphor for refusing to desecrate something pure.

Yes, I do think that last paragraph saves the story. I remember an incredibly heavy snow as a child when we were living in Kent, going out in my gumboots and being enchanted. The field was so pure I didn't want to walk on it.

You've said elsewhere that 'To and Fro' is one of your favourite stories, perhaps because it's rather personal. Could you say something about it, because many readers do find it a bit obscure?

It's fairly simple really. A man lying in bed beside his lover, imagining himself at work pursued by a colleague who seems to crowd in on his identity. Celebrating the sleeping lover, dreading the obtrusive colleague – these are the simple oppositions.

Was 'First Love, Last Rites' in any way written as an allegory of your own experience? It is perhaps your most heavily symbolic story; it's about a relationship and pregnancy, and it includes fishing for eels, which you have at some time done.

Oddly enough I had no sense of its symbols when I was writing it, none at all. I certainly wasn't inserting symbols into the story. I was remembering and changing certain events in my own life. I think the story is about pregnancy. The narrator has a sure sense of the girl's power as she kneels by a dead rat. I've always thought it was an affirmative and tender story, as I do 'In Between the Sheets', and that was part of the source of my astonishment at the sensational copy reviewers made out of the stories. Reviewers seemed to be fixated by things that weren't central.

I agree with you there: 'First Love, Last Rites' seems to me to concern the characters purging themselves of false images of an as yet unsatisfactory relationship. Whatever is macabre in the story works towards a positive resolution.

I also had a simple–silly desire to end a story with the word 'Yes'. I was dazzled by the end of *Ulysses*. My problem was how to get to this 'Yes'. The problem almost preceded the content, and when you concentrate on that sort of trivial puzzle you find yourself drawing quite freely and unconsciously on surprising material: you come upon an eel in a bucket and it's not a symbol – it's a *memory*. When the eel is set free, I was not thinking of it as a thinly disguised phallus, nor did I think of eel traps as vaginas. One doesn't think about symbols, though there comes a time when one can't deny that they are there.

But another story, 'Butterflies', concerns a man abusing and finally killing a child, and that is an appalling subject.

Yes, 'Butterflies' is appalling; it's a story written by someone who had nothing to do with children. I couldn't possibly write that story now, it would frighten me too much. As children come more into your life the possibility of their death is not something you can play with lightly.

Since your more recent work has made a change of gear into greater social and political awareness, can you say something about what caused this shift?

It was something I intended, because I had begun to feel rather trapped by the kinds of things I had been writing. I had been labelled as the chronicler of comically exaggerated psychopathic states of mind or of adolescent anxiety, snot and pimples. My relationship with Penny Allen, who is now my wife, was a rich source of ideas and I had wanted to give them shape. In writing *The Imitation Game* I stepped out into the world – consciously to find out about a certain time in the past and to recreate it – and at that point I felt I had made a very distinct change. But when I came back to *The Comfort of Strangers* I found myself immediately being drawn again into a very private world, without quite intending it, where psychological states once more become more important than relationships between, for example, individuals and their societies. These things are not entirely within one's control, and I don't think they should be. I am aware of the danger that in trying to write more politically, in the broadest sense – trying to go out more into the world, because it is a world that distresses me and makes me anxious – I could take up moral positions that might pre-empt or exclude that rather mysterious and unreflective element that is so important in fiction. I also think the changes I've been through are quite possibly related to form itself: it's when I have to collaborate with other people that I find myself writing about a larger world.

Do you mean that in writing for film or television you don't have the space to invest in detailed expositions of psychological states?

Film seems to suggest a large canvas to me, the novel a smaller one. That is how the forms have affected me so far. Of course other writers have found the novel the ideal form for describing a whole society, and there are film-makers, like Tarkosky, who have successfully used their chosen form to make inner journeys. I would like to write a less claustrophobic novel. It may be something to do with confidence.

And yet there is an allegorical dimension to your novels which does suggest a larger frame of reference beyond the psychologically hermetic.
Yes. I am just daydreaming my way into a novel now, and I write all sorts of messages to myself about what I would like to do. I can already feel that something is emerging, and it is not quite what I intended. So I hope that moral concerns will be balanced, or even undermined, by the fact that I still don't have complete control. Some element of mystery must remain. I know novelists who talk quite freely about the novel they're going to write next. I envy them to some extent, because I can get depressed between writing things. But I know that for me there has to be some silence, and that silence often means getting very fed up.

I know that you now have some reservations about The Imitation Game, *your film for television. Do you think with hindsight that it was oversimplified?*
It was a first film both for Richard Eyre and for me, and it has longueurs and a certain kind of linearity: it pushed forward along one front all the time. But this was its strength too.

You feel it was pace rather than content that was wrong? The plot is straightforward, being the story of a young woman in wartime England in 1940 who tries to challenge and enter the man's world . . .
And more broadly it is an allegory of a person against the system. The problem I encountered in the writing was that as soon as you had a woman at the centre she stands there as a representative of her *sex*; a central male character, on the other hand, is understood to be talking for humankind. The play wasn't only about the way in which men oppress women, it was also about the way systems exclude individuals. I think that got lost, and if it were to be done again I would try to make the heroine representative of things that men understood. I wasn't only concerned with why women see themselves as a repressed class, but the way it turned out it does have a one-dimensional feel.

Given that the play is set in 1940 the figure of Cathy Raine does come over as a unique example of rebelliousness and confrontation. What The Imitation Game *didn't appear to offer was a context for her thoughts and actions as a feminist.*

Virginia Woolf's *Three Guineas*, from which *The Imitation Game* draws something, was published in 1938 and went through three reprints during the war. As feminist scholars have pointed out, women's experiences have constantly to be rediscovered – there's no tradition. A lot of women were discontented then, but they would not have articulated their discontent in terms of being a woman or sharing their experiences with other women at the time. I think that element should have been in the film, because otherwise it does suggest a kind of anachronism, and I did wince when people said I had put a 1978 heroine into a 1940 drama. I felt it was untrue, but I do feel I should have given it a little more context. I went to see a number of women who had been in the ATS, and they certainly had strong things to say. These were now very conventional ladies living polished suburban lives – rather lonely, with children grown up, houses sterilely clean – and they felt a strange wistfulness for that time when they had paradoxically more freedom because they had their own careers and an interesting lack of security. I think Cathy Raine should have been more related to other women, rather than being just a rather bolshy middle-class girl not getting a big enough slice of the action. I am being rather crude and dismissive of the play's procedures, but I think the same points could have been made in a more complex way. It was my first crack at a film. But I still think it is moving.

You would have no doubts about the polemicism of the play?

No, I would hold by that.

Do you have any misgivings about the way you portrayed the men as stereotypes or caricatures?

The men certainly were stereotypes in *The Imitation Game*. I think people objected to the idea that it was possible to make stereotypes out of male behaviour. We have accepted for a long time that women can be made into dramatic stereotypes, and I felt it was possible to have a solid, rounded female character moving against a cardboard background of very familiar but nevertheless stereotypical forms of male behaviour. Men's behaviour is somehow invisible; we don't see ourselves as having a behaviour that is identifiably male – we're just *human*. So the cry goes up that you cannot caricature men like this, and that men are more complicated, and my reply is that of course I have a polemical purpose.

While I was writing *The Imitation Game* two women were thrown out of a pub in Camden Town for knitting. The publican said knitting was what his customers had come to get away from. The next day, in a way that was silly but right, thirty women turned up at the pub with their knitting, and the publican was well within his legal rights to call the police and have them ejected. That confirmed my view that male behaviour can reach incredibly comic and stereotypical limits. It was farcical and delightful that the power of the state had to be invoked to remove these women.

Women's liberation, I think, properly requires not only social changes but also radical psychological and emotional alterations in men's attitudes and behaviour, and I think that would be an area that would continue to involve you as a writer.

The problem is, what do you do about it once you've said it? There are ways in which you clearly have to address your own behaviour in private life, but after writing *The Imitation Game* – having escaped the label of being the chronicler of adolescence – I was then suddenly the male feminist, which really made me shrink. I found myself being co-opted into attending various types of convocation on 'Sexism in the Media' or 'Writers against Sexism'. It was very gratifying to see the enormous amount of attention *The Imitation Game* received, but I found I wanted to back off the subject. I didn't want to be used as a spokesman for women's affairs. I didn't want to be a man appropriating women's voices.

Were you happy about the way you treated the crisis in The Imitation Game, *where Turner, the intellectual mathematician, fails to make it in bed with Cathy. He feels betrayed and hates the woman, and he avenges himself. It struck me as very brave of you to have come so close to delivering a piece of melodrama and yet to have brought off the real truth of the situation and its nightmare consequences. The danger seemed to lie in relating Turner's impotence to his intellectuality.*

I hadn't thought of the polarity as being to do with intellectuality and impotence. It had more to do with his sense of total competence in the outer world, and therefore his fear of failure in the inner world. What blurred the issue was that in an earlier scene a dispatch-rider tells Cathy that Bletchley is full of homosexuals, and there is also Turner's description of his dominating mother, so that some gays though I was saying he couldn't make it and was vicious because he was homosexual. This was a false trail I had made here, one that was not relevant to the argument of the play.

There is among men a fear of women and of their power. What is meant to be clear in the scene is that once Cathy is sexually excited she becomes very demanding, which is very frightening for Turner, and so his anger seemed to be dramatically in order. Once she had made the journey to the centre of official secrets, the other secret – the secret in the private world – creates the same response: she meets the masculine defensiveness that won't admit weakness. I see this defensiveness as a burden for men, and not just as the thing men do to women. I would not like to say who is unhappier in that scene, but it is quite clear who is the more powerful.

Did you move straight on to The Comfort of Strangers *after finishing* The Imitation Game?

Yes. It sounds easy, but in fact there was a break in time: it was a good year later.

To what extent did Nicholas Roeg's film Don't Look Now *influence you in writing* The Comfort of Strangers?

I was aware of the film but I hadn't seen it. Nor had I read the book on which it was based. I felt sensitive about it, but then I saw it on TV a couple of years ago, and I thought no sweat.

Penny Allen and I spent a week in Venice in 1978, at the height of the tourist season, and something of our visit found its way into the book. I can't really describe the book as setting out with any clear intention. After being to Venice I came back and wrote some notes about it, which I lost, and then I found them a good one-and-a-half years later; it seemed to me that I had already been describing two characters who were not quite like either myself or Penny, and already it seemed to be describing the city in terms of a state of mind, and vice versa. So the novel took off from the notes. Those notes contain the phrase 'self-fulfilling accusation', as well as the first sentence, so I must have been thinking about a novel even then.

I found it terribly difficult to write, and it is a book I find very hard to understand or talk about. It seemed to be saying something either true or so true that it was banal. It was an elaboration of an argument in *The Imitation Game*. This again brings up the question of form, since it wasn't enough to talk about men and women in social terms, I had to address myself to the nature of the unconscious, and how the unconscious is shaped. It wasn't enough to be rational, since there might be desires – masochism in women, sadism in men – which act out the oppression of women or patriarchal societies but which have actually become related to sources of pleasure. Now this is a very difficult argument to make.

I recently attended a *Marxism Today* conference about eroticism and the left, and I made an *extempore* speech – very clumsily – about eroticism not being totally amenable to rationalism, that it wasn't just a matter of talking out a programme of the feminist left. The conference was a broad coalition of socialists and feminists, and I got on to incredibly dangerous ground when I suggested that many women probably have masochistic fantasies and that many men probably have sadistic fantasies, which are acted out in private but never spoken about in any kind of public debate. And then I said that it would be far better in a relationship to embrace this than to deny it, and that true freedom would be for such women to recognize their masochism and to understand how it had become related to sexual pleasure. The same was no less true for male masochists. I was talking here of sexual fantasy. The whole room exploded, and I came away feeling terribly bruised because I had been very inarticulate, as one is when speaking against such hostility. But I was attacked for providing a 'rapist's charter' and for poaching on forbidden territory – women's experience.

That goes a long way to explain the characters of Robert and Caroline in The Comfort of Strangers. *Robert obtrusively recounts his intimate childhood experiences to Colin and Mary, who are strangers to him. What he tells them amounts to a threat, and yet the young couple retreat to their hotel and curiously do not speak about their extraordinary encounter. But they do respond to it unconsciously, in their behaviour towards one another. You mention their 'conspiracy of silence' and – in chapter 7 – the way they start to 'invent themselves anew' and to make up sexual fantasies.*

I felt they had become mesmerized by Robert and Caroline in ways they could not speak about. Robert and Caroline were for me simply a sort of comic drawing of a relationship of domination, and when this decently liberal and slightly tired couple, Colin and Mary, come in contact with that relationship they find it has a sway over their unconscious life, and they begin to act out – or rather speak to each other – these incredible masochistic and sadistic fantasies while they are making love. By example, as it were, their very carefully constructed rational view – he being a mild feminist, she a rather stronger one, and their sort of balance – becomes undone, because they haven't ever addressed the matter at a deeper level of themselves; they've always seen it as a social matter.

What I was trying to say at the conference was that there is a certain sort of silliness attached to talking about eroticism if you are just talking about it in terms of domestic relationships. There is something intractable about the sexual imagination, and what you desire is not very amenable to programmes of change. You might well have grown up deciding that you accept certain intellectual points of view, and you might also change the way you behave as a man or as a woman, but there are also other things – vulnerabilities, desires – within you that might well have been irreversibly shaped in childhood. People of our generation, who grew up in the 1950s, grew up in the time of the fathers, and I made the point that there are many women for whom the figure of the father lies very deeply and powerfully within their sexuality. I got into incredibly hot water, but I still think I was right. I came away thinking that the left was actually bristling with taboos, almost as many taboos as there would have been at a synod of clergy in the late nineteenth century. Everyone was so used to a kind of likemindedness, that it was stirring for them to see me as an enemy in their midst.

In The Comfort of Strangers *Colin and Mary take unconscious refuge in indulgent self-involvement, what you call a 'rhetorical mode, a means of proceeding', and it's as if they can agree on the politics of sex because they avoid discussing the social confrontation which drove them into collusion.*

Yes, the one thing they don't talk about is Robert and Caroline, and they interiorize it instead. In order to collude they mustn't talk about Robert and Caroline, and so they become Robert and Caroline.

I think of it as an old-fashioned novel about the head and the heart: two creatures of the head meet two creatures of the heart, and the head goes a bit haywire as a consequence. Robert is a sort of cartoon figure of extreme patriarchal domination, and he cannot tolerate the existence of Colin, who represents a threat to him. Colin becomes useful grist to Robert's ultimate fantasies of cruelty, wherein Robert can exercise his full sadism and Caroline can identify with it.

One of the interesting scenes on the way is where Mary goes swimming. Colin thinks she is drowning and he exhaustingly swims out to rescue her. When he reaches her he finds that she is in fact quite safe and happy, but his care for her is never communicated . . .

There is also another current involved there, as it were, in the sense that if you are so wrong about something you have to question whether your desires aren't involved in your judgement, and maybe Colin wants Mary to be drowned and sees her in that way. But for me the dominant feature of that scene is the notion of swimming out too far, which is what they are about to do.

*Christopher Ricks wrote a very interesting review of the novel (*London Review of Books, *4:1, 21 January–3 February 1982), in which he talks about the incorrigibility of certain manifestations of evil, that they just cannot be explained. Yet it is the case that Robert enters very full evidence about the aetiology of his perversion. He explains the source of his sadism in a way which is not otherwise questioned in the novel, and I found that because of that unquestioned ratiocination apropos of Robert I was much more taken up by the subtle and exploratory treatment of Colin and Mary.*

I think of Robert more as a cipher than as a character. People either buy Robert or they don't. He is part of the premise of the novel rather than an entirely convincing character.

But still you chose not to leave him as an unaccountable figure; you wanted to show how much he understands his sadism.

Yes, the violence that Robert does to Colin, which is a violence that is in the air – people do murder each other, wars do break out – has a lot to do with people's perceptions of their own exercise of power, and the pleasures they find in exercising power. What is interesting is the extent to which people will collude in their own subjection, which is true not only of Caroline in relation to Robert but also of Colin. There is something about Colin's behaviour which suggests from the beginning that he is a victim; he goes along with Robert and is easily manipulated, which suggests an unconscious contractual agreement. I think such an agreement can exist between oppressor and victim.

Ricks interprets The Comfort of Strangers *as a tragedy.*

I didn't think of it in those terms, but I did think there was a sense in which Colin and Mary had agreed about what was going to happen to them. The city, and their relationship to it, was littered with notions of possible death. In the first chapter I posit a *stranger* for whom they're getting dressed, so that they conjure him up, and that was long before I had a title for the book. So it had a fatalistic element in it from the start which I suppose tragedy shares. A lot of readers were so infuriated by Colin and Mary that they couldn't enjoy the book, and I think there has to be an act of recognition: the ideal reader has to recognize within himself or herself that area of lack of freedom in a relationship.

I wonder if the development in your writing towards greater political awareness was fostered by reading and seeing the plays of David Hare?

I certainly feel that David interests me more than most of my contemporaries.

Is that because he relates the private life to the political life?

I think that message – the necessity of relating private and personal behaviour with what you do in broader relationships – has come to me through the women's movement. David Hare has an ambivalence towards his subject matter which I find very interesting, and in a way I've been dogging his footsteps. Long after David has written about the state of England now and a certain sense of betrayal, I'm still toiling away in that particular field in *The Ploughman's Lunch*. I went to see *Licking Hitler* before I wrote *The Imitation Game*; they're linked, but there's no direct influence, and they come from very different viewpoints. I like *Licking Hitler* enormously, and I engage with David's work.

You have written that before you came to write the oratorio Or Shall We Die? *you had tried a novel and a filmscript on the same theme.*

The novel hardly got off the ground, it seemed too programmatic. It had something to do with family relationships which were being soured by things happening outside. The film was much more apocalyptic, a survival fantasy with a cast of millions, but it had too many elements: disaster, thriller, love story . . . and no mystery.

In Or Shall We Die? *you rather simply oppose the male world and the female world.*

The male and female in the oratorio were really principles rather than genders: the elements of the feminine and the elements of the masculine, and how our civilization is heavily weighted towards the latter. Male and female should exist in balance within individuals and within society. The oratorio makes a point about tendencies of behaviour. It was in one sense an ethereal polarity, but in another sense the mother and child seemed to me the most powerful and central image of what civilization has to protect – children are its major resource, which nuclear war threatens.

The development of nuclear weapons shows the dissociation of science from feelings, science run amok: this can be usefully described in terms of the male principle, active and aggressive, without the compassion or a sense of nurture. Newtonian physics seems to encapsulate a certain male principle of detached observation. But within the New Physics there are theories like the Uncertainty Principle where the observer cannot exclude himself and faces the limits of what can be known. And just as Newtonian physics slowly found its moral correlative, I think there is hope that various forms of holism, for example, are very tentative expressions of the New Physics moving into moral positions.

I am emphatically a unilateralist; I think this country makes itself a target by having nuclear weapons, and we pervert our economy and our democracy. The position is different for the US and Russia, who clearly have to negotiate between themselves. My view is not idealistic but practical; I want to survive, and I feel great sadness and anger that we devote so much of our national resources and half our scientists to projects of destruction. We have made no democratic decisions about these weapons; the first Labour government after the war took a decision on them without consulting Parliament. All kinds of democratic principles have been subverted by the apparent necessity of having nuclear weapons. I believe quite passionately in the democratic procedures.

Did you have any hesitation about using an oratorio to serve your political – what some critics have felt to be tendentious – arguments?
I think I'm one very small part of a massive sense of revulsion. There is a vast anxiety which inevitably finds its way into works of art. It's impossible to keep this preoccupation out, because it is so personal.

*Some years ago, in an interview with Christopher Ricks (*The Listener, *12 April 1979), you said that you felt elated by your work, and that you did not feel threatened or disturbed by the content of what you wrote . . .*
There is always that paradox about any work of art: it will finally have something optimistic in it because it is an expression of desire or will or energy. I was walking on air the day I finished the oratorio, although I had brought together terrible things. I found it very painful while I was writing *The Comfort of Strangers*, but I did feel terribly happy when I had written a good page.

What sort of pain did you feel in writing The Comfort of Strangers?
I felt very strongly identified with Colin, as if I was writing my own death in some strange way. I felt terribly sickened by it. Part of me did not want to go on, and another part of me was ambitious . . . and delighted by the writing.

You achieve a terrible coolness in both The Comfort of Strangers *and* The Ploughman's Lunch.
I get pleasure from the feeling that I have found more truth in detachment than if I had written self-directed or passionate prose.

The Ploughman's Lunch is a film which builds up a large number of layers and perspectives. Did you begin with that idea of making a panorama of England roughly a year ago?

Yes, but it started in March 1981. I had the idea of writing a film that was set in contemporary England, but I had no idea who was going to be in it. For a long time I thought it was going to be about royalty. It was the year of the royal wedding, and as that intensified I realized just how everyone was transfixed, even the dissenters: there was no way out of it. Even indifference had to be furiously cultivated. I thought maybe one could look at this fixation through the eyes of an inebriated pressman; and for a long time I thought along those lines, but I got sick of it. I thought you could look at it like an anthropologist, and see it in terms of the powerful myths of kings and queens and princes. After a while I began to wonder if it was so relevant.

But all the time I had the title, *The Ploughman's Lunch* – an invented meal which had been incorporated as a fake past – and so the metaphor was always there. Then I drifted around to what turned out to be the different locations. At the Labour Party conference I met some women who had just set up a peace camp, so I went to visit them at Greenham Common, when they were still struggling to get it together. I also spent some time in Norfolk, thinking that this harsh and beautiful area of England was never represented on film, and I went to Poland. Then I saw how it might all fit together.

It sounds as though you were taking samplings of places rather than of contemporary attitudes.

The two were really indistinguishable. Going to Greenham Common, for example, was to visit people who had a very clear sense of value and attitude.

In this process of moving around, were you actually taking the measure of your own commitments and attitudes?

Yes. I became very fascinated by the two women at Brighton. They were clearly dedicated to a set of ideas. I had to measure the extent to which I had ideas and the extent to which I would live them out, and I felt great admiration for the women at Greenham Common. At the other end of the scale, I witnessed the law-and-order debate at the Tory Party conference in Blackpool in 1981, and I came to understand something of the real violent hatred that exists among the people who now predominate in the Tory Party. I was with a number of journalists, who see it every year and talk about it remotely and funnily, since the law-and-order debate is always a high point of the circus. But it was extraordinary how people, delegates, were so animated by negative ideas: a political party whose members were brought to their feet by the idea of punishment – longer prison sentences, arming the police, thrashing vandals. The negative passions whipping people into such a frenzy really did shake me. Strangely enough, though, I wanted a film in which people would move quite cynically and calmly among all this, people who would take it for granted the way a lot of journalists did.

The conference scene in The Ploughman's Lunch *certainly does bring home the eerie reality.*

Yes, we sneaked in under the auspices of another organization. The Tory Press Office, who had asked to see the script, were initially friendly and said we could film there, but a few months later so many hard-news teams had applied that our permissions were revoked – but not for reasons of ideology. We eventually got in another way, quite legitimately. Our crew had technical passes and our actors had press passes, so we were virtually invisible among all the journalists and camera crews. We also had quite strenuously to avoid getting two other film teams into frame. I was amazed at how easily we could insinuate our actors. Jonathan Pryce was very bold in walking under the platform when Heseltine was speaking (no one recognized him as an actor), and doing it about six or seven times, since we had to do several takes.

It's a very dispiriting film. In the beginning we may be beguiled by the character of James (Jonathan Pryce), but we soon realize that he is selfish and self-deceiving. You seem to have gone out of your way not to provide any character the audience can identify with, and I wonder if that policy of alienation was with you from the start?

Yes, there is a great tradition of having sympathetic characters in films, whereas in novels anti-heroes are acceptable: you travel with them. In films you stand outside characters. I suppose it *is* a pessimistic film; it was meant to be addressed to something of the spirit of the age, and to the way in which private deceptions and national deceptions are not entirely disconnected. James's rewriting of the history of the Suez crisis is constantly linked with his deceits in the pursuit of Susan. I do feel we live in dispiriting times, but I also hoped the film would give narrative pleasure and be funny, even though the humour is meant to be rather awkward.

In your interview with Ricks you mentioned that you were wary of putting 'gratuitous optimism' into your stories. Did the film medium solve a certain problem for you, in that you could be sincerely pessimistic?

Films generally end optimistically, don't they? I think people often don't have the courage of their pessimism. But I thought of the Greenham Common women as a kind of measure of moral certainty. When I researched for the film the women constantly complained about not getting enough publicity, so people will have to remember that they're watching an historical film. The ground has been rather pulled from under our feet since making the film, but Greenham Common was not in the news during the Falklands crisis.

The purity of the peace-camp women in the film seems to go along with a kind of innocence, an apparent unawareness that people could shrug off their appeal in the way the character James does.

Yes, by travelling with James you assume his urban and urbane values, so that people camping out in a field can look silly, just as earnest people at a poetry reading can look silly. I wanted not simply to watch James with distaste but to enter his world.

And yet the scene at a poetry reading might appear to be rather gratuitous. It helps the audience to reckon a little more with the extent of James's cynicism, and how he can casually condescend to his decent friend, the poet, but unfortunately the cinema audience will laugh along with James.

Yes, the scene is a sort of dog-leg, but we found in cutting that virtually every scene is relentlessly pushing ahead with Suez or the pursuit of the girl. I was very fond of the scene. It is a digression, but I also wanted to keep the sense of a diverse world, and the scene has the effect of getting you on the side of James and Jeremy, his friend, in a horrible and invidious way, to make you giggle at your friend's poetry reading. When you can afford to be so *louche* and cynical, then everyone around you seems too earnest, damned by their earnestness; it is a seductive and lazy viewpoint, one that can prevail in literary or journalistic London, and it's fuelled by drink too. I wanted people both to be sucked in and to be left cold . . .

With a nasty taste?

Yes, because England under Mrs Thatcher leaves me with a nasty taste.

James comes over finally as a ruthless character. We see him seizing all his opportunities, and yet he doesn't seem to show much self-awareness, so that he is portrayed as both opportunistic and naive.

He is obtuse, I think. He is quite aware of professional self-promotion.

But his obtuseness extends to not understanding the even more worldly characters of Susan and Jeremy. It comes as a shock to him that they are also self-serving.

Yes, there is a kind of horrible innocence about him, which does perhaps fit uneasily. But then I wanted so many things: I wanted somebody practising deception and being deceived at the same time, and also the other people being deceived. One point is that the unholy alliance between Britain, France and Israel over the Suez affair is matched in the characters of the film. One fortuitous point of colour matching occurs, for example, when Richard Eyre dissolves through James's map of Suez into a Norfolk field. Similarly, at the end, Jeremy says about Susie and himself, 'We're old allies.' Everybody is taking pleasure in taking each other for a ride. At the centre of all that it does need a certain gullibility on James's side. But I don't think it's implausible, because when you want something a lot you tend to think it must be clear to everyone else why you want it.

What sort of metaphor or parallel did you see between Suez and the Falklands crisis?

The Falklands business blew up when I had finished the first draft, so I let it bubble along in the background of the second draft, knowing full well that when we got to Brighton to film the Conservative Party conference they would be talking about the Falklands. While there are clear differences between Suez and the Falklands crisis, I still think they have their roots in the same illusion: a Churchillian dimension, and also war as serving a certain rallying function for the right. It's another form of self-delusion. I can see the case for taking back the Falklands, but I think the case was not really the point; there were more marginal and emotional reasons for sending out the fleet.

I find the historian, Ann Barrington, a complex and sympathetic character in The Ploughman's Lunch. *She is treated ambiguously, of course, as a compromised character who is emotionally wounded and has thrown in her lot with a commercial film-maker. She looks for private consolation, and yet her political beliefs are still vital and creditable.*

I always thought of her as very sympathetic. It's only lately that I've begun to feel that she's slightly less than totally sympathetic. For me she expresses something very honourable about the educated English middle class, which doesn't go to Tory Party conferences and bray for more punishment. She does have a sense of history, but she can no longer make an opposition to this prevailing spirit because she herself is tired; the time, she says, is past, so there's no hope to be had. She has a great deal of decency and compassion, but no position of strength.

What about her efforts to act vicariously through James's writing about Suez?

That is a monstrous piece of self-delusion. I gave her all the things that many people would desire – a beautiful house, and access to what I think of as a magnificent piece of English countryside – and who could resist her compromises at a certain age? I don't want to make a cruel point against her, simply a human one – that very few of us could occupy a position of total radical opposition without becoming bitter. If you spend your whole life in opposition it must shape your character; you are giving so much of your energy to what you think is bad or evil that you become almost in league with it. I think there is a time in your life when you have the energy to do that, and then you hope another generation will come along to take up the task. What is important is history and memory. So I do still see Ann Barrington as a sympathetic character, one based loosely in her ideas around E. P. Thompson, but with the great difference that

E. P. Thompson has in fact moved in the opposite direction, from theory into practice.

The final impression one has of Ann is that she is rather pitiable, both psychologically hurt and yet still believing that James actually shares her ideological integrity.

Yes, I wanted to give her a motive for being taken in by James. I've always been fascinated by the way in which people like James who don't say much are often considered to be profound, and can go a long way by being silent.

When he is asked to articulate a defence of socialism and property-owning he comes up with a platitude.

Ludicrous, yes. I like that scene . . . partly because similar things happened to me when I was about 20 and first began to meet people who had intellectual parents. I would visit their houses in the role of the boyfriend who had to be tested for my opinions. Everybody had a debating-society style, coming up with things like 'As Macaulay says . . .', and I used to find it absolutely terrifying. It was as if the size of your penis were being measured just because you had come in the door. At least, that was my paranoia about it. My parents were always very kind to people I took home, and they certainly weren't interested in gauging the megawatts of their intellects.

Do you think there is much of that sort of thing in your work: I mean, not exactly getting chips off your shoulder but in a way shriving early occasions of embarrassment?

Only in terms of tiny bits of oneself going into unsympathetic characters.

Is there now a sense in which you think of your early stories as a kind of apprentice work?

I like to think that I can come back to writing short stories, but I do have a feeling that I might not be able to write them as well as I did when I was younger. I don't know. The form itself is a good laboratory. I took the stories very seriously and worked on them very slowly, and I would always want to stand by them. I wouldn't want to lose the concentrated exploration of the short stories, nor to feel as I grow older that my sole duty is to address the nation on public themes: that would be arid and arrogant. I would always want to keep the excitement and mystery of writing, but I would find it harder to achieve that young man's easy swipe at life. A lot of the early stories concern initiation, things to do with becoming an adult.

If you are going to write a novel the subject has to be very appealing: it really has to be something that draws you, even if it is painful, because you are going to have to live with it so long. I have no idea what my next subject is going to be, but I feel very free in doodling at the moment.

· IRIS MURDOCH ·

In a period of less than thirty years Iris Murdoch has published twenty-one (mostly substantial) novels, as well as three works of philosophy – *Sartre: Romantic Rationalist* (1953), *The Sovereignty of Good* (1970) and *The Fire and the Sun* (1977). The list of her fiction begins with *Under the Net* (1954), and includes the widely acclaimed *The Bell* (1958), *A Severed Head* (1961), *The Nice and the Good* (1968), *The Black Prince* (1973) and *The Sea, The Sea* (1978), which won the Booker McConnell Prize.

Born in Dublin in 1919, Iris Murdoch was brought up in England. She was educated at Badminton School, Bristol, and took a degree in Classics at Somerville College, Oxford, in 1942. After two years as an Assistant Principal at the Treasury, she worked for a further two years (1944–6) with the United Nations Relief and Rehabilitation Administration in Belgium and Austria. She held the Sarah Smithson Studentship in Philosophy at Newnham College, Cambridge, for a year, and in 1948 returned to Oxford, where she was for fifteen years a Fellow of St Anne's College and University Lecturer in Philosophy. In 1956 she married John Bayley, who is Warton Professor of English Literature and a Fellow of St Catherine's College, Oxford.

Many readers have had the experience of feeling at once excited and exasperated by Murdoch's fiction. The mixture of apparent bizarrerie, excogitation and anagogical implication is altogether too heady, they find, but they are none the less – albeit reluctantly – absorbed. Martin Amis, who has long pondered the prose and haruspicated the nature of the Murdoch product, wrote of *Nuns and Soldiers* (1980):

> Miss Murdoch's novels are tragi-comic, in the sense that about half her characters live happily ever after, while the nuns and soldiers soldier on alone. They all inhabit a suspended and eroticised world, removed from the anxieties of health and money – and the half-made feelings on which most of us subsist. . . . It is breathless, gushing, and hopelessly uneconomical – which perhaps suits its theme. Miss Murdoch is very addictive, however. As with 'Nuns and Soldiers', so with the condition of love: you want to know how it will turn out, but you certainly don't want it to end. (*The Observer*, 7 September 1980)

'The style is contagious,' Victoria Glendinning wrote of *The Philosopher's Pupil* (1983):

> *Can* one combine a grand metaphysical fable with a situation comedy set in a provincial town and hope to get away with it? *Is* Iris Murdoch's controlling mythology powerful enough for us to go flailing after her as she 'swims lengths' indefatigably, sometimes absurdly, in pursuit of the Good? The answer to that last question is yes – unwillingly. (*The Sunday Times*, 1 May 1983)

Peter Ackroyd, on the other hand, was less reluctant to recognize the strengths of the novel:

> Miss Murdoch's writing is continually interesting because it works on so many levels at once and has a range which few other contemporary novelists possess. Passages of moral reflection are followed by demotic dialogue or by historical narrative, and long chapters of apparently realistic description can culminate in an expressly allegorical scene. She can create chaos and then allow it to disperse into a formal and lucid pattern. . . . It is altogether a quirky and precarious world, which remains credible only because of Miss Murdoch's extraordinary intellectual control of her material. (*The Times*, 28 April 1983)

For Iris Murdoch herself, writing fiction is a religious activity: 'all art is a struggle to be, in a particular sort of way, virtuous.' The art of the novelist may be mystification and fun, but it is equally truth-seeking and truth-revealing, she believes; it requires the novelist to make moral judgements. Her books seek to overcome the formlessness of experience by composing patterns and myths – 'the interaction of "the mythical" with the ordinary stuff of human life' – since 'we live in myth and symbol all the time' (*Spectator*, 7 September 1962). Since form can also falsify reality, however, it is dangerous to look for consolation from art. 'Only the very greatest art invigorates without consoling, and defeats our attempts, in W. H. Auden's words, to use it as magic' ('Against Dryness', *Encounter*, 16, January 1961).

Murdoch's deepest concerns are certainly ethical and spiritual – the complex natures of egoism, evil, enchantment and virtue, as well as the operations of chance – but her novels allow that the manifestations of uninsistent goodness are as obscure and deceptive as the negotiations of spurious human power. A character in *Bruno's Dream* comes to recognize that 'good art comes out of courage, humility, virtue', and it is just so with Murdoch's fictions: the allusive, mythopoeic and sometimes Gothicizing shapes of her imagination are at once generous and stringent.

Iris Murdoch is a moral philosopher as well as a novelist, and she is happy to have in her novels what she has called 'idea-play', but she does not use fiction to serve a determined philosophical programme. In so far as her philosophical preoccupations are relevant to her work as a novelist, it is still necessary to point out that she submits them to the test of the artistic imagination. Her novels do not prove anything; they attend as much to what is intricate and ambivalent in experience as to what is absolute and unambiguous. She relishes the free and expansive complexity of the world of human purposes, interweaving the stratagems and surrenders of such a multitude of characters that her novels can take on the appearance of overpopulated chess-boards. (Malcolm Bradbury has parodied the 'accidents' of her work in his piece 'A Jaundiced View', *Who Do You Think You Are?* (1976).) But the complicated web of her plots is properly a function of the chaos and contingency of experience rather than of choice conceptualization or thesis-making. The 'austere and unconsoling love of the Good' which informs her own religious sense is examined through the drama (and sometimes melodrama) of bourgeois behaviour – the graphically involved substantiality – of her fiction.

Iris Murdoch has a house in Steeple Aston, Oxfordshire, and a compact top-floor *pied-à-terre* – hung with much-loved pictures by favourite artists – in London, where I talked to her in March 1983. I began by asking about her most recent novel, *The Philosopher's Pupil* (1983), to which Kay Dick has given the credit it surely deserves: Iris Murdoch, she wrote,

> manifests an exuberant passion in her creation of an English spa peopled by the immediately recognisable Murdochian characters . . . hugely funny, although the deeds it illustrates are dark, dialogue which has those brain cells renewing themselves *en vitesse*, luxurious in its range of personality, motive and counterpoint. . . . *The Philosopher's Pupil* is a feast of possibilities to entertain. I can only say thank you, Iris Murdoch. (*Spectator*, 30 April 1983)

★ ★ ★

The Philosopher's Pupil *is a powerful story of dark obsession and love, riveting reading. It's the first novel in which you've placed a philosopher at the centre, almost as if you are outfacing critics who have labelled you a philosophical novelist.*
This novel really has more to do with a pupil–teacher relationship, which I've been involved in all my life – in both roles. I think it's interesting and moving, and I made the character a philosopher because it came along with the package, as it were. I am writing philosophy at the moment, but of course in *The Philosopher's Pupil* the character talks philosophy *en passant* rather than as part of the story.
And yet the character, John Robert Rozanov, has covered something of the same ground as your own work in philosophy, including Platonism . . .
In a very rough way, yes, but that's not particularly significant.

You didn't intend the novel to be an indictment of a certain kind of philosopher?
No, but I think philosophy is a subject which does lead some people to despair, it's much too difficult for the human mind. If you are an ancient historian or a linguist there is always something you can be doing which is part of your job, but if you're not doing philosophy pretty well you're not doing it at all.

Do you mean that philosophy requires a rigorously disciplined mind, a mind which can live with the knowledge that the ultimate quest of moral philosophy – for the good, that is – can never be completed?
It is impossible to do moral philosophy without asserting values of your own, and – as you say – virtue is unattainable. It's a very deep subject and can't help being a metaphysical subject, and that's what interests me most.

There's one passage in the novel which may be very difficult for the reader who hasn't followed your earlier work, and that's when the philosopher has his first long and crucial conversation with Father Bernard, who suffers his own doubts.
Yes, I think that conversation is important. It's about real issues, but of course it is very inconclusive. It's important in relation to the characters, or else I wouldn't have it as part of the story.

John Robert can be seen as a kind of Prospero figure who attempts to dominate and to decide the destiny of other characters – particularly of Hattie and Tom, who are hopeful innocents – while the flailing and angry George, his former pupil, takes the part of Caliban. I wonder to what extent you deliberately assumed The Tempest *as the myth of the novel?*
I've always got *The Tempest* in my head, just as I had in *The Sea, The Sea*: the idea of giving up magic, the relation between religion and power, and so on. John Robert is a power figure, he can't help exercising power. I don't think too much weight should be put on the notion that the book is about the nature of philosophy; it's about the nature of power in human relations. The teacher is a powerful and potentially destructive person. Of course Rozanov acts wrongly towards George. He should let George off, be nice to him, and become a bit less absolute; but a certain kind of philosophical mind is very absolute in relation to

philosophy. This could spill over into real life, as it were, the feeling that you must have perfect truth and never fudge things. John Robert hates messy and emotional situations. George behaves in exactly the way to enrage him, which is what George partly wants: he wants the emotional drama which will make a bond between them.

George is looking for salvation from the mess of his own life, and so he constructs for himself the myth that John Robert should be his redeemer.

He's been obsessed and dominated by this man; it's a love relationship of a special kind.

The question of whether or not George did actually try to kill his wife, Stella, is never actually answered, is it?

It's an extreme fit of rage (and he's had plenty of such fits before), and it comes up when Stella mentions John Robert. It happens again later, as the narrator points out, when George thinks he's about to go off with his mistress, Diane, and he asks Stella what she is going to do. She says that she might go and see John Robert, and that remark sets off another frenzy.

I know that you write at least two drafts of each novel. Can you explain how you set about writing this novel?

The drafts come after I've finished the novel. The invention is what's difficult; everything is over, as it were, when I've finished inventing it, because I invent it in such enormous detail. So that the drafts come at a fairly late stage of the proceeding.

Before you actually start writing you have set out for yourself every character and incident?

Yes. It's all very strongly related, they all come into being with a kind of necessity in relation to each other.

I am interested in the way you use an omniscient narrator who also plays a part in the story. N, as he's called, is resented by John Robert, and he's slandered by other characters – once for being what someone calls an 'impotent voyeur'.

But are they right to describe him that way? Perhaps they're not.

There seems to be a slight structural problem with the role of Stella, George's wife, who has to be removed from much of the action in order that George himself should become the focus of attention. His private and public turbulence requires him to be set apart from his wife, and the reader may be rather sceptically surprised to discover that Stella has in fact been harboured by N.

Yes, I think Stella is not a very successful character. I never solved the problem of Stella. She had to be put off the stage for a while, and it occurred to me later on that she was with N.

Did you have a real spa in mind in creating the town of Ennistone?

No, it's entirely fictional, and inventing it gave me great pleasure.

But the baths do reflect your own passion for water.

Yes, there is water in all the books. Thinking of the background of the drowning of John Robert, one image printed on my mind is from a film I saw a hundred years ago, *Les Enfants du Paradis*, where there is a murder in a swimming bath (though the character in the film is not drowned but shot, I think). When I was in China I visited a bath establishment, which also struck my imagination, and in Iceland I have been in warm pools where it is a great joy to swim on a cold day. I do love swimming. I used to be absolutely fearless in the sea, but I nearly drowned once, and I'm now much more cautious. I used to think the sea and I were great friends, but one must fear the sea.

The character who is known as 'Emma' is in some ways the purest part in the novel.

I adore Emma, but it took me a long time to invent him. He was originally an Icelander, but I couldn't make him work as an Icelandic boy, and to make him Irish was the solution to the problem. The idea that he should be a singer did come first.

He certainly comes over very naturally, but one scene I felt unsure about was when he goes to visit his mother in Belgium. I don't think I picked up the function of that encounter.

Does a scene have to have a function in that strict sense? It's just to show him in another place, with this charming woman. We see another aspect of his character, in relation to his mother. It's a sort of magic scene, a magic picture.

The Slipper House in which John Robert virtually imprisons Hattie – along with her companion and guardian Pearl, who also fancies herself to be in love with John Robert – does seem to figure as a sort of enchanted castle containing the fairy princess, and yet again it may suggest to the reader a kind of Prospero's island.

Yes, but don't overdo *The Tempest* here, because the relation to *The Tempest* is terribly shadowy. The fact that George thinks himself Caliban is part of George's myth.

Would you then resist the notion of the novel being diagrammed by allusion to The Tempest, *with Hattie standing for a kind of Miranda and Tom being the person whom John Robert designs to be Ferdinand?*
Yes, absolutely. I not only resist it, I abhor it. *The Tempest* is very deeply in my mind, but it's not what the book is about. The book is about what it's about.

I know you have felt the strain between determining the form of a novel and allowing the characters to have an open and contingent life of their own.
The determined form I'm frightened of is certainly not anybody else's form. It has nothing to do with being dominated by Shakespeare or anyone else; it has to do with being dominated by myself and by my own mythology, which is very strong. This book is very scattered, and has a lot of people in it, and that's good. I think there are a great number of points of serious interest, and I hope the characters exist in their own right.

Is it a great effort for you to claw away from the proclivity to impose myth and pattern?
It's a problem which used to be a great difficulty for me, but now I feel less worried about it, either because I may have got better at doing both things at once or because I don't care. At a certain point one becomes less anxious.

The question of self-expression is relevant here, I think, in the sense that the novelist may have an absorbing interest in other human beings or use the novel as a forum for his own personal concerns and obsessions.
It begins from an interest in human beings, but any writer is inevitably going to work with his own anxieties and desires. If the book is any good it has got to have in it the fire of a personal unconscious mind.

Which of your anxieties and desires came into this book, do you think? Is it to do with the tension between philosophy and art?
No, I don't feel any such tension. The only tension involved there is that both pursuits take up time. This book has much more to do with power – being isolated by power, and John Robert's misuse of power – together with the despair of the

philosopher. The anguish of the philosopher comes about because philosophy touches impossibility. I think it's something all philosophers feel. I'm sure Plato and Kant felt it, that you can't get it right. It's impossible for the human mind to dominate the things which haunt it. There's the impossibility of being good, and the way in which the human being is doomed to be bad and even evil, and the impossibility of stating the basis of everything. Kant and Plato, my personal gods, come near to doing this: their god-like minds make these patterns, but that isn't quite right either, since one can't really do it.

Is the philosopher seeking power?

Yes, you want to be God, you want to see the whole thing.

Is there a sense in which writing novels is therefore a relaxation for you?

No, writing novels is my job, and it's a serious undertaking. I always wanted to be a novelist, but there was a time when I thought I wanted to be an archaeologist and art historian, when I was at Oxford. I couldn't go on with the art history because I was conscripted as soon as I left Oxford; I was working in a government office, the Treasury, just ten days after I took Schools. My path took me away from the academic world, but then I was taken over by the desire to be a philosopher by the end of the war. I would very much like to have been a Renaissance art historian, and at one time I wanted to be a painter. I think I would have been a moderate painter if I had given my life to it, but that is an absolute hypothesis without any basis to it! I do sometimes try to paint, but I haven't got any training. So this is just a dream life. I envy painters, I think they are happy people. The painter lives with his craft the whole time: the visual world, which I adore, is always present, and the artist can always be thinking about his work, being inspired by light and so on. Painters can have a nice time.

Do you have a nice time writing novels?

Yes, I very much enjoy writing novels, but the beginning of a novel is a time of awful torment, when you're dealing with a lot of dead pieces and you have to wait and wait for some kind of animation.

Writing is also terribly solitary, and prevents you from observing and being with other people.

That's what sometimes makes me want to write for the theatre: you can have company! I very much enjoyed being a teacher, and I enjoyed college life. But I don't co-operate with anybody in writing novels.

You mean you don't discuss your work in progress with anybody, not even with your husband?

No, he reads the novels only when they're absolutely finished.

Do you think you've been influenced by his work as a critic?

I don't think I've been influenced as a novelist by him, but obviously if you live with someone for many years your mind and his mind become very closely connected. But he doesn't do any sort of critical job on the novels.

How did you get on with your parents?

Perfectly. I'm an only child, and I lived in a perfect trinity of love. It made me expect that, in a way, everything is going to be like that, since it was a very deep harmony.

My darling mother, who is still alive, was a marvellous singer – Dublin, as you know, is a great singing city – but she got married when she was 18, which was silly of her from the point of view of a possible career! She had a professional teacher in Dublin, and then again when we moved to London.

My father was an extremely good and clever man, and we used to discuss books when I was very young, the *Alice* books and so on. He comes from County Down and grew up in a sheep-farming family. His family were admirable people, but Protestants of a very strict kind, and I think he wanted to get away. He joined a territorial unit just before the war, and went through the entire First World War in the cavalry, which saved his life. Although the cavalry did many dangerous things they weren't in that awful holocaust of the trenches. When he wasn't in France his unit was stationed at the Curragh, and one day in Dublin when he was going to church on a tram he met a pretty girl who was going to the same church. So that was that; they got married and he removed her to London where he joined the civil service. My father was a very good civil servant; he started at a low level and rose to the top. We settled down in London – where we knew nobody – and I grew up as a Londoner, and it's only lately that I've imagined how strange that was. I never had any family apart from this perfect trinity, and I scarcely know my Irish relations. I feel as I grow older that we were wanderers, and I've only recently realized that I'm a kind of exile, a displaced person. I identify with exiles.

Your work in the United Nations Relief and Rehabilitation Administration at the end of the war must have been quite harrowing?

Yes, it was extraordinary. It was concerned with displaced persons, lots of Yugoslavs and Poles, every sort of person who had to be identified and looked after. A number of them, particularly Yugoslavs, didn't want to go back to their homeland. It was absolutely front-line stuff, and much of the time one was simply preoccupied with feeding people.

What impressions are you left with from that time? Is it mostly a sense of hassle and anxiety?

Yes, chaos, and the sadness of the old people. I did help some younger people to come to England. But in general the problem was so enormous that one couldn't do much, other than feeding them and being nice to them. There was an utter breakdown of society. At least it was instructive to witness that.

One of the interesting aspects of your novels is that you often depict characters – such as Hilary Burde in A Word Child, *and Charles Arrowby in* The Sea, The Sea – *who are repressed or in some way fixated by their past lives, by certain events or situations they cannot escape.*

It's a salient thing in human life, one of the most general features of human beings, that they may be dominated by remorse or by some plan of their lives which may have gone wrong. I think it's one of the things that prevents people from being good. Why are people not good, and why, without being evil or even having bad intentions, do they do bad things? Schopenhauer, whom I admire, is good on this topic of tragedy. Some people who are not bad find themselves so situated that they are unable to stop themselves from doing the greatest possible harm they can to others. It's an evident feature of human psychology that people have secret dream lives. The secrecy of people is very interesting, and the novelist is overcoming the secrecy and attempting to understand. Readers sometimes say to me that I portray odd characters; but the secret thoughts and obsessions and fantasies of others would amaze one, only people don't tell them, partly because they're ashamed and partly because secrecy is very natural and proper.

I think you've remarked elsewhere on the inadequacies of psychoanalysis.

Yes, but not in any theoretic way. It's not as if I've studied Freud and found him wanting, though I have read a lot of Freud. I love reading Freud, because one gets all sorts of ideas from him, and he's a great and interesting thinker. But one effect of psychoanalysis is to make you concentrate enormously on yourself, to think too much about yourself, whereas the best cure for misery is to help somebody else. I think analysis can help people as a sort of first-aid. The analyst is in a sense a blunt instrument, but he can work as somebody who cares, and I think a good analyst makes the patient feel that he has value. People can easily feel that their value is lost or blackened, and the analyst can fulfil a priestly role in making them feel there is hope. I don't think the theoretical stuff quite explains what the analyst is doing, but a good analyst knows that the theory is something suggestive and perhaps helpful to him. What is really happening is a very private and emotional thing, a relationship between two individuals of a secret kind.

Do you have any qualms about the fact that as a novelist you are revealing secrets?

I reveal other people's secrets, not mine, except in the sense that any artist reveals himself to some extent in his work. But it's the secrets of my fictional characters that I'm giving away.

Do you think you reveal your theoretical if not your personal preoccupations?

My theoretical preoccupations don't come in much. They sometimes come in through the characters, who might want to discuss certain things in a theoretical way. Putting in too much theorizing is an obvious danger, but it's not a temptation I especially feel. One could paralyse a book by putting in a lot of theoretical stuff. But knowing things is vital for a novelist. Cleverness and thought and understanding a lot of things are a great benefit.

What areas of Freud's work do you think valuable?

Well, there's a bit of deep truth in certain things like the notion of the superego and the id. What I agree with in Freud is what he frankly says he's pinched from Plato. The doctrine of anamnesis is a doctrine of the unconscious mind, and the idea of eros as fundamental energy, a drive which includes sex and which can be good and can be bad: that's all in Plato.

I wonder what you think of Freud's explanations of dreams? After all, Freud himself writes packaged stories, solved and shaped . . .
I think dreams have a great many sorts of explanation. Once the Freud virus has, as it were, got into you, you keep on looking at things in that way. But surely there's a lot of pure accident in dreams. One has kinds of obsessions and fears that can't be given a sexual meaning. I think the inventiveness and the details of dreams are amazing.

Do you ever record your own dreams?
I sometimes do. One invents amazing things in dreams which one couldn't invent in real life. One cure for insomnia is to make yourself dream. I usually sleep extremely well, but if ever I find myself waking I invent a dream, which starts off consciously and goes on unconsciously.

Can you give me an example?
I don't think I will.

Have you experienced lucid dreams?
Yes, one can guide a dream, and that's very exciting.

You have written that it's always a good question to ask a philosopher what he's afraid of, and I would like to ask that question of you.
I think I'm afraid of somehow finding out that it doesn't really matter how you behave, that morality is just a superficial phenomenon. I don't think one could find this out, it's just a bogey; the impossibility of finding it out is very deep in moral philosophy. I don't believe in God, but I think morality is fundamental to human life.

In The Philosopher's Pupil, *of course, John Robert determines on the possibility of passing beyond good and evil.*
Yes, he's interested in this question, and George tags on to it.

What do you say to critics who think you take a dismal view of marital love and of fulfilment, and that you dismiss characters to happiness?

Well, of course a novel is a drama, and dramas happen when there is trouble. A completely harmonious life might not produce the drama. But the books are full of happiness; I feel they are shining with happiness. In spite of the fact that people have a bad time – this is true of the novel in a general way – the novel is a comic form.

But comedy can be a consequence of form, which might be illustrating the risible divisions between people's self-images and what they find themselves doing.

I'm not mocking my characters. The comedy is very deep in the form. The vitality and energy of art make you happy whatever its subject matter. In *The Philosopher's Pupil* Hattie and Tom are radiant and happy people; they have the sort of energy that destines them for happiness, and I think that's true of Emma too. But one tends to be impressed by the people who are demonic.

Yes, you've said elsewhere that demonic characters have a sort of 'illegitimate charm'.

That's true in real life as well. To dramatize your life and to feel that you have a destiny represents a very general human temptation. It's a magical element in life which is so dangerous, and which is the enemy of religion and the enemy of goodness. I think one identifies with the demonic characters in books, since it's a deep notion to feel that the devil tempts you and gives you power in return for giving up goodness, which is after all often dull.

I imagine you feel dubious about imposing form on the novel for both artistic and ethical reasons, in that form might become a libel on real life?

A strong form tends to narrow the characters. I felt it particularly about *A Severed Head*, which was the end of a certain road, because a strong mythology can issue in a mechanical and unsurprising sort of writing. Good writing is full of surprises and novelties, moving in a direction you don't expect. The idea of the myth and the form have got to be present, but one has brutally to stop the form determining the emotion of the book by working in the opposite direction, by making something happen which doesn't belong to the world of the magic.

But when you first map your characters and plot you may in a sense be pre-empting the contingent openness of it.

No, because that has to be invented too, the way in which one destroys or blocks the myth. I am very conscious of this tension at the start, and I play it to and fro.

You have written that art is the 'great clue to morals'. I assume you feel that there must be some educational or even didactic thrust to the novel, whereas some theorists believe that the novel can be no more than conjectural play.

Yes, there is a sort of pedagogue in my novels. I think a novelist must be truthful. Bad novels project various personal daydreams – the daydream of power, for example, or of being fearfully sexually attractive and so on – and this can be horrid. But the contingent nature of life and what human failings are like, and also what it's like for somebody to be good: all this is very difficult, and it's where truthfulness comes in, to stop yourself from telling something which is a lie.

And yet it might seem presumptuous for a novelist to aspire to truth-telling, when there are so many ingredients and variables in a novel, including characterization, pattern of events, myth, as well as ethics.

All these things are mixed up. A bad painter is lying because he hasn't really *looked* – in the way that Rembrandt has looked. Truth and justice are involved there, because the artist has to have a just judgement. I think it's not presumptuous; it's a humble occupation if it's pursued properly. But then, you see, one is also carried away by the eros of the thing. Truth and happiness are ideally frolicking together, so that it is a happy destiny when it's working well. Works of art make you happy. Even *King Lear* makes you happy, and yet it comes near to the edge of the impossible – that you could be made happy by a work of art which is about something terrible.

Your good characters – Tallis in A Fairly Honourable Defeat, *for example, or those who aspire to good behaviour like the Count and Anne in* Nuns and Soldiers – *can turn out to be ineffectual people, moral touchstones which verge on the symbolic. A virtuous character acts in a disinterested way and therefore, as you suggested earlier, can become uninteresting.*

Yes, that's the paradox. But Tallis is allegorical, he is supposed to be a sort of Christ figure and is recognized as such by his arch-enemy, Julius. Tallis is a symbolic character; it's his job, as it were, to be good. You tend to think that a good character is not strong, but Tallis is strong. The count, on the other hand, is an innocent and noble character; he's not exactly a good character in any strict sense, but then good characters in a strict sense are not met with in ordinary life.

I want to ask about your evidently deep response to Simone Weil . . .
Yes, I love her.

. . .mainly because it might be thought that her prescription for a kind of hopeless waiting (which is involved in the concept of amor fati*) could be regarded as life-denying.*
Not at all. It requires the most enormous spiritual energy to decreate yourself in this sort of way. Ordinary life is a kind of dreamy drifting, defending yourself all the time, pushing other people out of the way. I think things like meditation and prayer help you to grasp the unreality of ordinary states of mind. I don't like the idea of *amor fati*, which seems to be the opposite of what I think. Simone Weil does sometimes use the term *amor fati* – which I connect with stoicism, a doctrine I don't at all embrace – but I think her notion of obedience is rather to be understood as breaking the current of the ordinary egoistic life and feeling as if you might as well be anything. I am very much against Jung, who is the enemy here. I think you realize your contingency when you break this current, and not that you have a great sense of destiny – because you don't *know* the myth, you don't know what's happening. It's rather that you relate yourself to your surroundings in a different way, and you relate yourself to other people in a selfless way. It's an exercise in self-denial.

Does this connect with your interest in Buddhism, which has the idea that at death you should feel both fulfilled and mortified?
It seems to me that some kind of Christian Buddhism would make a satisfactory religion because of course I can't get away from Christ, who travels with me; I was a Christian as a child. But I don't believe in the supernatural aspects of Christianity. Buddhism is a good picture of the thing – not, of course, its

mythical ideas about reincarnation, but that the aim is to destroy
the ego. Schopenhauer plays with this idea, that one's task in life
is to be aware of the world without the ego. It's not at all an
other-worldly religion, it's absolutely this-worldly, here and
now: this is where it's all happening and there isn't anywhere
else. But to deny the ego is the most difficult thing of all. It
would be a condition of goodness when you then respond to
your surroundings in an appropriate way because you are not
blind. Painting is an image of the spiritual life; the painter really
sees, and the veil is taken away. You see the world in a much
more clarified way, which would be at its most important where
one is thinking about other people, because they are the most
difficult and complicated things you ever come across. I think
people who are good – it sounds romantic, but I think I've met
one or two – make a sort of space around them, and you feel you
are safe with them. And there are certainly people who are
menacing, who breathe up all the air so that you can't breathe,
and who diminish you. This is why a good analyst would have
to have this quality of making a large space – someone who is
reassuring without bolstering up in an illegitimate way, because
the good person also comes to one as a judge. Buddhism has
very much to do with understanding these things about human
life, together with the notion that it is absolutely important. I
want there to be religion on this planet.

*But what is worrying is Buddhism's radical ruling that all existence is
ultimately evil, and should perhaps be annihilated.*

It depends how you understand this. I think nirvana should be
taken as a mythical idea; there couldn't be such a thing as
entering nothingness. Nirvana means that the selfish world is as
nothing to the spiritual, and vice versa. Sophisticated Buddhism
is very conscious of conceptual limitations, that these myths are
saying something which has to be understood in another way.
The total obliteration of your present being would mean that the
world would exist and not you. This is an idea that Simone Weil
expresses – that you want the world and God to be alone
together and to remove yourself – and it makes sense to me. I
think that in this sense death is happening all the time, and not
that one soldiers on through life and then there's something

terribly special at the end, which seems to me to be an old-fashioned religious mythical idea.

Some critics have felt that you have a very limited view of the human capability for improvement.

I think anybody would have it if they looked around. Perhaps one can improve a little bit, but egoism is so fearfully strong and so natural. One is demanding something which goes contrary to nature if one thinks of attaining goodness, or even of improving oneself markedly. Do you know anyone who has improved themselves much?

Yet it does seem that there is a sort of sub-text in some of your novels, positing an impersonal love which is impossible – quite beyond human happiness, niceness, decency, sexual love . . .

Yes, I think one is haunted by this idea. How far it can change one's life is another matter, but I think it's worth having it there. That's why I feel much closer to Christianity now than when I was younger. If you are fortunate enough to have Christ in your life, it's something you should hold on to.

What do you think is the true function of art? Is it consolation, education, pure pleasure?

The phrase you've used – pure pleasure – is good, I think. One should live with good art and not get addicted to bad art, which is demoralizing and disappointing. Good art is a pleasure which is uncontaminated, it's happiness. One also learns a lot from art: how to look at the world and to understand it; it makes everything far more interesting. It's a mode of reflection, and this is why it's a terrible crime for totalitarian states to interfere with artists. Artists must be left alone, and critics must leave them alone too. I think artists are often in the situation of being bullied by critics, which is monstrous. Artists are essentially free individuals. Art is a great hall of reflection, and that's why it's important from a political point of view that there should be a free art, because art is a place where all sorts of free reflection goes on. It's a mode of thought, a mode of knowledge. Good art can't help teaching you things, but it mustn't aim at teaching. The artist's task is to make good works of art. A novel is a mode of explanation; you can't help explaining characters and scrutinizing their motives. The novelist is the judge of these people –

that can't help emerging – and it is most difficult for the novelist to be a just judge. In the traditional novel, which is what I'm talking about, the novelist is *ipso facto* revealing his own morality, and he should be doing so.

· V.S. PRITCHETT ·

England's premier short-story writer and literary essayist, V. S. Pritchett is equally renowned as autobiographer, biographer (Balzac and Turgenev), and travel writer. His many books include *Collected Stories* (1982), *More Collected Stories* (1983), *The Myth Makers* (1979), *The Tale Bearers* (1980), *The Spanish Temper* (1954), and novels including *Mr Beluncle* (1951) and *Dead Man Leading* (1937). An invaluable collection, *The Other Side of a Frontier: A V. S. Pritchett Reader* – 'It's wonderful, isn't it? It makes me sound like a Latin primer' – appeared in 1984.

A master both of the short story as a form and of English prose style, Pritchett writes stories which are true revelations of character, with an instinctive sense of compassionate comedy, and – as Walter Allen has pointed out – he is a connoisseur of lower-middle-class puritanism. Claire Tomalin has acutely described his *Collected Stories* in remarking, 'V. S. Pritchett catches something about the English character that no writer since Dickens has seen: its obsessive and excitable nature, its exoticism in love and melancholy. Pritchett's phrases breathe like living things; his book gives intense and lasting pleasure' (*The Sunday Times*).

Educated at Alleyn's School, Dulwich, London, Pritchett worked first in the leather trade in London, then in the shellac, glue and photographic trade in Paris. From 1923 to 1926 he was a correspondent in Ireland and Spain for the *Christian Science Monitor*, and for many years afterwards he wrote criticism for the *New Statesman*, of which he also became a director, 1946–78.

He has been a visiting professor at several American universities, and in 1969 he delivered the Clark Lectures at Cambridge University (published as *George Meredith and English Comedy*). He is President of the Society of Authors, an Honorary Member of the American Academy of Arts and Letters and of the Academy of Arts and Sciences, and an ex-President of PEN. He was knighted in 1975.

Short, twinkling with geniality, immaculately courteous ('Would you like a pee-break before a tea-break?'), a man of modesty and pride, Pritchett is as old as the century and works as hard as ever. His wonderfully happy second marriage is going on fifty years. Temporarily badgered by a neighbour's building repairs (which somehow managed to knock a hole through one party-wall), Sir Victor and Lady Pritchett live in a handsome terrace to the north of Regents Park, London; a taxidermist's triumph – birds in a large glass case – dominates one end of their first-floor sitting-room.

'It has all been very damaging to the ego, talking about myself', he remarked at the end of this interview, which took place in the summer of 1984. 'I'll be in a terribly inflated state; I shall have to puncture myself.'

* * *

Judging from the tone and approach of your first volume of autobiography, A Cab at the Door, *it was obviously written without any view to the sequel,* Midnight Oil. *Can you tell me how you came to write two volumes?*
My brothers and sisters and I all felt we'd had a most extraordinary childhood: we half-deplored it and half-laughed at it, and we could not stop talking about it. Our father was an endless source of interest to us, and he was a story in himself. The second volume was very much about wanting to become a writer, and I could only write about my life in so far as I was a writer – almost in technical terms. *Midnight Oil* is otherwise an account of how the son becomes the father of the father: the roles were reversed, and that was nice. I wrote it under a strong sense of restriction: since I had become a writer I was running very fast

into what I had already written – about Ireland, Spain and so on.
I was up against my own work, which was a great problem to
me.

A Cab at the Door *seems to be much harsher on your father than*
Midnight Oil.

Very likely. We naturally made all sorts of harsh judgements
about him. But when I got to the point of leaving home I slowly
realized that there must have been another side to his character,
or that he must have valued it in some other way. I began to feel
that the writer had to justify the characters he's describing, and
to see them – to some extent – as they see themselves, or at least
to understand that they can and do see themselves in another
way. One has to let them have a voice, to see what it is that
makes them distinctive in their own eyes.

There were certain virtues about him which I remember
strongly and which still appeal to me: he was a natural craftsman, and was only moderately fit for the business world. It was
interesting to see him designing something, and to see how
tremendously he valued the materials of his trade: he had a great
feeling for the surfaces of silks. But his dream life was so odd,
and his extraordinary optimism issued in a dreamlike form.
How on earth could it have arrived, why was it there, what was
its nature? I came to the conclusion that he was a man with no
imagination, only a very strong sense of fantasy. My mother,
who was a real cockney realist, was much more imaginative,
and she had almost no sense of fantasy.

In A Cab at the Door *you describe him as a bumptious cocksparrow*
and a domestic tyrant.

In many ways he was a passionately affectionate man, but in a
hard Yorkshire way he wasn't going to let anything pass. He had
a good deal of self-conceit, and would put anyone right. He
perhaps assumed more dignity than a cocksparrow has; in his
merry moments, on the other hand, there was a good deal of the
cocksparrow about him. I think he must have been very shy, for
in public he had somehow to make himself into a person visible
to all. In restaurants he was a mixture of the obsequious and the
bumptious; he would speak to the manager in a very pretentious
way.

There's an interesting strategic difference between the two books in the way you talk about your father's death. In A Cab at the Door *you remark that his last coherent words were 'That woman meant well but she did not give me enough to eat,' whereas in* Midnight Oil *there's no mockery when you describe how he died of cancer: '"Not the knife. I won't have the knife," he gasped. He said he was hungry. Then he died.'*

That's very true. I think that he himself had more dignity as he got older. My earliest memories of him are of a dressy man with a shiny suit and a cigar in his mouth, boastful – as it seemed to me then – in a mysterious way. Later in life he lived in another kind of imaginary personality. I think I also got tired of the fact that when we were young we had treated him as a comic character . . .

Comic but also hateful, I think. In A Cab at the Door *you depict him as a kind of villain, and it comes as something of a surprise to find you calling him a 'hero' at one point in* Midnight Oil. *I felt that you had made an artistic decision to see your father in the aspect of a hero, when that aspect had been missing in the first volume.*

He was a kind of dream to us when we were young. The story about him dressing up in order to seem like a yachtsman is absolutely genuine, and he became very much worse for a period, but that side of him became rather more sophisticated as he grew older. He wanted to identify with any enormously successful person he met, and therefore his demeanour took on the character of other people.

When one is young one is very much in collision with other people, but growing older makes one revise one's views and see the other aspects: you become more reflective.

Do you think there is something disingenuous about writing autobiography, since you must inevitably compose and shape your memories (I ask this question because you have somewhere recorded the fact that you have an 'associative memory')?

Yes, I think I'd agree with you, but on the other hand practically anyone could write well about their childhood. One's observation is so sharp at the age; detail is everything to a child. I can remember even now exactly how my great-uncle smelt, but I couldn't say that about any person I meet nowadays. It is extraordinary, for example, how children watch hands.

Was there anything you consciously excised or underplayed in writing your autobiography? In various places you mention the idea of parricide, and at times you must have felt murderous towards your father.

Yes, but that should be taken as a kind of joke. A great friend of mine, Gerald Brenan, had been on frightful terms with his father, and we used to laugh and say that we clearly belonged to the Parricides' Club. We would talk about Stendhal as an example, and it was a comic way of referring to the tension between father and son, with a side-glance at the Oedipus Complex.

My mother was really illiterate; my father was not illiterate but not very literate. People often say that I derive my literary talent from my grandfather, who was a preacher, but I have come to think that it's not so at all. My mother's narrative gifts were enormous; although she only wrote a letter to me about four times in her life, she was fantastic in talk.

The autobiography is clearly patterned in one way: you see in yourself both the truculence and pride of your father and the moodiness of your mother. You seem to give a lot of credit to that sort of genetic equation, how you combine in yourself the characteristics of your parents.

I do see that very much, yes. I think my brother who died became almost a caricature as a man: he was most tenderly affectionate but also a caricature of my father; my brother had all my father's affectations, but he transferred them to a world of his own. I was the bullying elder brother, and I used to regard him as being almost unspeakably soft and silly, but he turned out to be extremely able.

I also think there is a vast, almost racial difference – which is strongly emphasized in my family – between someone who comes from the south and someone who comes from the north. My mother represented all the virtues and vices of the south, and my father the other side of me: we would look for it in each other. My very youngest brother surprises me by being almost completely the Yorkshireman, but he also has this curious streak of fantasy in his nature. Being the youngest, he was the most free of the family and never had any troubles with my father. He stood up to my father and made fun of him, whereas the rest of us were much too frightened to do that.

Whenever I've done something unwise or extremely silly, I think I've made an incompetent bid to live out of character.

It sounds as though you can see very few special qualities or peculiarities in yourself other than those you have isolated in your forebears . . .

I don't understand or even think of peculiarities in myself. I'm sure I must have them, but I would find it very hard to portray myself. I suppose one can't describe oneself.

Your autobiography draws on a great deal that has otherwise gone into your short stories: were you ever fearful that in writing it you might leave yourself short of fiction, so to speak?

I thought it was going to be something quite different, and in fact I never particularly wanted to write the autobiography. I was rather nagged into writing it, particularly by people with sociological curiosity. Someone said to me that I had sailed through all sorts of English society, and that I'd gone from world to world much more than other people. It had never really occurred to me. But I knew I had this obsession – I believe very strongly in the value of obsessions to a writer – and I had to get it out of the way, just as I had to grow up when I got towards the age of 30. I reached a crisis in my life at about the age of 27, and thought I had had an arrested development in many ways.

You have often written about writing as being fertilized by recovering an emotion, that nothing in literature is an 'exercise', only fact transmuted . . .

One's own history is a kind of bank account which tells you a lot not only about yourself but also about society. I often think of my great-uncle in this context. As a child I never knew anything about him except that he looked very strange; but when I came to draw his portrait I considered him as a sort of social being, a thinking man in his own way, and he became much larger in my mind. I would revert to him as an example of a craftsman, a man whose mind worked in a certain way. He used to take me around York Minster, and far from being an ignorant worker he understood every damn thing about the building; he almost said he had built it and might even revise it (he always had a ruler sticking out of his pocket).

In Midnight Oil *you describe your travels and work in France, Spain and Ireland, with wonderful portraits of your encounters with the famous and the not-so-famous, but you speak very little of the anguish and solitude you must have experienced.*

I did enjoy being lonely. If you've been brought up in a crowded family with no time for yourself, and if you have an enquiring mind and want to know about things, the only way you can know them is by not talking to someone. I was in a way terribly deprived. I was never bored in the least; I was constantly interested, for example, in walking down the streets of Paris: I simply loved doing it. I was very much on my own: I lived on my own, I ate on my own, I didn't belong to a gang of people. I felt completely outside any group of friends, and I very much wanted to be outside. I used to think of myself as the lonely poet who only speaks to sheep or looks at nature: it seemed the thing to go in for, my consolation. I always felt that everything happens to everyone else, but nothing happens to me: I was very priggish as a young man. I did feel terribly the fact of being deprived of choices when I was young. It was a great blow to me to have to leave school just before I was 16. I had no objection to work, but it wasn't my choice: I thought I was done for. I found myself among people who made assumptions which would never occur to me: I never thought of going to the south of France, for example, since I had to earn my living.

So your first travels were in no sense epicurean exploits . . .

No, my epicureanism was confined to what I could afford.

Were you conscious of struggling against an inferior social position?

No, I didn't feel that. It has never worried me, I think. My father had the good Yorkshire characteristic of thinking of himself as himself, and that was a great protection. I never suffered from class envy. I didn't feel I had to join something in order to become a person. My youngest brother had a strong sense, I think, of buried inferiority which he rapidly compensated for by becoming rather snobbish and joining things. I thought I had talent, but I didn't know whether it would ever come to anything: I felt terribly compelled to dig it out.

In your Clark lectures, George Meredith and English Comedy, *you carefully point out that an obsession with class has seriously limited psychological penetration in fiction. Did you mean that any writer who is bugged by class inhibits himself from being open to the multifarious experiences of other kinds of people?*

I certainly had schoolboy snobberies: I wished I had gone to a more classy school and so forth . . . but it was not at all the thing I lived by. I could never have imposed a false personality, simply because I think I was too self-centred, too engrossed in myself, too egotistical.

In my generation so many young men who were going abroad on government service, for example, were immensely British and extremely hostile to foreigners and rather rude to them. I never felt that contempt for foreigners, and I really rather hated the British Empire for producing that kind of person. Although I was inclined to think of the British Empire as the most beneficent thing in the world, I didn't want to belong to it. I felt I ought in some way to unself myself and to become a foreigner, and that was always important to me. It has lasted to the present day, and in my ordinary life I want to be the people I see.

That would also seem to be the aesthetic which governs the way you write short stories.

I think it is, yes. I just want to become someone else, and at certain points I have to create the impression that they are justified, which is the most difficult thing to do. Most people don't think that way about other people, they just think they're wrong; but as a writer one has to think they are right, even if they are obviously wrong.

Is that part of the 'moral seriousness' you have often mentioned in your criticism? Do you feel it's your duty to vindicate other people's lives, with all their illusions, vanities and hypocrisies?

Very much so. It's the moral purpose, though there are also other purposes including entertainment and suggesting enquiry. People are in the end very much alone, and they act alone to a great extent. One has to be very careful of making a judgement. Each person is of course part of society, but in the end I think he feels he could always be the exception.

In A Cab at the Door *you relate how your interest shifted from poetry to writing prose, partly because prose provided 'common experience and solid worlds were judgements were made'. Yet what you seem to be saying is that in writing fiction you are intent on withholding judgements of your characters.*

I try not to extinguish temperament – the sort of free being which has a temperament, a temperament which will live even against its own feelings and judgements and interests. I have to be interested in temperament, the ways in which – because of temperament – a person could not live in any other way.

In some stories it must be quite painful to have to recognize what is unpleasant in yourself in order to show other characters.

Yes, it is. When I wrote a short story called 'Sense of Humour', for example, which is about a commercial traveller – it is based on a commercial traveller I once met, and I have known many others – it was his language which interested me, how awful his language was: it was a mixture of the comic and the second-rate, and it indicated a temperament which was rather coarse-grained or muddled, things which I hoped I wasn't. I thought that kind of person was both funny and painful, and I felt he was living by some sort of principle inside himself which I had to accept, although it was very hard to accept it.

Does it require much self-denial for you to depict such a character, when you have to offer yourself to a character which might be vulgar or crude?

I suppose I have an eye for certain apparent extremities of human behaviour. I am very conscious of how often one comes across people who are so self-absorbed that they are entirely insensitive to what they should be feeling. They are inarticulate in a way. It always strikes me that the French are absolutely determined to analyse every possible sensation they have, and in fact this acts as a sort of purgation – according to them, it makes human relationships better.

Do you think the writer of fiction has to be a psychologist? I am thinking here of a writer such as David Storey, who sets great store by allowing his material to unfold, without apparently searching for psychological insight or explanation.

I haven't thought about it much, but I do think the writer should be a psychologist. I'm not sure it's an entirely good thing: it removes a certain amount of drama from the writing. It's hilly rather than mountainous writing: you are unlikely to write a

Himalayan psychological novel, though you might write a nice little hilly one.

But do you feel you have to understand your characters, or at least to have interpreted for yourself exactly what makes them tick? Or is it a matter of showing the extraordinariness of the ordinary?

I think I certainly feel that, but on the other hand in writing it I can often become aware that it is something much larger than it appears to be. One of the things I enjoy in my writing about people is that to describe what they do and say leads to points of enquiry. That is the moment at which something entirely poetic comes into writing prose, when you are left at the point of enquiry, a state of mind or feeling which only poetry can deal with.

One discovers what one wants to do in the course of writing. I very often set out writing a short story and come to a full stop, realizing that I am just about to go wrong: I have to reconsider the whole thing, and I rewrite enormously. I so much admire Chekhov's stories because they're open-ended, and I try to be as open-ended as possible, leaving things hanging: it's terribly difficult for English writers to do, since some sort of practical or responsible sense works against it. We tend to lack the courage to leave it like that, and we don't know what 'that' is.

Is that one important difference between the short-story writer and the novelist, that the novelist continues the enquiry, pressing on to renew it and renew it?

Yes, that's right. Writing short stories is like writing sonnets or a lyrical poem: it's strictly disciplined, it has to be highly concentrated, and it has to suggest a world much larger than it appears to be doing in its space. It would be quite easy to write a short story on the theme of James's *The Wings of the Dove* – if only you had thought of that idea. I have always wanted to pursue intensity, and a long time ago I became infatuated with the idea of 'essences' – essences of behaviour – which I got out of reading Croce in Spanish. Croce made a great impression on me as a young man, and I thought: 'Yes, I don't want the whole cake, I want the essence.'

The curiously double quality of the mind also interests me. Somebody once said that I was always writing about liars. But people do live more than one life as they go along. Someone's 'essence' might appear, for example, when they're in a temper: another being sprouts out of them, which is just as real as the patient being.

This connects, I think, with your idea of the self-inventing character, the myth-maker . . . the idea that each person is living the myth of their life.

Yes, and your personal myths in a way justify you. It is all defined for me by hearing two men in Hampstead: they were friends who hadn't seen each other for some time. One of them said that he was living down in Chichester, and then he announced to the other, 'I'm a well-known character there.' It seemed to me an extraordinary remark to make, to describe yourself as a 'character'. It happens over and over again that people have another personality which they are enacting.

In a bad fiction-writer that recognition could lead to the indulgence of malice or superiority, but you have the artistic discipline and generosity never to do that.

Well, on the other hand, when I wrote 'Sense of Humour' some American students said they hated the story because it was so cruel, and I can see their point: it could very well be thought a heartless story. But the story itself came from a number of experiences I'd had in Ireland, where I realized that there were certain people with an element of absolutely amoral cruelty in them. Usually the British sentimentalize it and think that it's Irish-funny; but it's not Irish-funny, it's Irish cruelty. The whole character of the girl in 'Sense of Humour' springs entirely from an Irish background, though I transported the story to the Midlands when I wrote it. I've often discussed this with some of my Irish friends, who have great theories about the cruelty of the Celts: it is really something historical. Sean O'Faolain wrote a remarkable article in the *London Review* about how hunger-striking was enormously popular in Ireland in the eighth century. It's also connected, I think, with a certain feyness in the Irish: I distrust fey people, I think they've got a knife somewhere or other . . .

You've written five novels – Dead Man Leading *and* Mr Beluncle *being outstanding – although your achievement there has been insuf-*

ficiently recognized. But a large part of your critical writing has been in defence of the short story: you've written, for example, that the novelist has to be 'ruminative' and 'vegetative', which sound to me rather pejorative terms – as if you were suggesting that the novelist's procedures might be a vast, rather wasted labour. Do you suspect yourself of a sneaking envy of novelists?

No, I have great admiration for them. I can't understand why I didn't write better novels. At the age of 21 I would have loved to be Thomas Hardy. The publisher of my first book, *Marching Spain*, took it on condition that I would write a novel, which I thought was possibly beyond my powers. It baffled me, since I had no idea how to write a novel, so I fell back on the usual course of writing a rather autobiographical novel about my life in Ireland. I've never been able to read it since; it was tremendously overwritten, as if I were trying to enlarge my vocabulary.

Do you feel that any of your novels has been undervalued?

I think *Mr Beluncle* is quite a good book, and a number of reviewers thought so too.

The criticism I recall is that it seemed a rather static novel.

Yes, I found it hard to make the characters move: I had to get a furniture van or a bus to get them from one chapter to another. The business of making a novel move simply defeated me; it was cumbersome to a degree. But the reason why I think *Mr Beluncle* improved on the earlier novels is because I decided to write it in the form of a series of short stories, for which my model was Maupassant's *Bel Ami*. I thought the series of episodes would give an illusion of progress, just as there's only the illusion of progress in *Bel Ami*. To that extent I think it became a better novel.

Did your father really take to reading Mr Beluncle, *which is very much about him, as calmly as you suggest in* Midnight Oil?

Yes, he did. He had reached the stage of being frightened of me, and he really wasn't interested in reading at all. I think it probably bored him. He was very deferential to me in his later years. He was an egoistical man, so full of himself that other people fell away and became unreal to him: his wife and children became strange shapes which invaded his life in some way he could not account for. He thought that all of us were wrong about everything, and couldn't believe the amount of Error – in Christian Science terms – that he had generated.

Dead Man Leading concerns a son searching for a lost father, and I would guess that the obsessiveness of the novel says something about your investment of personal passion at the time of writing it. Can you recover for me what drove you on?

Dead Man Leading was a kind of protest against writing novels about England. I thought I had no novelistic skill in English realism: I would get rid of my inhibitions about novel-writing if I chose somewhere I had never been, so I chose South America. It's allied to my own passion for travel, the feeling that you see yourself more clearly if you get outside this country. People have an air of drama about them by the mere fact of being abroad. The other factor is that I was passionately interested in explorers – at the age of 18 I wanted to be Captain Scott – although I had no capacity at all for exploring. I did once meet the explorer Steffanson in America, and he made a very strong impression on me. I discovered among explorers a very peculiar attitude towards women . . . an extreme masochism which interested me deeply.

It strikes me as a novel of extraordinary immersion on your part, and yet you do manage to maintain an ironic distance through the character of Gilbert Phillips, the journalist who is caught up in this relentless quest much against his will.

I always thought I had no capacity for heroic physical endurance – I would be an encumbrance on any expedition – but I wrote the book at a time in my life when I was able to release great passion. I felt no masochism at all, but I had a deep and unfrustrated emotional experience: the book came from the force of that emotion. I felt I could involve myself with anything at that time, and I'm sure it was entirely due to meeting my second wife. Before then I had been frittering away in disappointment after disappointment.

In your autobiography you remark that 'writing has one of its sources in the sense of moral danger to which the writer is sensitive.' Can you explain what you meant by that?

A large number of characters are in moral danger – at the point of risk in their lives, or when they can't live without making themselves at risk. That kind of character, especially in women, is very interesting to me. Their temptation is to have two kinds of behaviour – to do what they want and yet to pretend that they're not doing what they want, or vice versa.

It sounds as if you are saying that women are hypocritical.

I don't think women are hypocritical, but I do think they have more than one life going on at the same time. They have a special area of emotional command in which they feel themselves to be absolutely free. I've once or twice written about women who take great risks and yet appear to be demure – the very pious woman, for example, who leads a loose life without noticing that she's doing it. It's not hypocritical.

'Handsome Is as Handsome Does' is a painful story about a woman.

It's very much an account of my first marriage, not literally but essentially. The characters were utterly different people – Americans, in fact – but the element of frustration in the woman interested me. My first wife was self-frustrated, I think. It was a very wounding experience to me, but I got rid of it by writing about it. The man contains about three characters, with nothing of myself in it, and in fact part of the character comes from a man I never met but whom I heard about from his mother: she disliked me very much, thinking that I was a rich young man having a marvellously good time while her poor son was killing himself in a factory in Birmingham.

The woman in the story yearns for what she supposes will be the satisfactions of an affair with a virile young man, who in effect rebuffs her. Towards the end the narrative voice comments, 'she knew she had not gone to Alex's room to will her desire to life or even to will it out of him, but to abase herself to the depths of her husband's abasement. He dominated her entirely, all her life; she wished to be no better than he. They were both of them like that; helpless, halted, tangled people, outcasts in everything they did.' It's a chilling indictment.

I had in mind an American woman, a southern lady of good family. I wrote the story when my first marriage was over, and the character of my first wife was in some ways, but only partially, like that of the woman in the story . . . masochistic, frustrated when very young.

It is a story where your judgement is made very clear, and in some ways it's an ugly story.

It is an ugly story, but what really made me want to write it was the business of rescuing the Frenchman from drowning, which was something absolutely straight from life. The theme of jealousy and accusation gave me the impulse in the story, and then it generated its own moral dilemmas. I often start with a real person, but he doesn't become real until you make him unreal, until you transport him to another environment or put him into a situation where he shows up. The language either exposes or covers up, and the writer must write in such a way that the reader can form an opinion. Dialogue has always been a great pleasure for me: it's such marvellously give-away stuff, a help and a discipline. Real dialogue can suggest three things at once.

You've remarked that your stories are in some sense about liars, and in A Cab at the Door *you wrote that your stories were always laments – though that was of course a tongue-in-cheek comment. But can you reconcile those two things in your own mind? Do you find human behaviour a sorry spectacle?*

It fills me with wonder in a way. There is a good deal of lamentation in life. Nothing could be less lamenting than Wells's *Mr Polly*, but it would be easy to write that story as a lamentation. My mother loved lamenting and got a tremendous kick out of it: it was half-funny to her. Lamentation is not a very high degree of passion, it's a very modest degree. Lots of awful things happen in the world which go beyond lamentation: you can't lament about Beirut, for example, you feel distraught and angry. The more I look at the state of the world the more I think this generation is jolly lucky: very few people have the experience of horror. There's a good deal of rough stuff in our society, but not that sort of spectacular destruction, which I would find very difficult to write about.

What you've called 'revelations of a nature' and exposing 'the illusions or received ideas by which people live' is evidently at the centre of your purpose in writing. You always try for more than life's little ironies, and 'exposing characters' must put an awful burden on you.

I suppose I've been guilty of exposing characters just because they're amusing, but I think I've usually gone beyond that. I wrote a group of stories about an air pilot called Noisy, for example, which were farcical stories, because I am a great admirer of Chekhov who could write any kind of story. I think a writer ought to be able to write any kind of story, and therefore I don't mind writing farce, which is irresponsible, and I don't regard myself as having any moral obligations to it. Farce is very often tragedy out of uniform. It's difficult to write, and it goes at a certain speed. I very much admire Feydeau, who turned Greek tragedy upside down, and there's no reason why a writer – if he has the skill – should not do that. I am always trying to think of a bolder or more dangerous idea.

Perhaps one of the boldest of your stories is 'The Camberwell Beauty', which is about possessiveness and covetousness, and centres on a man's obsession with an innocent young woman. It's a chastening sort of story, I think, and it says a lot about men's views of women. The moral riskiness of the story seems to me very acute.

Yes, it is. I started to write it simply because I once read in a Wiltshire newspaper a paragraph about an antique dealer who had got into serious trouble for keeping his young wife locked up in his shop. At one time I thought I had perhaps stopped being able to write – I couldn't think of anything to write about – so I took this story, and almost at once it leapt back into the past: I knew just such a girl when I was about 17 or 18 years of age. From then on I simply invented, and I realized I knew a lot about the antiques trade simply from walking down streets and seeing antique shops: you do know about life by looking at it.

Another remarkable story is 'Blind Love' – a story about pride, I think – where you confront the risk many short-story writers seem to take, of using physical disability as a sort of shorthand or metaphor.

Yes, it seems almost like cheating to write about the abnormal, doesn't it? I often wondered what goes on in the minds of blind people, so I tried to work it out intellectually. I met two blind people – Ved Mehta and Borges, whom I once had lunch with in Boston – and Borges did suggest certain things. Then somebody told me that people idealize the blind but that the blind are absolutely consumed with jealousy: their jealousy can be unbelievable, to a degree which is uncommon in ordinary life. I can't say that I've ever noticed it for myself, but I came to the conclusion that it must be so.

What most impressed you about meeting Borges?

I was very impressed by him. He amuses himself with you a lot, and his complete literariness – his being shut up in literature – is a very extraordinary thing. Almost any intelligent man of his generation in South America has literature at second hand – since South American literature was then based on French – and it established a very strong bookish attitude towards life.

Among all the distinguished and remarkable people you've met in life, who did you find the most engaging?

A Spanish writer called Pio Baroja, a very kind man who impressed me by being laconic and writing laconically – dry and hard. He wrote short sentences, which very much impressed me, and he had a sardonic and bruised nature. He was a very isolated man, and he thought no one told the truth: he told the brutal truth, not with any air of showing off but from deep conviction. Another Spaniard who impressed me was Ayala, who used to be Spanish ambassador here just before the Civil War, a high-brow novelist, brilliant and witty and a marvellous conversationalist: I found him very important.

Would you like to have been like Baroja, whom you describe in Midnight Oil *as manifesting 'disbelief and pity' in his writings?*

I couldn't be, really. The Spaniards have almost no inner life, whereas northern people are more sentimental and have an introspective life: it was one of the culture shocks which I found rather seductive.

The writer who nearly killed me was Meredith, whose style first intoxicated me, but I got out of that quite quickly.

Is that why you gave your Clark Lectures on Meredith, to get him out of your system once and for all?

I thought it would annoy Cambridge, and that someone ought to get back at Leavis for saying that Meredith was no good at all. *Harry Richmond* is a jolly good book, and so is *The Egoist.*

Do you acknowledge any Spanish pessimism or fatalism in yourself? I think it's in The Spanish Temper, *for example, where you observe that the thought of death is the 'individualist's thirst for a freedom that is absolute'.*

I rather responded to Spanish stoicism. I also admired the Spanish because they were so different from ourselves. I had to become like someone else. And Spain absolutely rid me of optimism: the almost total lack of metaphysics in the Spanish cured me of any kind of hangover from the notorious optimism of Christian Science. I can see that in the long run it may have cut me off from certain kinds of valuable speculations.

You oppose your own 'appetite for life' against religious beliefs?

Yes, my feeling nowadays is that the human race is almost mythological: it's a perpetuator of myths. I have no religious interests, except for the fact that religion is psychologically and historically very interesting. I know it's a lack of sensibility in myself that I lack a religious sense. But conventional religions have constructed fixed dramas which contain the meaning of life, whereas I think that life contains its meaning unaided. I should like to think a writer just celebrates being alive. I shall be sorry to die, but the notion of seeing life celebrated from day to day is so wonderful that I can't see the point of believing anything else.

I am a humanist, simply because that's my preoccupation. I didn't have any religious upbringing – although my parents were very religious they never sent us to church – until my father became a Christian Scientist, and then all hell broke out. I didn't know what communion was, for example, or baptism, and very often I was annoyed because I could see that it was rather interesting to have a scheme by which you understood things. I really was very ignorant, and I think I still am.

When you described writing your first novel in Midnight Oil, *you remarked that it could never have been any good because you 'had arrived at no settled view of life'. Were you implying that a writer has to acquire such a view?*

I think I have got the settled view I've suggested rather vaguely. But I haven't got a view of life such as the Greek tragedians had, which was rather grand. I meant I was rather lost in my attitudes when I wrote my first novel, split in two, with no standpoint other than the accident of my own temperament. I did feel very sceptical at a very young age, and I can remember the moment when I became sceptical – sitting up in a tree when I was about

227

15, reading Molière and thinking 'This is me'. I think a writer should have talent; I am not averse to any view of life that any considerable writer has, and I would never denounce a book on the grounds of its having the wrong view of life.

Here and there in your critical writings, as well as in your lectures on Meredith, you've remarked that comedy is not intellectual but cheerfully sociable. Is sociability the chief good of comedy?

Well, there are innumerable kinds of comedy. I used to like the writings of W. W. Jacobs, for example, who wrote a curious kind of local comedy, wry and penetrating. I think comedy is diverting to the mind; it sharpens the judgement, it doesn't take received ideas very willingly, it inspects, and it has a natural verve. I am attracted by the verve of comedy, which is why I tolerate quite a lot of farce – for its dash. Fielding is sharp and truthful, and very observant of society, and he has the benefit of intellectual or even philosophical assumptions which were workable in his time. Comedy does not depress or lower: it absolutely shuts out despair.

One of the weaknesses of English comedy seems to be a certain whimsy . . .

Yes, and cosiness, a feeling that words are not enough. One should try to see that words are enough.

In the Preface to your Collected Stories *you say that 'When My Girl Comes Home' is your favourite, and indeed it strikes me as being a tour de force, almost a novel in little, with a large number of characters.*

It's my favourite because so many people have said that you couldn't write a short story about a large number of people, and – just like taking a bet – I thought it must be possible. It's awfully difficult to connect the people and events in a way that is natural, without intervening to tell the reader what is happening, and I found a way by luck. The rather Meredithian notion of people reporting on each other suddenly came to me, and I managed to prevent myself from closing the story. I had accumulated a sense of the neighbourhoods I'd lived in, and the fact that the story occurred just after the war – when people were coming together in a most peculiar way – was a great help. For once I seemed to have created a small community, which I'd never done before.

The reader can be rather foxed, of course, because there is no single viewpoint to share.

It seemed to me a story about not knowing, which is a very common experience. The fact of not knowing is thrilling. The character of the woman in the story is created by the people around her. I often wish I could write another story like it, but I don't think I could. It belongs to its time. As far as I was concerned it had the explosion of post-war feeling in it: there was a very strong public sense of not knowing what was going on, a feeling of rumour.

In spite of your relish for life, do you see in yourself a dark side? You wrote in George Meredith and English Comedy *that 'the important ordeal is spiritual.'*

Like any writer I have natural depressions when I think I'm writing badly. At the moment I feel very much outside society because I'm old: there is a gap. I must say that politically I'm very pessimistic. I try to hope there's a sporting chance for the world, and to take a cheerful view of change, but I'm terrified for my grandchildren. I don't feel alienated, and I'm not quite sure what people mean by feeling alienated. I can see that in countries like America where everything is open there is alienation, which means that there is no society to be alienated from, and to the extent that it percolates here it depresses me. I think anyone who has lived up till now has been very fortunate, but whether we shall be fortunate from this moment onwards is doubtful. The decline of England is rather depressing.

In writing about Borges you said that the real test of a writer is a distinctive voice. What do you think is the distinction of your voice?

I don't know what it is in myself, but I'm sure it's there. I'm sure it's in writers I admire. I recognize a good short-story writer by a pitch in his voice, some sort of nervousness. From the first sentence the voice is pitched as though someone said it aloud to me. D. H. Lawrence, for example, is recognizable anywhere, as in that wonderful opening to 'The Rocking-Horse Winner' – 'There was a woman who was beautiful, who started with all the advantages, yet she had no luck' – which is a brilliant sentence. No novel could begin like that.

There is obviously an intimate connection between your eagerness for

travel – which you've called 'immolating' – and your willingness to
unself yourself in order to portray character in your stories.

Yes, there is, and I *seek* to be a non-imposer. I obviously do
impose, but I try not to. I think very few people really do have a
philosophy of life. I feel delinquent in not having created the
society I'm living in: that faculty seems to have escaped me.

But any art shows what is keeping people alive. I feel that very
strongly when I'm looking at pictures. I don't know a great deal
about painting, and I have a terribly literary view of it, but I love
looking at pictures. I have a taste for all the English watercolour
painters of the nineteenth century, which I think are exquisite. I
once had to write about impressionism for the *New York Review*,
and I was entranced by it. I really would have liked to have been a
painter, but I only had a little talent. I always said I'd do it in my
old age, but I still haven't taken it up: I've even got a drawerful of
crayons I bought twenty years ago, and a box of paints I've
never opened. I enormously admire painters and the way they
work. And they have one incredible advantage: they have one
page and they can see it the whole time, whereas I have to turn
over pages and look back to see that I'm continuing what I did
before. I can't see what I'm writing, and the advantage of direct
contact with your subject is to my mind a form of enchantment
and a privilege, and most enviable. The business of getting at the
'essence' still very much preoccupies me.

· SALMAN RUSHDIE ·

Salman Rushdie's *Midnight's Children* (1981) won the Booker McConnell Prize for 1981, the James Tait Black Memorial Prize and the English-Speaking Union Literary Award. A fecund, dynamic, baroque, transformative fable of memory and politics – 'a commingling of the improbable and the mundane' – the book has been equally acclaimed on both sides of the Atlantic, and in the subcontinent. 250,000 words long, it has sold more than a quarter of a million copies in this country alone, and has been translated into twelve languages. After the critical unsuccess of his first novel, *Grimus* (1975), Rushdie 'went for broke' in reclaiming India for himself in his 'great, encapsulating' comic epic: 'There were times', he has admitted, 'when I was convinced that I was mad.'

His most recent novel, *Shame* (1983), shows us Pakistan in the looking-glass: 'however I choose to write about over-there,' he writes, 'I am forced to reflect that world in fragments of broken mirrors.' Its subject is truly shame – '*Sharam*, that's the word . . . shame . . . embarrassment, discomfiture, decency, modesty, shyness, the sense of having an ordained place in the world, and other dialects of emotion for which English has no counterparts' – and shamelessness. Malcolm Bradbury has written of the book, 'Like Márquez and Kundera, with whom he is so naturally contemporary, Rushdie shows us with what fantasy our sort of history must now be written – if, that is, we are to penetrate it, and perhaps even save it' (*The Guardian*, 8 September 1983).

Born in Bombay in 1947 into a Muslim family who emigrated

to Pakistan in 1964, Rushdie was brought up bilingually in English and Urdu; he was educated at Rugby School and at King's College, Cambridge, where he read History. 'I am an emigrant from one country (India) and a newcomer to two (England, where I live, and Pakistan, to which my family moved against my will),' he writes. 'And I have a theory that the resentments we *mohajirs* engender have something to do with our conquest of the force of gravity.' After Cambridge he became a professional actor, working with a multi-media theatre group, and then supported his creative writing by working for a time as an advertising copywriter. He is married to an Englishwoman, Clarissa, and has a young son, Zafar.

Occasionally interrupted by telephone calls, builders calling at the door to talk about roofing and pointing, and Rushdie's own eagerness to check the Test match scores on teletext, I talked to him in 1983 at his comfortable terrace house in Tufnell Park, London. (In 1984 Rushdie and his family moved to another address, though still in London.)

* * *

Many readers of Midnight's Children *have felt that the childhood of Saleem Sinai must approximate to that of Salman Rushdie. Speaking now* in propria persona, *can you say something about your early life and upbringing in Bombay and Karachi?*
I don't like Karachi, whereas I did like Bombay very much. But even Bombay has been more or less ruined as a city; it's now an urban nightmare whereas it used to be a courtly, open, hilly, seaside city. It has become a kind of Hong Kong, only more incompetent than Hong Kong. In Bombay nothing works. When I was there in February there had been a fire in the telephone exchange on Malabar Hill, which is the ritziest residential area, and they had still not got around to providing a telephone service four months afterwards. If I were to go back to India now, I would not live in Bombay, which is something I would never have said before. It still has the feeling of being my home town, but it is no longer a place in which I feel comfortable.

My family moved to Pakistan in 1964, when I was 17. I had come to school in England in 1961, but I went back for most of the holidays; and until I was 14 I had never left the subcontinent. I was a complete Bombayite until I was 17. Karachi I gradually got used to over many years; I have come to know it better and to feel more connected to it as a place, but it's not a big city the way Bombay is. Karachi is a city that has almost no urban life, because of the repressions in the culture. Very little happens on the street, and there is a problem with sexual segregation, which makes life odd. You see men holding hands – and that is not because they are homosexual, it has to do with the need for physical contact. I find society in Pakistan very closed, and that closed world is expressed in *Shame*.

Was your father a businessman?

Yes, he was: business covers more or less everything in India. He's now retired, 73 years old. He and I have a good but sometimes explosive relationship: we have the same kind of bad temper. My mother and I also get on very well . . . and I have three sisters, not one like Saleem.

Is your father at all like Ahmed Sinai in Midnight's Children?

No. But he was the one member of my family who was a little worried by the book, not because it gave a portrait of him but because people might think so. Obviously there has been a certain assumption about the book being autobiographical, but that has faded away. My mother could never see what the fuss was about: she could see that they were not the characters in the novel. In actual fact my childhood was relatively uninteresting, though it has certain superficial similarities to Saleem's in so far as the school is the same, and the house is the house I grew up in. But my childhood was uneventfully happy. Saleem's childhood is tempestuous and disturbed, and in that respect we're not the same at all.

You went to school at Rugby, where I think you had a bad time?

The first half of my time there was very bad, the second half less bad, but the whole of it was bad enough to make me not want to go on to Cambridge, and I had to be more or less bullied by my parents. I had my place at Cambridge, but there was a six months' interim during which I went to Karachi and told my parents that I did not want to go back to England. My father was appalled because he had gone to King's, and in the end I think I went to Cambridge because they wanted me to do so.

Did your schoolmasters persecute you as much as the boys?

No, to be fair to them, it wasn't the masters. I had a pretty hideous time from my own age group: minor persecutions and racist attacks which felt major at the time, the odd bit of beating up. But I grew to my adult height very young – which meant that I was for a long time taller than my contemporaries – so there were not many physical attacks. People would go into my room and tear up my essays or write slogans on the wall. I found it odd because I had never thought of myself as foreign before – largely because I had never left my own country before, but also because I had been educated in an English mission school in Bombay. For a long time I had been taught by English and Scottish teachers, and I knew quite a lot about England, so I did not feel strange in coming here. I went home for the holidays, but I didn't tell my parents what a bad time I was having, I only told them when I left school. I remember very bad moments when I felt very depressed, but it did get better as I got older. I never had any friends at school, and I don't know a single person I was at school wi·h: when I left school I consciously determined never to see any of those people ever again, and I never have, I just wiped them out. I did decide to be cleverer than them – which wasn't difficult – and Rugby did have brilliant teachers. Obviously, it helped to be in classes of six or seven, and I certainly had the impression of being better taught at Rugby than I ever was at Cambridge. Although Cambridge had the great historians – I was studying history – not many of them were great teachers. I think my real problem at school was that I wasn't good at games; other Indians and Pakistanis at Rugby had no trouble if they were good at games: everything was forgiven them.

Did you lack interest or facility?

Both, really. I liked the games that weren't glamorous – table tennis and chess – and I was reasonably good at both of them, but they didn't count. I hated rugby football, although I was made to play quite a lot of it because of my early size.

I had somehow assumed that you must have read English at Cambridge, since you are well read.

Well, with huge gaps. I made the mistake of going on a TV quiz show and admitting that I'd never read *Middlemarch* . . . and I don't think I'll ever live it down. When I saw I was in trouble I went out and bought it, and I'm planning to read it. I hear it's good.

Did you have any mentor in your life, someone who inspired you to write?

No. My father never wanted me to be a writer, and I never had any encouragement to write. My grandfather – my father's father – was a writer, but then I never knew him: he died before I was born. He was a good poet and published a couple of volumes of Urdu poetry, and he is the only literary ancestor I have. Apart from that, there was no reason for me to become a writer, but it was the only thing I ever wanted to do; I never had any other ambition, except – briefly – to act.

And going to Cambridge did revitalize you?

Yes, it was a great pleasure to know that the persecution was over, and to be surrounded by intelligent people, so that intelligence ceased to be a factor in one's encounters. It was nice to know that you didn't always have to be in the company of idiots whose idea of literature was the *Daily Mail*. Public schools are basically composed of philistines. It was an exciting time to be at Cambridge, from 1965 to 1968: it was a very politicized period. There was the Vietnam war to protest about, student power to insist upon, drugs to smoke, flowers to put in your hair, good music to listen to. It was a good time to be young, and I'm very pleased to have had those years: there was an energy about student life then.

How did you catch the acting bug?

I had done a little acting at school in Bombay, then some at Rugby, and quite a lot at university. I enjoyed it without ever being outstanding at it. After Cambridge I worked for a while as an actor, mostly at an extraordinary place called the Oval House in Kennington which had an enlightened administrator. It began as a youth club, with a huge room he turned into a theatre, and a great many groups flocked there. A lot of the people who are now mainstays of the British theatre were beginning there, stretching their wings in different groups, and you knew that this was the most interesting theatre being done in London: the people involved had great originality. Most of the people were unemployed, living off the pittances we earned, and I had no other source of money. The standard was very high – professional productions on no money.

I remember a Brecht production . . . and a rock play called *Viet Rock*, a musical written by Megan Terry: we did that, with certain parts being improvised. I also remember what was probably the worst thing that ever happened to me in a theatre, one night in 1969, at a time when it was an interesting thing to insult the audience every so often. During one sequence each member of the cast had to take a section of the audience, which was arranged in a horseshoe, and abuse them for their complacency about Vietnam. But this night we saw that the first two rows of the audience was composed of a coach party of paraplegics, and we were panic-stricken. I was in a cold sweat, but the producer said we had to do the show, so we had to abuse those cripples while being mortified at what we could hear ourselves saying. At the end they came rushing around in their wheelchairs to say that they'd never had such a good evening in the theatre. They felt wonderful to have been sworn at as human beings, because normally everyone treated them with excessive respect or assumed that they're deaf because they're crippled.

And after the acting?

I was starving, and I got a job in advertising for a year. Then I gave it up to write a book that nobody published; then advertising for another year. I worked for Ogilvy and Mather, and more recently for a firm called Charles Barker, which is the oldest advertising agency in England. At both firms I eventually got a deal where I had to work between two and three days a week, and that effectively gave me between four and five days a week to write for myself. I thought it a kind of luxury I wouldn't find anywhere else. I thought of it as industrial sponsorship. That was how I wrote *Midnight's Children*. It is possible to write commercials which are not dishonest, without telling lies, and I don't remember writing anything which I don't think was true or at least arguable. But the people you have to deal with are mostly appalling, and they make you feel suspicious of what you're doing. I never really enjoyed it, and in fact it got worse and worse. When I finished *Midnight's Children* I simply ceased to be able to write advertisements; it was as though – quite without my volition – something in me had pulled the plug out. I was disillusioned with the process of advertising, but it was odd that it happened that way. When I realized that I couldn't do it any more – this was before *Midnight's Children* was published – I told my wife to prepare for poverty. So I left in the spring of 1981, and I was fortunate when the book came out. There were some press reports that said that I had won the Booker Prize and then left my job, when actually I had done something much more risky.

Fay Weldon believes that working as a copywriter did influence her style of creative writing.

I can see that it does in Fay's case, but I don't think it taught me anything other than self-discipline and regularity. It also taught me self-criticism, the ability to edit myself. With so few words at your disposal in advertising, you have to condense. It seems odd to say this, after I've written three long books, but one of the things about *Midnight's Children* is that it is actually condensed. I felt that a book of such length had to feel almost too short for its length, not prolix, and *Shame* is also an attempt at density.

In writing Midnight's Children *did you feel any element of compensating to yourself for the lack of tempest in your own early childhood?*

No. When I began the book it was more autobiographical, and it only began to work when I started making it fictional. The characters came alive when they stopped being like people in my own family. You see, my grandfather was a doctor but he never lived in Kashmir, he never met my grandmother in that odd way, nor was he particularly involved in politics. One of the discoveries of the book was the importance of escaping from autobiography.

Your first draft was 900 pages long, and written in the third person.

It was messier, much more direct. It was a very uneven draft, because I was discovering things as I went along. The character of Saleem in the draft was not the same at the end as it was at the beginning; I was learning about him as I was writing the draft. At the beginning of that draft he was probably quite like me, or quite like what I thought I wanted to say about me.

Did the pattern of incidents change much as you revised?

No, although a certain amount didn't happen until Saleem took over the narrative. One couldn't have those discursive passages until the first-person voice took over. I thought that by putting the book in the first person Saleem's voice would organize and hold together the material. But basically the sequence of events and the structure of the story didn't change, except that a lot of it got left out, and some things that were very long in the original draft either vanished completely or became very small pieces. All the sentences changed, because in the first draft I wasn't too worried about the actual words, I was trying to get the story down. I use first drafts in a very rough way, almost to find out what's happening. Some passages do survive, but almost all the sentences change, and in the case of *Midnight's Children* it was almost inevitable that they would change because of the switch from the third person into the first. *Shame* had three complete drafts. I tinker between the second and third drafts, but there's not much change of substance then, mostly technical things.

Do you now feel at all dissatisfied with anything in Midnight's Children?

I do feel that it's no longer my property. The reaction to it in India has been so enormous that it belongs to hundreds of thousands of people, and in a way my view of it is now no more or less valuable than anyone else's. I also feel quite detached from it, since I finished it more than three years ago, and I started it in 1976 – seven years ago – and one simply forgets. I can remember feeling alarmed at the size it was turning out to be – frequent feelings of panic that I was losing control of the material and that what was happening was no good – and also being nervous that nobody might wish to publish it . . . and having to proceed in spite of that. What I can't remember is the day-to-day process of discovering the story.

Was there a time-lag between writing the first two Books and the third, which seems to be written with a different sort of moral energy?

It wasn't written at a different time, it was deliberately written to
be quite different. I think the book would not work without
Book Three, it would be much less unusual – a kind of *Bildungs-*
roman – and that part puts the rest of it into perspective. Book
Three grows so naturally out of the earlier stages, it was essential
to have it. I personally think Book Three contains some of the
best things in the novel – the jungle chapter, for instance, which
is the passage that divides the book's readers most dramatically:
readers dislike it intensely or they like it enormously.
Because it is a phantasmagoria?
It seemed to me that if you are going to write an epic, even a
comic epic, you need a descent into hell. That chapter is the
inferno chapter, so it was written to be different in texture from
what was around it. Those were among my favourite ten or
twelve pages to write, and I was amazed at how they divided
people so extremely.
Yes, it is quite a short section in the context of the book as a whole, yet it
seems to be an eternity of disintegration and mania.
I like that: a lot is imagined to be happening by the characters. I
also very much like the magician's ghetto. The jungle section
and the magician's ghetto are two parts I still feel very affectionate about in the book. There are things in Book Two which I
don't like so much any more, although, by and large, that
section has been most praised.
Do you feel there were more gimmicks, as it were, in Book Two, more
opportunistic details and excursions?
It's not that, though I put in some things just because they were
stories I remembered. But one of the deliberate efforts in the
book was to leave loose ends; I was very interested in the idea of
implying a multitude of stories in one's structure, through
which one picked one narrative path. There are stories you just
happen to bump into and that you never see again, or stories that
are just fragments of themselves and not completed. It was
structured to contain that kind of waste material in it, because
that was part of what I was trying to say.
One of the things that slightly puzzles me about the book is the question
of tone. The book is fundamentally about the destruction of potential in
a new, independent India, and one might have expected more overt

anger to have emerged from that context. Did you feel you needed to establish a consistency of tone geared to that impetus?

The tone is basically comic and remains so even when it darkens: I thought that was a kind of constancy.

A black comedy, do you mean, almost like Candide?

There is a comedy that doesn't always make you laugh, and in that sense it is a comedy . . . even at its worst moments, and that is one of the elements *Midnight's Children* has in common with *Shame*. The moment when Sufiya is discovered surrounded by decapitated turkeys is a comic moment, but black comedy of that sort doesn't make you laugh. I think of *Shame* as a comedy, although in a way it is even nastier than *Midnight's Children*, or at least the nastiness goes on in a more sustained way. Kafka can unite comedy and tragedy, and I was interested in doing that.

Did you none the less have to make deliberate efforts to countervail the anger you must have felt at the real events which lay behind the action of Midnight's Children, *consciously to translate it into the genre of comic epic?*

The book was conceived and begun during the Emergency, and I was very angry about that. The stain of it is on the book. The Emergency and the Bangladesh war were the two most terrible events since Independence, and they had to be treated as the outrageous crimes that they were. I was in India near the beginning of the Emergency, but not throughout it; I felt the shock of having it imposed. Fortunately I wasn't in Bangladesh, but I know a lot of people who were there – on all three sides. It is a complete fallacy to believe you must always experience what you put into a book, what matters is whether you can imagine it or not; there is no automatic connection between experience and imaginative writing.

It must have taken some nerve to write such a spirited novel, full of anecdotes and divagations, while taking as your context a series of horrific and devastating public events. The perilous paradox seems to me that one of your impulses in writing both Midnight's Children *and* Shame *was an urgent political one, and yet you compose the subjects with such inventive bizarrerie . . . as entertainment, in fact.*

It didn't strike me as being too difficult to achieve, since it is a matter of ear: you just have to listen to whether or not you're overdoing it. There is a danger that things which are fun to write about will take over from what you're trying to say, but it is a matter of craft: you can hear the strained applause if you take too many encores. I find it much more of an effort of nerve to write without jokes. The first draft of Shame was much darker, oppressively and unremittingly gloomy, and I thought nobody would ever get through it if it was that sad. But I also felt that the characters involved didn't deserve high tragedy. Although the relationship between Raza and Iskander is basically tragic, the actual figures are clowns – gangsters, hoodlums – and not people who deserve Shakespearian tragedy. So you have to bring comedy into it – you have to write black comedy, because they are black-comedy figures – and I rewrote the entire book, changing the tone, making it lighter. I find, in a book where the plot is dark and the characters unsympathetic, that if you can make it comic it doesn't lose the tragic content – the story is still the story – but it gains an extra dimension which makes the characters more human. Even when the characters are not sympathetic, you find a way of seeing what they're thinking.

In Shame I found that the characters of Iskander and Raza, because they are in some sense buffoon characters, become palatable, almost sympathetic, and yet one knows that they are based on Bhutto and General Zia of Pakistan. I felt uneasy as to whether that mode of burlesque was right, the one you felt it appropriate to hit.

I was trying to say that there are moments when both of them are sympathetic characters. When Raza stakes himself to the ground, for example, one does feel on his side. When Iskander gives up his mistress, he tells his daughter that men are bastards and that she should never have anything to do with them; he's talking about himself but she takes him literally, and I felt quite warmly towards him at that moment. If one is not going to make cardboard characters it is important to say that even people who do terrible things are not unrelievedly terrible people, or at least that they are not always terrible: there can be moments when they behave well.

Which is not to say that their stupidity redeems them, but it humanizes them?

Yes, nothing redeems them. I didn't want just to make hate-figures, I wanted to make people. Although there is clearly something of Bhutto in the one, and something of Zia in the other, I have no way of knowing whether the personalities of Iskander and Raza are actually like those actual personalities. It really wasn't my purpose to invent portraits of them, but what I took from them was that kind of tragic connection – of the one being the protégé of the other and ending up as his executioner – that was what interested me, that was the given from history.

There were two or three starting points which glued together. Another was the title, *Shame*: I kept finding instances of that emotion or concept at work in societies, at all different levels from the private to the public, and I began to think that it was one of the most central means of orchestrating our experience. The more I looked for it in human affairs, the more central I discovered it was, and I wanted to explore that area. When the book starts, the shame is private and sexual – to do with being pregnant when you don't know who the father is – and the book develops by building variations on that theme, showing how shame is part of the architecture of the society the novel describes, and perhaps not only that society. I have a feeling that it is not peculiar to the east, but I didn't explore that; I thought that if it were universal the only way of showing that was to be concrete and particular. People who read the book can decide whether or not it has applications outside the society under discussion. It seems to me that it does exist elsewhere.

In Midnight's Children *you acted, as it were, as the recording angel of the experiences of India since Independence, whilst in* Shame *you seem to be more sternly controlling a story about an alienated place, Pakistan . . .*

. . . as the exterminating angel, if you like. That felt partly good: I felt in charge of the material, probably more so than I had ever felt before – except at the end of *Midnight's Children*, where I felt great relief that I had somehow managed not to fuck it up. I felt with *Shame* that I knew what I was doing from a much earlier point. It is a harder book, and it's not written so affectionately, although – as I say somewhere in the book – Pakistan is a place I've grown to have affection for, so that it's not written entirely without affection. The episode of the wedding scandal may be satirical, but it is affectionately written. But by and large it is a harder and darker book. And that's because of its subject matter: Pakistan is very unlike India.

To my mind there was more satire in Midnight's Children. Shame *seems to be composed in parts with a fierce sarcasm.*

There were parts of *Shame* that disturbed me to write, because they were so savage and I wasn't quite sure where that savagery was coming from. The later sections of the book were very disturbing: they disturb me to have written them. It's a book which comes from a very different place from *Midnight's Children.*

Did you think of Midnight's Children *as proposing a continuous allegory – the allegory of Saleem's body as being the mirror of a disintegrating state, for example, or the allegory of the Midnight's Children's Conference?*

There are those allegorical elements, but I always resisted them in the writing. Allegory comes very naturally in India, it's almost the only basis of literary criticism – as though every text is not what it seems but only a veil behind which is the real text. I quite dislike the notion that what you are reading is really something else. The children in *Midnight's Children* become more a metaphor than an allegory, a representation of hope and potential betrayed. They are not developed along any formal allegorical lines, and when they operate in the plot – like Parvati the witch – they don't operate allegorically but just as characters. Similarly, although Saleem claims to be connected to history, the connections in the book between his life and history are not allegorical ones, they're circumstantial. Although the book contains those large allegorical notions, it tries to defuse them.

You've said elsewhere that the book is written from the point of view of a child who feels responsible for everything that happens in the larger sphere, and yet it seems to me that the form you gave the novel suggests something different, that things that happen in the public domain just happen to answer to states of collapse in his own being.

What I meant was that Saleem's whole persona is a childlike one, because children believe themselves to be the centre of the universe, and they stop as they grow up; but he never stops, he believes – at the point where he begins the novel – that he is the prime mover of these great events. It seemed to me that it was quite possible to read the entire book as his distortion of history, written to prove that he was at the middle of it. But the moment at which reality starts to face him it destroys him: he can't cope with it, and he retreats into a kind of catatonic state or he becomes acquiescent and complacent.

A number of critics have found it a rather despairing book, but perhaps nihilism is the better word. Nihilism supposes that there was no possible rectification of the events that have taken place – they're something appalling and absolute – whereas despair would imply that things could have gone better, with a programme or strategy which has failed in a desolating way.

I wouldn't really accept either word. The book wasn't written as a social tract, it was written as a fiction which forces you to obey the rules you've laid down. It seemed to me that the Emergency represented the dark side of Independence, and that there was a progression from one to the other – from light to dark – and that was going to be the progression both of the book and of Saleem's personality. It never occurred to me that people would read the book as showing the end of all hope. It's the end of a particular hope, but the book implies that there is another, tougher generation on the way. The book exists to be a reaction to events as the author has reacted to them. It was written in the light of a very dark time.

Saleem offers us a hope for the next generation, as you say, and yet we have learned to look ironically at his narration, his self-illusions and delusions, and we might therefore judge that his hopes are frail and ill-founded. Authorial irony has made us sceptical.

Yes, you are supposed to be sceptical, but what I'm saying is that the book does not present the end of possibility . . .

. . . *which would be a cynical view to take.*

Yes, and actually stupid, objectively disprovable, untrue. It has somehow been taken that way, but I think it's a misreading. People in India actually say much worse things than anything *Midnight's Children* says; it's an optimistic book by comparison with present Indian attitudes about the future, which are much bleaker. The book contains nothing that people in India don't say every day, and my point was to put it down. People chicken out of saying things; they become optimistic and talk about rays of hope, but at the time of writing there didn't seem to be much hope. First of all there was the Emergency, and when that ended the world got taken over by 80-year-old urine drinkers, and that didn't seem to be much improvement: they proved to be just as corrupt and more incompetent.

Is it true that Morarji Desai drinks his own urine?

Yes, every day. He lives on urine and pistachio. He calls it 'taking his own water', and he thinks it's very good for him. Maybe he's right: look how old he is – he's endless, immortal.

Your first book, Grimus, *is a sustained work of fantasy, with a plethora of characters and incidents. The story concerns a group of people who perpetuate their mortal lives and discover that the intrigues and jealousies of life go on, so that the final endeavour of the hero – Flapping Eagle – is literally to explode the arrangement. Did you find it difficult to control a fantasy of such length and complexity?*

It was easy in the sense that it was the only book I've written which had its source in another book, a twelfth-century Sufi narrative poem called *The Conference of the Birds*, which is the closest thing in Persian literature to *Pilgrim's Progress*. The characters are all birds, which is why the central character of *Grimus* is a bird, Flapping Eagle. In the poem twenty-nine birds are persuaded by a hoopoe, a messenger of a bird god, to make a pilgrimage to the god. They set off and go through allegorical valleys and eventually climb the mountain to meet the god at the top, but at the top they find that there is no god there. The god is called Simurg, and they accuse the hoopoe of bringing them on – oh dear – a wild goose chase. The whole poem rests on a Persian pun: if you break Simurg into parts – 'Si' and 'murg' – it can be translated to mean 'thirty birds', so that, having gone through the processes of purification and reached the top of the mountain, the birds have become the god. Although the plot of *Grimus* is not that of the poem, it has it at its centre, and that gave me something to cling on to. I was trying to take a theme out of eastern philosophy or mythology and transpose it into a western convention, and I think it didn't really work. I find the book difficult to read now: the language in it embarrasses me.

Yet you obviously wanted to say something about a hell on earth in it.
Yes, I think the interesting part of the book is the town where nobody dies, and the horror is that life goes on. I thought that if one was going to transpose something as rarefied as Sufi metaphysics into a western context, one needed consciously to use a genre in a way that now makes me cringe.

Since you use fantastic and fabulous elements in both Midnight's Children *and* Shame, *I wonder if you draw any distinction in your own mind between fantasy and fable?*
What I didn't like about *Grimus* was that it seemed too easy to use a fantasy that didn't grow out of the real world, a kind of whimsy. I don't even really like the word fantasy as a description of that kind of non-naturalistic material in my books, because fantasy seems to contain that idea of whimsy and randomness, whereas I now think of it as a method of producing intensified images of reality – images which have their roots in observable, verifiable fact. Except for the character of the girl, Sufiya Zinobia, *Shame* is somewhat less fabulated than *Midnight's Children*. When Bilquis's father is blown up in a cinema there is a kind of hallucinated sequence; but then she is in a state of shock, so that there is a naturalistic basis for why it is hallucinated. I do think that one thing that is valuable in fiction is to find techniques for making actuality more intense, so that you experience it more intensely in the writing than you do outside the writing.

You mean that any intensification should not become sheerly fantastic, it must have some political or social context to which it is the response?
Yes, I think so. It has to come out of something real, and in that sense I had to reject certain things about the way *Grimus* was written. I had to re-examine everything I had thought about writing and put it back together another way.

At one point in Shame *you actually call yourself a fantasist, and you write , 'I build imaginary countries and try to impose them on the ones that exist.' I would have thought that the usual definition of fantasist would be to abstract or extrapolate things from the real world and to pursue their imaginative logic.*
I think the writer has a kind of vision which he tries to project on

to other people, and the fit between that vision and other people's is the tension between the writer and the reader. As a writer I am trying to say, 'This is the shape of how it is,' and the more I can persuade you that that *is* how it is, the greater my success. In *Shame* the author sometimes knows less than a character, and he's obliged to say that there are things he doesn't know. Normally an author is omniscient or not, and to try to make an authorial voice which would shift between the two positions was technically one of the things I enjoyed in the book – sometimes the author is the writer of the story, sometimes he's the reader of the story, and I thought that was quite valuable in providing shading.

William Golding has written – specifically with reference to Lord of the Flies – *that the fabulist is a moralist: 'the fabulist is didactic, desires to inculcate a moral lesson.'*

He's right about the fable – *Aesop's Fables* or the *Panchatantra* – where the machinery of the tale is designed inexorably to reach that moral statement which the story is seen to have proved. It carries with it the dreadful warning against not behaving in the moral way the fable recommends. In that sense I think the term 'fabulism' as it applies to contemporary literature is false, though in the case of Golding it may well be true. What's happened recently is that writers are using the machinery of the fable but without wishing to point a simple moral. I don't think of either *Midnight's Children* or *Shame* as containing a moral. *Shame* is about ethics, about good and evil, but it doesn't tell you how to behave, whereas fable does. *Shame* is not morally didactic; it shows you something. Italo Calvino is described as a fabulist, but his stories don't have morals: they're shaped like fables, they have the characteristics of fables, but without the purpose.

I'm also very fond of myth, but it isn't possible to sit down and say that I will now write a myth. Myth is a cultural accumulation – a collective experience, not an individual achievement – and you can learn from and use its shapes, since they provide a strength in the work. The greatest compliment I received for *Midnight's Children* was when students in Bombay, and not only in Bombay, said that they knew everything in the book and that I had just written it down. I thought that was wonderful, because they really were saying that I had expressed a shared experience. Naturally, I had not made a conscious attempt to articulate the shared experience of my generation, but the students were saying that the book had some mythic content.

Do you feel that there's no place for didacticism in your work?

In terms of politics *Shame* contains certain political criticisms, which makes it didactic in that sense. If you're going to write about politics it is almost impossible to escape having a view about it. I have a simple view: I believe military dictatorships to be bad and that it's desirable to end them. But I was also trying to show in *Shame* that the last time there was an elected civilian government in Pakistan it actually did worse things than the Army is now doing, that the civilian government was a different kind of dictatorship. Just to have the ballot box doesn't automatically destroy totalitarianism, if the people elected are sufficiently unscrupulous, which – both in the case of the characters in the book and in the case of history – they were.

In his essay on fable, Golding also says that 'the writer has to have a coherent picture of the subject; but if he takes the whole human condition as his subject, his picture is likely to get a little dim at the edges . . . literary parallels between the fable and the underlying life do not extend to infinity'. That strikes me as an interesting comment on what you tried to do in Midnight's Children, *where Saleem speaks of swallowing a world. Golding regards fable as dealing with a much more contained and demarcated area of experience.*

I think that's a difference between Golding and me. Golding's books do take small metaphors, an island or a ship. But what I was trying to do in *Midnight's Children* was to make a plural form, since it seemed to me that I was writing about a world that was about as manifold as it's possible for a world to be. If you were to reflect that plurality, you would have to use as many different kinds of form as were available to you – fable, political novel, surrealism, kitchen sink, everything – and try to find an architecture which would allow all those different kinds of writing to co-exist.

So that what you produce is a kind of kaleidoscope without insistent purposiveness, whereas Golding would insist on a moralistic purpose in his novels?

If *Midnight's Children* had any purpose in that sense, it was an attempt to say that the thirty-two years between Independence and the end of the book didn't add up to very much, that a kind of betrayal had taken place, and that the book was dealing with the nature of that betrayal. To that extent there was a kind of public purpose.

I also had an idea about personality. I was trying to write about one person, and finding – as he says – that in order to do so you have to swallow a world. In order to create one character, you would theoretically have to create the universe. I was interested in what it meant to be an individual in the middle of that many hundreds of millions. The normal response would be to say that it means less to be an individual in the midst of the billions, but I thought it could mean the opposite. The book therefore made a kind of comic inversion: instead of being one speck on the beach, Saleem became the speck which contained the beach. Now that's not really a purpose in the sense of having a message, it was a way of examining personality. Once upon a time you could have written novels in which the public world and the private world were discrete from one another – Jane Austen didn't have to mention the Battle of Waterloo, and that was all right – but it seemed to me that one of the things we've learned about ourselves as a species is that we are very closely interconnected. Originally the first line of the book, which is now buried somewhere, was 'Most of what matters in your life takes place in your absence,' and that was a central idea. An important idea for me was that people leak into each other – 'like flavours when you cook', as Saleem says at one point – and I was trying to write about how people are pieces of each other. It's not just that public life affects private life, but separately lived private lives can affect each other quite fundamentally: things which become a central part of you can actually have happened three stages away from you, and have been passed on to you through successive leakages.

Some critics regard the form of a novel as being the pattern of an author's personality. Do you feel any discrepancy in yourself between the free-wheeling and exuberant personality we feel in Midnight's Children *and your social self, which seems on first acquaintance to be urbane and intellectual?*

I think, like most writers, that I am most completely myself when I write, and not the rest of the time. I have a social self, and my full self can't be released except in the writing. *Shame* is a different sort of book from *Midnight's Children*, and that's me too. Books are interim reports from the consciousness of the writer, and that changes. I don't think I could write *Midnight's Children* now.

Midnight's Children *has been compared to novels like* The World According to Garp *and other large-scale, potentially absurdist books, and of course it has strong affinities with a tradition stemming from Sterne.* Shame *also fits the modern form of the reflexive novel – you take pains to draw attention to yourself-as-author and to the fictiveness of the book. To what extent did you decide your literary pedigree when you began writing* Midnight's Children, *or to what extent did you take any models – Márquez, Gogol, Kundera . . . ?*

I don't like *The World According to Garp*, I don't think it's a good novel. I didn't consciously think of a single writer as a model. Even the correspondences with Sterne were for a time unconscious, and I only realised that *Tristram Shandy* had gone before me when I was some way into the drafts. When I remembered it, I did little bits of stylistic underlining, to make sure that people knew that I knew.

Gogol saw Dead Souls *as being a book which might reform Russian society.*

Actually Gogol got that into his head at the end of volume one, and fortunately not much of volume two got written. I was under no illusions that *Midnight's Children* could change the world. But I did think that there were certain kinds of conversation which were not taking place in India and Pakistan, because certain things had been swept under the carpet. I had not read Kundera when I wrote *Midnight's Children*, but the point he makes about the connection between memory and politics is, I think, relevant to what I was doing. I thought that because I write about these things people who read the book will be obliged to think about them. So I did want to say how it was, so far as I could remember; and when your version differs from the official version, then remembering becomes a political act.

Would you subscribe to Kundera's concept of the novel as 'investigation into human existence'? That definition comes from an article he wrote in the New York Times *(24 October 1982) about his novel* The Joke – *I suppose the emphasis should be put upon the word 'investigation' – and he also says that the novel proclaims no truth, no morality.*

Yes, I think so, though that formulation actually says very little. *Midnight's Children* is very orchestrated, full of architecture – it's as though the skeleton is on the outside and the flesh on the inside – but I felt that *Shame* was much more of a voyage of discovery. When I had the Iskander–Raza plot, for instance, I thought it was a very *macho* kind of book – all about careerism, coups, politics, revenge, assassinations, executions, blood and guts – but then I kept discovering more and more in all the peripheral characters, particularly the female characters. It became very interesting to me to find that I was writing a book in which the central characters almost never took the front of stage, and that in a way there were no central characters: there were a dozen or so major characters, and they would sometimes step into the centre of the plot and sometimes move to the edges of it. That struck me as an enjoyable thing to do after writing a novel in which the central character had been so dominant. Omar Khayyam in *Shame* is constantly described as the hero, but he's clearly *not* the hero. That was a piece of deliberate fun. Omar Khayyam is not important, except as the person who brings Raza Hyder to the killing ground.

He's described as Iskander's confederate in debauchery, and he marries Sufiya.

Yes, he has peripheral roles all the way through the plot, and I wanted to have a peripheral man as someone I called the hero. He's central to none of it, and he's not important enough to arouse real rage. After Saleem in *Midnight's Children* I wanted to have a kind of nonentity at the centre of *Shame*, a zero who happens to be rather a good doctor. During his nightmare towards the end of the book he confesses that 'Other persons have been the principal actors in my life-story.' What he is saying, and what I was saying, is that the sum total of the events of the book adds up to his life. There can be people who are peripheral to their own lives: that's what his character is about, that there can be people whose lives are led entirely as spectators, and everything that's interesting in their lives is done to them or by others in their presence.

Do you feel any emotional identification with that position? I ask because of what you said earlier about your uninteresting childhood.

No, I'm not very passive, really. Saleem has been accused of being excessively passive, and I don't think that criticism is fair in his case: he finds it difficult to act as an adult, but he's not passive in the way Omar Khayyam is passive . . . and even Omar Khayyam is not entirely passive – he saves a girl's life, for instance, and later marries her, without which there would be no plot. But he is an irritating character, and irritating to write about – because there's nothing there.

Your mention of passivity reminds me of Saleem's remark about making oneself grotesque in order to preserve individuality. And yet his grotesqueness happens to him, either by inheritance or circumstances. He purports to be taking control of his life, when in fact he can't and doesn't.

Yes, he tells his story retrospectively, and I'm not sure I believe him. One of the problems with *Midnight's Children* is the almost complete impossibility of pointing out that there are moments when Saleem and I don't think alike. I accepted that as the price I had to pay for his narrative voice, which was very useful to me.

Do you identify with Saleem's remark about establishing a 'philosophy of coolness and dignity-despite-everything'?

I probably did then. I think I was a less relaxed individual when I wrote that book than I am now; I've been gradually calming down. At the time I had many more uncertainties about my writing and therefore about myself. There's nothing like the fear of doing the work and not having it see the light of day; I don't think it's a constructive fear, it's something you have to banish in order to have the energy to do the work. Not having that problem calms you down, makes you feel a little less frenzied.

Shame is the first book I've written with the expectation of an audience.

Do you find that you can now write with less self-consciousness . . . or perhaps more?

Less rather than more. There's less performance in *Shame* than there is in *Midnight's Children*. But then performance is usually regarded as showing off, at least in western criticism. I don't see it like that. One of the things about the Indian tradition is that the performer and the creator are almost always the same person. The idea of performance as being central to creation is present in all Indian art. The dancer is the artist, for example, and not simply the exponent. But *Shame* seemed to be a book which forbade the kind of display in *Midnight's Children*.

Perhaps one of the keys to your transition from Midnight's Children *to the more harsh treatment of* Shame *rests in Saleem's observation that whereas India embodies alternative realities, Pakistan consists of falsenesses and unrealities.*

I hadn't remembered that particular opposition. The first part of the statement – that India has multiple possibilities – seemed to me to be true, whereas contemporary Pakistan seems to represent a closure of possibilities, a loss of possibilities. That affected not just the tone of voice in the book but also the plotting, because I thought that this time I couldn't write an open-structured book. The plot became like a clamp in which everybody is held: they can't escape from it. Instead of saying, as in *Midnight's Children*, that here is superabundance, one was saying that here is constraint. But it's also wrong to see *Midnight's Children* as the India book and *Shame* as the Pakistan book, and actually the Partition section of *Shame* – in Delhi – is one of the sections I'm most proud of, because it is still very difficult to write about the Hindu–Muslim troubles in 1947. It seemed to me important to write about it because that sort of communal tension is starting up again in India – quite apart from the difficulty of writing about something that happened when you were unborn or just born. I showed the typescript to Anita Desai – she was about 10 years old and living in Delhi at the time of Partition, and she has memories of it – and I was pleased that she liked that chapter very much. So the book is not just an attempt to slam Pakistan, because the book is not just about Pakistan. I discovered that I seemed to be writing about the nature of evil, and that isn't exclusive to any part of the world, but it acquires more external resonances when you remain concrete about the place you're writing about.

Did you feel more nervous in writing Shame *than in writing* Midnight's Children?

No, in a way I felt more relaxed, partly for this feeling of having got into control of it at an earlier stage. The moment of control happens, if I'm lucky, at the end of the first draft. I have abandoned two novels at that stage because they didn't seem to be going anywhere.

And at that stage in writing Shame *you found out how important it would be to refract the story through peripheral characters, and that you had come to be writing a story of malign familial crises rather than a political allegory?*

I discovered bits of it in writing the first draft, and then I saw that the most interesting things were in that area. I didn't want to write a political allegory, though it is a political story: it's a book about the private life of the master race. In Pakistan the numbers of people who settle the fate of the nation are very small, so that it is a kind of domestic story about kitchen tyranny.

Sufiya Zinobia, the demon child, is perhaps the most discomforting character in the book. She personifies nemesis, incarnating all the shame and vengefulness of the family. She's both alarmingly real and a metaphorical agent which explodes the tyranny of her father, Raza Hyder. The last image of the book, which encapsulates that phantasmagorical dimension of Sufiya's character, suggests the explosion of a nuclear bomb. I wonder why you felt compelled to bring the novel to a conclusion by toppling the military–bureaucratic dictatorship through a metaphorical–fantastic mechanism?

I wanted Raza to fall, and it was also – having set up the idea of the nemesis – in the logic of the plot. One of the interesting things is that Sufiya does not get Raza, although she is the instrument of his fall. I find she is the most disturbing thing in the book, and she was very disturbing to write because she more or less made herself up. For instance, I hadn't originally thought of her as being mentally retarded, but it suddenly became clear that that was the only way in which she would operate. I hadn't fully understood in the first draft the way in which she would develop into this completely monstrous being. I thought that the reason why she and Omar Khayyam arrive as opposite figures in the final moment is that in their different ways they are both the repositories of the society, and that's why they are married.

Originally I wanted her father, the military dictator Raza, to end up in exile in Gloucester Road, as many fallen figures might – not to die in that appalling way but to be living in a Kensington flat, with no pictures on the walls, stick furniture from Pontings, curtains that are never opened, lots of lights and heaters on all the time. I felt quite anxious to get him out of the country and into England – the first draft didn't have that final carve-up – but it then became clear to me that the characters were refusing to leave the country; it was as though they were saying to me that they had an imaginative life but only within the frontiers of that world, and that if I brought them to Gloucester Road they would cease to exist: they would crumble like characters coming out of Shangri-la. I tried several ways of getting them out of the country, but they wouldn't go.

So you had to take your chance with melodrama, with this incredibly alarming and literal image of the feral girl?

Yes, it is a bloodthirsty ending. I find it very affecting; she did frighten me. I think it's unusual to be frightened by one's own creations, but she did make me worried about her. I worried about what she meant. Why is it that the character who is the most innocent in the book is also the most terrible? In the end I thought it would be dangerous to go on asking that sort of question – since that unresolved ambiguity was obviously at the centre of her, and it is what makes her moving.

One incentive to your creation of her was clearly the anger you felt about the white boys who set upon an Asian girl in the London underground, as you mention in the non-fiction part of chapter 7, entitled 'Blushing'.

Yes, I know where she comes from and the process of making her, but she seems to transcend her source material. There is a dark area at the centre of her, and the book is about that dark area.

Is Sameen, to whom you dedicate the book, your sister?
Yes, the one of my sisters who lives here.
And she was the girl who was beaten up?
That was actually much exaggerated by the press. She had some trouble on the tube during the time of the Brixton riots. Three kids began to be abusive – I think one of them slapped her once – and a black man in the next carriage came to her rescue. It was upsetting and it made me angry, but it was a very small thing. It was exaggerated when it came out in the papers, and she was furious with me. I mention it in the book in the context of saying that the girl is not one girl but many, so that the instance in the book is not just my sister.
Can you say something about the enjoyable but ultimately sinister complex of the three mothers of Omar Khayyam?
They came about more or less by chance. The book is partly about the way in which women are socially repressed. I think that what does happen in that state of affairs is that women become very close to each other, and there is a female network of support which is very powerful. There are various expressions of that in the book – the telephone link between Bilquis and Rani, for instance, a connection in which the power relations shift, and eventually that umbilical cord is cut by the intercession of the men. Omar Khayyam's mothers are another instance of female solidarity, which is really brought about by the way they are obliged to live in the male-dominated society. The group-baby was an intensification of the idea that if they wanted to share everything they would even want to share a child. I like them very much, but for a long time – even before I wrote the first draft – I wasn't sure whose mothers they were. I even tried to write it so that they were Raza's mothers (Omar Khayyam was already present, as an adult), but they clearly didn't belong there. I didn't want to lose them, because they seemed a very strong image. Eventually they discovered their son, and I structured things so that the book began with that curiously fabulated chapter.
To a western reader Omar Khayyam's betrayal of his mothers might seem perfectly understandable, and even right in the circumstances. After living for so long in their perniciously claustrophobic environ-

ment, we can see how he would want to get away and never come back, disavowing his family.

Yes, and even to eastern readers it would seem like that, but they would never completely forgive him.

Since Shame *says a great deal about the position of women, do you anticipate that the book might be used as a women's text or tract?*

Books have authors and readers, and it seems to me that the sex of either is of minor interest. I don't think anybody could use *Shame* as a tract, because it contains too many ambiguities.

Do you have any sense of having used the fiction to enunciate your own view of political change in Pakistan?

It has to change, but I try very hard in the fiction to avoid saying what I personally would like or dislike. I think that if the society does not change it will explode. If Zia is to fall, he will fall by a palace revolution. But at some point – since the stresses inside the society are so great – unless something is done to defuse the bomb, it will blow up. Whether that is a good thing or a bad thing is not my point. It will be a bad thing in the sense that a lot of people will die. Whether or not it is desirable or undesirable that Pakistan should exist is really a question that the book doesn't discuss. If you ask me, I don't think Pakistan has a long-term chance of surviving.

It's difficult to see the military regime being displaced all the while Pakistan is a client nation of the USA, neglecting democratic rights and the federal aspirations of its peoples.

Yes, the military will be kept there as long as the west chooses. But there is a tendency in Pakistan – and I do it myself – to blame the west for all the problems, and I thought it would be worth writing a book to say that there's no point in blaming other countries, because actually we're doing it to ourselves. The point I'm making is that these plants – tyranny and so forth – are not grafted on, they grow naturally in this soil.

Do you mean, for example, the way General Zia uses Islamic fundamentalism as a political weapon, a device that seems particularly alien to a western audience?

It's actually very alien to the Pakistani audience as well. One of the things I say in the non-fiction parts of the book is that Zia cloaks what he does in the language of the faith, and because people respect the faith they don't want to question what he does: that's the way religion legitimizes tyranny, the way Islam is *linguistically* protecting Zia. I don't think Zia will destroy Islam, but he may well destroy the basis of the state.

Are you religious yourself?

No, I'm not formally religious. But it's like being a lapsed Catholic: you don't lose it – you have that intellectual tradition, and it's an important part of what you are. In that sense I'm a Muslim, but not in any practising sense.

I found that reading Shame *had a useful educational purpose for me, in so far as it prompted me to go away and read some books about Pakistan, to refresh my memory – including Tariq Ali's Book* Can Pakistan Survive?, *which struck me as setting out the issues clearly and conclusively.*

That's interesting, because he sent that book to me quite recently, long after I'd submitted *Shame.* I found there were really quite a lot of meeting-points between the ideas in the two books. Although we had never discussed it, we had both – in a position of exile – reached the same conclusions.

Would your wishes for Pakistan be the same as Tariq Ali's – a secular–democratic, socialist state?

Yes, certainly, and at one point in *Shame* I talk about the possibilities of the country disintegrating – once the Islamic myth has been devalued as a basis for the state – and the book then says that we could replace it with different myths, such as liberty, equality, fraternity. I do think that if the state has a chance of surviving it has to remove religion from itself, and when it does that it has a chance of removing the generals.

I do think that in a way the question about Pakistan doesn't matter to *Shame*, because the book has to make its own world. Whether or not you know anything about Pakistan shouldn't be a factor in reading a fiction, because the book has to tell you what you need to know, and if it doesn't it fails. You make a world, and you try to make it cohere and mean something about the world that you don't make, the actual world.

Midnight's Children *is a rich and elaborate concoction obviously rooted in your early love for Bombay and for India in general,* Shame *more of a dark decoction. Since you have never lived full-time in Pakistan, did you feel at all parasitic in writing a novel based there?*

Certainly my relationship to the material is different. I feel more detached, but not in the sense of feeling like an outsider – because in fact, in the last two decades, I've known Pakistan rather better than India. Still, you couldn't write that kind of exuberant, affectionate book about Pakistan, it would be a false book; and there will be plenty of people who won't like *Shame* because it is harder and sometimes cruel. But I don't think *Shame* is just unrelieved darkness: I went to some trouble to provide that light and shade we've talked about. In a way, I can write the book from the outside because I can stay alive; nobody in Pakistan could write the book, because they'd die.

Is there any danger to your family from the fact that you've written it?

Not as far as I can see. It's only a novel, after all, written in the English language – which most people can't read – and it will be stopped from entering the country. I now have a British passport, so in that sense they can refuse me entry to the country or they can deport me if I get through, but that's about it – given that I haven't broken any law in Pakistan.

But that's a risk you felt morally obliged to take?

Yes. When I started writing *Midnight's Children* the Emergency hadn't ended, and at the time the idea of writing a book which might prevent me from going to India ever again was very sad. But it hasn't happened.

Has Mrs Gandhi read Midnight's Children*?*

Of course she's read it, she's a very literate woman. She doesn't like it very much; she hasn't commented in public, but she's let her displeasure be known. It would have been amazing to me if she had not been displeased, because it is very rude about her.

When you return home to visit your family, do you feel any tension in yourself about re-accommodating yourself to their way of life . . . or just to Pakistan?

The first few days require a certain shift, but after that there's no strain – except that I do find Pakistan a strain. My parents speak very good English, but we don't speak that much English at home because they prefer not to.

Does your wife speak Urdu?

She understands a lot, but she hasn't acquired the courage to speak the language, and I don't blame her. Her vocabulary is not small, but I don't think she's mastered the syntax.

How did you meet your wife?

I met her in 1969, in London, through a mutual friend. She used to organize publicity work for a charity, and then she went into the publicity department of a publisher, but she stopped working a year or so ago.

Did you have any difficulty from your family when you chose to marry a white English girl?

I think there's no doubt that my parents would have rather I had not, but fortunately they both got on with her very well – very quickly – so there's never been a difficulty. And, to be fair, there's never been any difficulty from her family about her marrying me.

Are you active in working for race relations? You've written a strong article – 'The New Empire Within Britain' (New Society, 9 December 1982) – about racism here.

The background knowledge for that article came out of about five or six years of doing voluntary work in race relations – I was involved with the local community relations council, here in Camden – but now I simply don't have the time: it's sad but true. I've resigned from the executive council simply because I could never get to the meetings any more.

Your conclusion to that article is that 'Racism, of course, is not our problem. It is yours. We simply suffer the effects of your problem.' I think many people would consider it a joint problem, to be mutually overcome . . .

The victims of racism are the people who suffer from the effects of a problem which exists in the minds of the racists and in many of the institutions of this society. The argument began when the second generation grew up: it makes them bad-tempered when they are treated as foreigners. It would make me bad-tempered.

At least I know that I really am a foreigner, and I don't feel very English. I don't define myself by nationality – my passport doesn't tell me who I am. I define myself by friends, political affinity, groupings I feel at home in . . . and of course writing. I enjoy having access to three different countries, and I don't see that I need to choose.

· DAVID STOREY ·

David Storey is author of eight published novels, the first of which was *This Sporting Life* (1960, winner of the Macmillan Fiction Award and filmed by Lindsay Anderson, who has also directed many of Storey's plays): it was actually the eighth novel he had written, but it was turned down by more than a dozen publishers over a four-year period before it was recognized as a masterpiece. Storey's first play, *The Restoration of Arnold Middleton* (1967), similarly suffered nine years of neglect before it was produced on stage. But his work has not lacked enormous critical acclaim since those early years. His further publications include the novels *Flight into Camden* (1960, John Llewelyn Rhys Memorial Prize, Somerset Maugham Award 1963), *Pasmore* (1972, Geoffrey Faber Memorial Prize 1973) and *Saville* (1976, winner of the Booker McConnell Prize), and prize-winning plays including *The Contractor* (1970), *The Changing Room* (1972) and *Home* (1970).

Born in Wakefield, Yorkshire, in 1933, he is the third son of a mine-worker, though he was brought up on a large housing project and not in a rural mining community. Like another child of Wakefield, George Gissing, whom he admires for his 'mordant puritanism' – 'which I share in a way' – but not for his 'perverse pessimism', Storey quit the north at an early age. Taken aback by the fact that he achieved only 17 per cent in his English literature A-level, he still felt determined to extricate himself from a society in which he felt 'a total spiritual outcast': it was 'ignorant, vicious and ferocious', he has said. His ambition compelled him first to become an art student (he studied at the Slade School of Art, 1953–6) – in which he supported himself by playing professional football for Leeds Rugby League Club – before he pressed on to establish a literary career.

Storey is committed to the tradition of the English social novel. He regrets what he calls the 'new philistinism' of many misbegotten contemporary novels, which skip 'real life' and offer only a commentary upon life. He writes with 'the empirical view of letting the content shape its own form and the form finally declare itself', he has said, preferring 'a recital of facts rather than feelings or ideas and attitudes' (quoted by Ronald Hayman, 'Storey's stockpot', *Books and Bookmen*, July 1978). His work is commonly true to that standard: it interprets but refuses to psychologize experience – an activity which he finds deeply suspect.

The themes of his novels are to a certain degree autobiographical, and it can readily be inferred that Storey feels obliged to pay his emotional dues to a background which he found hostile to his sensibility. But in so far as his fiction may be called autobiographical, the important fact is that it imaginatively transforms the experiences it narrates. 'Art is a liberating experience – from yourself. You make it accessible to other people through a sort of fictionalized commonality,' he has said in an interview with the *New York Times* (28 August 1977). *Saville* – a novel which has invited favourable comparison with D. H. Lawrence's *Sons and Lovers* and Arnold Bennett's *Clayhanger* – characteristically relates the early life of 'a boy whose growing-up in the forties and fifties forges a powerful conflict in his nature, and a destructive resistance to his environment', as the publisher's blurb properly described it. That theme of estrangement and self-division in a youth whose temperament and gifts force him to challenge and betray a working-class context is in many ways the theme of Storey's own life, but Storey rigorously effaces himself in adapting it to the imagination. Although his stern narrative detachment paradoxically obliges the reader to share the experience and viewpoint of his central protagonists, the advantage of the method is a precise and passionate realization of place and character – a delineation which achieves an almost documentary authenticity. Storey honours the struggles and tenacity of his protagonists, and his writing is able to impart intense and honest observation. His fictions are understated and unsentimental but genuinely moving, and all the more disturbing for what is portrayed without intrusive analysis.

David Storey married in 1956, and has four children. He now lives in a roomy house in Hampstead – 'the working-class end' of Belsize Park – where he works a solid seven days a week at his writing. He has in fact written far more than he has ever seen fit to publish – 'It's a liability of the way I write,' he explains disarmingly – more than twenty-six full-length novels and nearly thirty plays in all. He is unlikely to write an autobiography, he told me. 'It would be difficult for me now to know truth from fiction.'

I talked to him in October 1982, shortly after the publication of *A Prodigal Child*.

★   ★   ★

A Prodigal Child concerns a working-class boy who dreams of a special destiny for himself and realizes it through the favours of an older woman. It shows great care and tact, and received a good critical reception. Are you pleased with it yourself?
No, I can't stand it. It started out as one kind of book and ended up as another, and I was really preoccupied with the original conception. In the original plan, the boy was in fact an orphan.
The last three chapters arrive unexpectedly. You present what appears to be an optimistic scene in which the boy acknowledges his father and background. Bryan seems not to have been damaged by the ambiguous tyranny and growing eroticism of his relationship with Mrs Corrigan.
I think the conclusion was willed, and to that extent false. I got so fed up with the characters that basically I jacked it in. The book was supposed to show how the working class has sold its inheritance, and the end was supposed to be ironical. The boy comes back in a rather cursory and distanced way. I think the irony can't be picked up by the reader because of the peremptory nature of the ending; it becomes specious. The allegory of working-class life in this country is stymied at the end. I think in

years to come, if I can bear to look at it again, I might put in the second half of the book, and the end might then become the natural consequence of the narrative. The second half concerns the sexual relationship of the boy living in Mrs Corrigan's house, the gradual disintegration of that relationship, and his return to the clapped-out working-class life – but as an outsider, an artist, who can make only a token return, no real reconnection.

But the published version does compose the relationship with great subtlety, every careful nuance . . .

It was that I found so difficult. In the original version the sexuality came in almost at the beginning, it was a given part of the relationship, and I found that it obscured a great deal of what was supposedly of greater interest. So I took it out and kept it implicit until the end of the book, where it becomes overt. His social position was more interesting to me.

Mrs Corrigan is none the less a fine achievement. On one hand you show her as vacuous, snobbish and sexy, and on the other hand there's a tremendous pathos about her attempts to manage a relationship with the child, to fill up her emptiness.

I became terribly impatient with her. I felt that she could only work in the book if I kept her distanced, and it was very difficult to keep her at arm's length. She became very intrusive, and I rather wearied of holding her off. In the second half of the book she really goes to seed. Her husband caves in, but she's such an egotist that she becomes more and more compulsive, insatiable, outrageous.

So you really felt very unsympathetic towards her?

No, I rather liked her, but she became more and more monstrous.

A Prodigal Child is meant to be a punning title, is it, implying not just that he returns home as a prodigal but that he's also precocious as an artist?

Yes, and also his sexual precociousness. I think I could keep it objective as far as it goes, and the second half became too subjective; I couldn't keep a control.

The parable of the prodigal child has always struck me as being very suspect. It seems to me a very gratuitous return, because the only motive for the son's return home is totally mercenary. You feel that he's as big a bastard when he comes back as he was when he left. He comes back for material reasons, not because of greater understanding. This absolute shit returns home and the ox is roasted . . . I really feel for the other brother.

Throughout your work you've mined the vein of your ambivalent feelings towards a working-class upbringing in Yorkshire, with antagonism and unhappiness, and I wonder how you now feel about it?

I don't think I will ever resolve it, my attitude will always be ambivalent. But it's really a locked-up period of history, and there's no connection when I go back now. The past has been disassembled, it's a different place.

Are your parents still alive?

Yes, they now live in a bungalow near Scarborough. My father was about 61 when he came off the coalface with pneumoconiosis, and he was given six months to live. So I took out a mortgage for them, and now twenty years later he's still going, getting fitter and fitter. I keep tapping my wallet as a reminder that he's overstayed his six months!

How do you get on with your parents?

Very well. For many years there was a great deal of pain because I was doing something to which they were actively indisposed: they sacrificed themselves to bring up a professional man.

But what about the anger you must have felt?

My anger never demonstrated itself, it really came out as withdrawal. It came out as a determination to succeed, to prove the world wrong. When I played football the other players thought I was homosexual, and at the Slade they thought I was a yob.

In one or two places you've mentioned your admiration for Wyndham Lewis's autobiography, Rude Assignment. *Given Lewis's well-known arrogance and often fascist attitudes, it's always struck me as strange that you should respond to him.*

I think it was his panache, but mainly his paranoia. He rationalizes paranoia into a political pose, and that was probably a reflection of my own unacknowledged paranoia. It seemed to me a compelling and romantic notion of the artist as someone beleaguered within society rather than outside it. That has certainly been my personal experience of trying to be an artist. I tried to be successful in two totally different and irreconcilable worlds, as a professional footballer and as an aesthete in London. What was odd was the struggle of trying to be effective in both areas. So when I came across Lewis as the belligerent protagonist who was irreconciled to everything, it raised a powerful echo. He was certainly a remarkable artistic personality. When I read *Rude Assignment* now, I wince all the way through; that sort of self-destructiveness in Lewis is transparent. I was also captivated by his style of writing. His literary criticisms and *America and Cosmic Man* are very readable, but I'm now very distracted by his affectations.

Twenty years ago, in an article called 'Journey through a Tunnel' (The Listener, *1 August 1963), you said that you admired Lewis's posture as an 'armoured protagonist'. Your own instinct was to take on protective colouring . . .*

The way I did survive was to adopt a kind of belligerence – which wasn't really my cup of tea – in both worlds. I was aggressive as an art student and extremely morose in the north.

Do you think the belligerence was at all self-pitying?

I think it was certainly self-pitying, and a self-commiserating device. But I also feel it had a more objective basis to do with class. I decided to become an artist when I was 17 or 18 almost as a political act, as a recoil against everything I was being directed towards. That kind of belligerence developed then, as the only way I could actually keep my morale going, since I was disowned by everybody. I wasn't even really sure whether I wanted to be a writer or a painter, I just wanted to be an artist – someone who had no practical function in society. The football world became the acceptance world I'd set aside, and the art school became the maverick world to which I was directing all my deepest energies. It developed the schizoid situation I described in *The Listener*. The more I struggled with the two worlds the further apart they became. I was absolutely desolate the two years I was at Wakefield Art School. They wanted me to become a commercial artist and absolutely refused to submit my work or write a testimonial for my application to the Slade. I pointed this out to the Slade, and then I got in, thank God. I don't know what else I would have done . . . My parents also refused to sign my application form, and in fact my auntie forged their signatures because she thought she had a moral right . . . and she had a similar name. So I found that everybody was actively indisposed to me being an artist. There was no social support for the idea of painting pictures, and then I had the huge emotional problem of being a muscled giant painting bloody pictures with a father who worked down the pit and crawled home prostrated. It seemed absolutely ridiculous.

In Celebration *portrays three sons who briefly return home to their working-class family, and their father is a miner. What seems curious is that the most outspokenly derisive character, Andrew – who might in some sense be taken as a spokesman for your personal point of view – is at the same time the most perversely destructive figure in the play.*

The parents' genuine love is shown to have its virtues. I think *In Celebration* did achieve some kind of balance. I split it into three: the reclusive son, the accommodating son and the maverick son; I thought those were the three elements involved, and they created different types of tension and conflict. I was disappointed by the play because I think the resolution it was building towards didn't really materialize. I thought when I was writing it that there would be a confrontation, but it came out as a token reconciliation. I couldn't see how a catharsis could be achieved in that play without it becoming melodramatic.

In The Farm, *on the other hand, the father's truculence and swingeing comments are very funny, to the point where he becomes almost endearing. And yet we're supposed to recognize that what he stands for has horribly oppressed his family.*

He is a comic character, and on the other hand the rather sour-faced son who can't accommodate him is no great shakes.

It is embarrassingly pathetic that the son can't bring himself to introduce to the family the woman whom he says he's chosen to marry, a woman twenty years older than himself.

Yes, it seems he's almost chosen the very woman he knew would antagonize his family the most. That's the perverse element, that he would deliberately or unconsciously choose the course that would do him the least good; that's his weakness.

I see all the plays as comedies really. What is interesting was

that the film of *In Celebration* came out as very remorseless, like
A Long Day's Journey into Night, whereas the audiences always
laughed heartily at the live productions.

What prompted you to write Mother's Day, *which is an out-and-out
farce?*

I wrote it at a time when I became aware of how ridiculous
everything is in this country, of how everybody is the inverse of
what they're supposed to be. I thought I'd write a family which
shows the *modus vivendi* of every family . . . everybody is trying
to screw everybody else . . .

And committing incest?

Yes . . . that became the everyday life of this family, not the
undercurrent.

*You've often said that you write the plays so quickly that you never
prefigure what's going to happen, and that only later do you realize the
themes and metaphors in what you've written. I wonder if that's not
really a slightly disingenuous account of how you go about writing your
plays?*

No, and in fact I find it a frustrating limitation. I've often
planned a play beforehand – plot, character, situation, and the
great scene that's going to illuminate everything – but then,
when I write it, it comes out as a turgid illustration of a theme.
With *Mother's Day* I thought I was going to write a serious play
to do with murder, a play as dark and brooding as a Dostoievsky
novel, but it just became more and more hilarious. All my
intentions were totally disconnected from what I was actually
writing.

What goes wrong, then?

I think it's an inability, a naivety. Most of my plays were written
with virtually no theatrical experience at all. Before I had a play
put on, my experience was confined to six or seven visits to the
theatre. Apart from the period when I was an adviser at the
Royal Court Theatre, where I was obliged to read a lot of
scripts, I never go to the theatre. It was seeing *Arnold Middleton*
on the stage which triggered off the other plays, and they were
written over three or four months, each in a period of three or
four days.

Does it disappoint you that the plays have received much wider critical

acclaim than the novels, when the novels take so much longer to finish?
They certainly seem more important in the sense that they take more time, and I personally get less out of writing the plays – largely because of this frustrating facility.

But that's not to say that the critics discern things that aren't there?
No, I think they've spotted the right things . . . I think it's rather like writing poetry. Whenever I read or see Shakespeare, which is very rarely, everything in the plays inclines me to believe that they were first drafts: it's a completely spontaneous facility, he doesn't think and conjure. I'm not comparing myself with Shakespeare, but there is a kind of creative temperament which hits it first time, and it's very frustrating. But I certainly linger over the novels.

There's a sense, isn't there, in which some of your plays lack a plot? I mean in the sense that you don't feel it necessary to lead up to an event or crisis which shifts the gear or changes the course of the action. What you do offer is a situation, an environment, and the meaning of the plays lies in the texture of dialogue and relationships rather than in a plot as such.
Yes, I find the plot is what I would like to have put in, but then I find the plot is melodramatic and always totally irrelevant to the experience that's being written about. I suppose you could describe the plays as evocations rather than as dramas, and there are themes which are identified and presented in that evocation. They don't have a dramatic plot in the conventional sense. And it's not that they fight shy of presenting one, they normally go out of their way – perversely – to avoid even indicating one.

Some of them are in a sense by-products of the novels, I suppose? I understand you wrote In Celebration, *for example, at a time when you found you'd stalled in the writing of* Saville.
The plays deal with aspects of that milieu which the novels don't or can't deal with, and vice versa. There's a superficial relationship, for instance, between *Radcliffe* and *The Contractor*, but in terms of the experience they present there's very little connection at all. In a way it's been a liability doing both plays and novels. It would be interesting if critics could relate the novels and the plays as a single imaginative world, but curiously they never do. The novel critics see the plays as superficial, and the theatre critics suspect me as a novelist. So again, rather like

when I tried to be a footballer and an artist, I've cut my cloth in the wrong shape.

In Celebration, *I think, explores psychological problems which for the most part you wanted to leave out of* Saville – *the psychology, that is to say, of the child as a compensation for the child who was lost.*

I saw the novel as a social rather than as a psychological novel, and the play became psychological. I found that I couldn't really write a psychological novel, that somehow the material didn't lend itself to what was coming out on the page. I stalled on the novel because it wasn't working, and then I thought I'd write a play to crystallize what I thought I was trying to do. When the play was done, I saw that I could take out that element in the novel, and it would be a social novel covering a particular period in the life of this country.

As you know, one or two critics have felt that the psychology in In Celebration, *the play, is in a way too pat.*

I think the psychology is self-conscious and intrusive in *In Celebration*, I don't think it's really been assimilated into the body of the play.

Was the psychology none the less true to you?

I think I wanted to unearth a particular truth, which was to do with my own life, and give it some kind of universal meaning. I think it bogged down in a particular experience, and the play didn't really free it into a larger experience. I think it was partly, in my case, being born in circumstances which were melancholic . . .

Because of the death of your elder brother?

Yes, and the ambiguous relationship that grew out of that – of being conceived of a woman who was suicidal and of growing into an environment where it was never actually acknowledged. You harboured an injury which could never be acknowledged. In other words, it was an untenable and unliveable situation. At that stage the experience was too close for me to be able to detach myself sufficiently to be able to write a play about it.

Do you feel that a novelist has to be something of a psychologist?

No, not at all. I think a rational understanding of experience is death for an artist. I find rationalization a bane. Real understanding comes when the rational and the intuitional are both engaged. Intellectual truths are only half-truths. I can only write intuitively, and it's frustrating. I would like to be able to plot a novel or a play and then sit down and write it.

A number of your works include characters who have breakdowns of one sort or another, and I wonder if you always regard those situations as metaphorical or if they spring literally from your own experience?

I've never actually broken down myself, but I've projected my potential to do so into plays and novels. On a personal level, if not as an artist, I've always been able vividly to evoke that catastrophe, and I've witnessed it in friends and colleagues.

The hero in Pasmore *experiences such a breakdown, which many readers take to be serious and disturbing, and yet you've always described the book as satirical or ironic. Can you explain that?*

Pasmore is a character who had been conditioned to represent a social attitude, the attitude of a conformist evolving out of the working class, and there are certainly markers throughout the book to indicate that he is to some extent a comic character. His emotions and sufferings are not basically comic, but the effect can be seen in a comic way: he's a working-class protagonist whose goal is the elusive fruits of middle-class security, which doesn't exist when he gets there. Pasmore was intended to be a representative rather than an exceptional figure in those circumstances. The unnatural allegiance he owes to his father's ambitions for him, and how he can't fulfil them, are really the core of his self-dissatisfaction. He's a compromised character.

It's extremely difficult in A Temporary Life *to see a perspective on Colin Freestone's actions other than what he tells us. Much of what he does and says seems very callous – his behaviour towards his mad wife, for example, or more especially towards her mother – and it might appear that you as author endorse his attitudes and behaviour.*

I thought the things he says to his wife were unkind in a helpful way, puncturing the illusions she has about the world and society. But yes, I thought the central character was too detached, he was outside the current of the book. He was supposed to be an imperturbable character who maintained his integrity through being imperturbable, only reacting in a conscious and deliberate way when he felt it necessary to maintain his imperturbability. But I think that because of his imperturbability he never seemed to be engaged with the matter of the novel itself. The only parts I found come alive are those to do with his relationship to his wife. I think what you call a callousness was supposed to be a kind of protean strength, a standing apart from the shit of society and a refusal to be compromised by anything, and it comes out as a cold-bloodedness. Again, in *This Sporting Life*, Arthur Machin refused to be compromised and basically used society for his own ends . . . to his own loss in the end. It's the attitude of an outsider preserving his integrity. If it had worked in *A Temporary Life*, Colin Freestone would have been the only sane element in the book.

Many of the women in your books seem to be oppressed or shadowy characters.

My own experience was of women who were oppressed almost to extinction by their circumstances . . .

Emotionally stultified?

Yes . . . or at least their emotional strength came out in per-verted ways; they were tyrants in a totally negative way. I wrote *Flight into Camden* from a woman's point of view. It was some-thing I felt I could identify with, writing as a woman and seeing society as an oppressive system which denied every kind of feeling and ambition she might have had. I felt it was my own experience, and it was true of what I felt was the feminine experience at that time. The moral blackmail of society and of her family were too much for her; her love for her family was exploited in order to imprison her. She took to another victim, another weak character, Howarth, whom she felt was as op-pressed as she was, and in the end he reverts to the masculine system. The irony is that at the end her family are discussing her as though she's the sacrificial goat brought back to the altar to be bled.

In The Restoration of Arnold Middleton *Arnie recites a verse about dying like 'a prince, a saviour, or a messiah', and it strikes me that several of your characters – such as Arthur Machin in* This Sporting Life *– set themselves up in such roles, as saviours . . .*

Yes, they have an evangelical ambition. They do have a clear view of society as being totally destructive of the individual. By their strength or pugnacity they somehow extricate themselves from those pressures, and yet by doing so they are isolated. They either come through or remain apart, but at the same time they never refuse to engage.

Arthur Machin tries to rescue an emotionally frozen woman, Mrs Hammond.

He found a woman who was very much like his own mother, and like many women in society at that time who were subjugated by domestic or emotional circumstances and lived basically a dog's life. He was insisting on a larger view of life in the evangelical sense of having a vision and wanting people to come to it. He felt he could transcend the circumstances into which he'd been born and the circumstances into which Mrs Hammond had been born.

He didn't reckon that his success as a footballer was a hollow crown?

Well, ambition in itself is not a hollow crown. Attaching value to the mechanisms of ambition is a hollow crown. You could say that his tragedy was that he got carried away by the mechanisms of ambition.

In one sense his vision became self-glory, an egotistical vision.

His means of achieving it became self-glory. It's rather like the artist who glories egotistically in his own gift, and yet he still has the gift. There are two things: what he gets out of his gift in an intrinsic way, which is probably offensive to other people, and what is objectively there in terms of what he expresses through that gift. So I always felt that the use to which Arthur applied his gift as a footballer was divided: in one way he was trying to save somebody and to introduce her to a larger and more expansive view of life, and at the same time he was trying to dominate and destroy.

What about the magnificent set-piece which ends the book, the football game itself: is physical valiance all that Arthur's left with?

I think it's rather like the artist painting great pictures in his ivory tower, it's marvellous and it's tragic. His isolation is unliveable but for the work he produces from it. The intent was to create a stoic view of life.

Do you feel isolated?

Yes, totally. I started in isolation and I think I've carried on in that way.

You speak of stoicism as though it's an unambiguous virtue.
I think that's the only alternative to despair.
Do you still feel, as you've said elsewhere, that life is essentially tragic?
I'm trying to get away from that. I find it more and more intolerable as I get older. You have to set it aside and take a more courageous view of life. Yeats says in a poem that tragedy is an affirmative thing. Stoicism is a step out of tragedy in the fatalistic sense, and in the end I think we're struggling towards grace – the ability to accept life and to live it at the same time. I think in the end you can't accept the despair which underlay my earlier writing.
You've said somewhere that the character of Proctor in Cromwell *ends up by making himself 'invulnerable to life': did you mean that he retreats from life or that he transcends it?*
I think he was probably giving up. His attempt to accommodate all the conflicting social aspirations is a self-defeating exercise, and he can either retreat or expand into some kind of spirituality. *Cromwell* is a play I absolutely loathe, I find it very pretentious, but curiously it's the play that gave me the greatest satisfaction in writing. I wrote it at a time when I couldn't take any more of the Vietnam war and of Northern Ireland, in a week when the horrors reached a peak. The protagonists on both sides seemed so totally justified in what they were doing that the imagination couldn't grasp it. The image I had in mind was what a soldier told me about a family carrying a rotting corpse around on a cart and refusing to bury it until they'd found a priest. It came out in what I thought a dishonest form of poetry, because there was no real disciplined structure to the 'poetic' writing. But it certainly gave me a great sense of relief to write it. Some people liked it, and others thought it a bag of bones, a load of crap: my own intuitions incline to the second view. I agreed to it being produced because I thought that seeing it done might lead me on to a different theatrical idiom, which it didn't. Seeing it done just confirmed my initial unease about the play. It seemed to be the illustration of a theme rather than a realization. There are a lot of labels in the play, and a novel like *Radcliffe* suffers from the same complaint.

What in fact possessed you in the writing of Radcliffe? *There must have been a huge emotional investment, since it teems with muscular metaphors and allegory.*

No, I didn't feel any emotional investment in it at all. The only emotion was an enormous sense of frustration and disappointment about the way critics had received the first two novels. *This Sporting Life* and *Flight into Camden* were accepted or dismissed as sociological symptoms. I thought I would get my own back and put into *Radcliffe* everything that discipline and intuition said I should keep out, and of course I completely screwed up the book. I see *Radcliffe* as an endless series of labels, and the style is blatant, so self-conscious and wilful; I can't see any grace in it at all.

For a long time your work did seem to go, in a sense, in two directions: one was the social determinism of the novels, and the other was the more psychological explorations in some of the plays.

The English novel is traditionally a social novel. The great momentum in society is social, not a psychological momentum created by individuals. The ideal is to show how the social element is informed by the psychological element, but in most cases it doesn't work.

Did you fully believe in determinism, that ultimately people cannot take charge of their lives?

It's something I started with, but I think that as a person I'm gradually working away from it. It's certainly the implacable element in everything I wrote to begin with.

Determinism can logically lead to passivity.

Yes, I think that's why I've tried to dig away from it, since it does lead to passivity and death.

Do you participate much in the rehearsals of your plays?

I never wanted to go to rehearsals. I tried my best either to sneak away or to stay away, but in the end it was almost impossible. There's always a point in about the third week of rehearsals when the actors actually take over the play, it becomes theirs; it's a very marked moment, and I feel at that point the author is a pain in the neck. Actors are on the whole suspicious of authors. But everybody is so insecure that if the author disappears they feel terribly uneasy – they think he's seen the light. So there is an element of being part of the band, maintaining a loyalty to the common venture. In the end I have to sweat it out.

The Contractor, *In Celebration* and *Home* were all written as a result of seeing *The Restoration of Arnold Middleton*, before I started working with Lindsay Anderson. I wrote *The Changing Room*, which is probably the most coherent of all the plays, after seeing *The Contractor*. The rest drifted out of my experience of working in the theatre.

The Contractor was only the second play I'd ever written, and there were enormous technical problems. I cut a lot of the play when we started rehearsals, but then I had to put it back in again because I realized that my instinct in timing the dialogue to the action had in fact been fairly accurate. The cuts had left a great deal of action to be done with nothing being said; in that sense it was purely magical that I'd got it right. The worst problem was to make the tent stay up; it was formidably difficult, and the first run-through took three hours and twenty minutes, almost twice as long as the production time. We never actually got the tent to stay up until the very first performance; before that, there was always some point when it would imperceptibly deflate like a balloon.

You obviously have an immense faith in Lindsay Anderson. Can you explain your relationship?
It's primarily intuition. It's very fortunate for me. There's absolutely no similarity between our characters or temperaments, and that enables a kind of objectivity which would be very difficult if there was an overlapping of aspiration or temperament. We came from opposite ends of the world; he was from a colonial–imperial tradition. But there were a number of coincidences. When I was breaking my heart at Wakefield Art School, Lindsay was in Wakefield making his first films at the factory on the edge of the estate where I was living, and he used the cinema at the end of our road to see his rushes in each day. One of the most remarkable films he made was called *Wakefield Express*, about the local newspaper. And then when we started working together we found that we never really had to discuss anything in terms of what it should be about. The only quarrel we ever had at the beginning was about his political sentimen-

tality. He had a sort of sentimental socialism, a middle-class socialism, which was based on a notion of the working class as a reservoir of spiritual life, when in fact the working class is the bourgeoisie bereft of its possessions. I always said: be true to the material and let the material dictate the theme; if the material is true, the theme will be there.

I think Lindsay's greatest strength is as a lyric artist. What he brings to the productions is an intellectual clarity and objectivity, which comes from his own intellectual abilities and also from his social experience – which precludes him from having anything personally to do with the subjects. He again is an artistically isolated character.

Is he your closest friend?

I think he probably is, yes, but we've worked so much together that I think we're relieved to disengage ourselves at times . . .

Was it ever unnerving for you to have a play taken over by the director and actors?

I take an empirical view of rehearsals. Since I never know what the plays are about, I've always been curious to see what's actually there. I've never felt personally involved in the text, I always watch as though it was somebody else's play. I know what I'd wished they'd been about.

What did *you wish for in* The Contractor?

When I was writing it there were various metaphors. Capitalism, the oppression of the workers, the dying empire, the artist creating a beautiful image which is never quite satisfactory and has to be disassembled at the end of the day: I hoped there were all those elements in it.

You're obviously very much engaged with the work ethic, and particularly with an ideal of communal work . . . as both a salvation and a refuge, perhaps?

The thing that has always interested me, at the deepest level, is that the novels and the plays are about groups, the relationship of the individual elements to the group – a football group, a group of people putting up a tent, or the family group. The group dominates the individuals in it, to the extent that they seek to escape from it but in the end are fetched back either to their salvation or to their damnation. I think it's largely because at an impressionable age I felt alienated from groups. All my works try to evoke the poetry of groups. *The Changing Room* was meant to have a double meaning: it was a room that changed because people came into it and also a room in which people were changed *by* it. That was one of the concerns I was aware of when writing it. Each character identifies himself as an individual when he enters and gradually acquires a new identity, just as the room acquires a new identity, and at the end the characters devolve into their individual identities and depart . . . in some peculiar way nourished by their complicity in coming there and going through their rituals. There's a kind of grandeur that stems from the comradeship of a joint enterprise and also the pathos of going off into the night as individuals.

In America there's an instantaneous recognition of the poetic content of the plays, and that's not the case in England. The critics here seem to like didactic theatre, grim and humourless. They have a rational, intellectualizing approach, and don't approach theatre in terms of life and experience and feeling. There's a huge new philistinism in the approach to art in this country, an attitude of thematic recognition. The theatre of ideas is a kind of philistinism. I think the theme has got to come out of the material, not the other way around.

Did you conceive the madhouse of Home *as a metaphor?*

I never thought it important that it is a madhouse. It seemed to me to be a close reflection of the everyday world. I felt *Home* was a picture of England, though *The Contractor* seemed to have a richer allegory.

Were you influenced by Beckett and Pinter in writing Home?

Curiously I'd never seen or read a Beckett or Pinter play when I wrote it. I've seen half a Pinter play since I wrote *Home*. When I was writing the plays my strongest feeling was a visual one. I always saw them framed like a painting, and the surface of the painting was to be kept continually mobile, both across and in-and-out: two-dimensional, a very plastic feeling. I find the proscenium arch very seductive, it is like a picture frame.

How did the evasive and inconsequential dialogue of Home *develop?*

I found as the characters were conversing that all the things they need to talk about and which tormented them the most were the things that they were most anxious not to mention. So that everything they *did* mention became a euphemism for this omission. It was by marking off the areas they couldn't refer to – like their loneliness, inadequacies and desolation – that they were more cogently expressed by omitting to express them. They constantly get to points where one character impinges on another's areas of non-intrusion, so that each character is constantly signalling and plotting a new line around them.

I felt it was a picture of our society now, and I found that the women were in fact the men, and the men were the women, because the women completely dominated. The women determine everything in the play, the direction of the dialogue, the intrusions upon sensitivity. They were much stronger characters, and that again seemed to be a reflection of the emotional life of this decaying country. Emotional momentum comes from the women. I always found that footballers had bravura and *macho*, but very little emotional reality.

Do you read a great deal?

Yes, enormously, mainly for pleasure. In an ideal world *Herzog* would be the kind of novel I would have like to have written: a novel where you are creatively in control. Many of Herzog's intellectual ideas are of course absolute bullshit, superficial and spurious, and there is an intellectual snobbishness in the book. Although the author sees the bullshit side to some degree, he covets the intellectual facility of his main character, since he goes on at such length in that intellectualizing effort – simply for its relish. I think that is the author's indulgence. But the great merit in the book is the enormous energy which Bellow has as a writer, his energy of language and his energy of projecting into language feelings of great diversity.

· EMMA TENNANT ·

One of today's most exciting novelists, energetic, quick-thinking, positive, Emma Tennant is a writer to whom easy labels will not apply. Her published novels include *Hotel de Dream* (1976), *The Bad Sister* (1978), *Wild Nights* (1979), *Queen of Stones* (1982; soon to be filmed by Channel 4 television) and *Woman Beware Woman* (1983), all of which have been praised for their poetic intensity, visionary power, wit and thrilling penetration of psychology. She has a large amount of the quality of mind and the talent she herself once described in David Hockney – that 'freedom lost by many people before childhood is out, a way of somersaulting'.

Born in 1937 into a famous family (Margot Asquith was her great-great-aunt), she spent her early years in Scotland, followed by an eccentric education which included a year at an idiosyncratic finishing school in Oxford, and then studied the history of art in Paris before becoming a debutante. She worked briefly on *Queen* and *Vogue*, before publishing her first novel *The Colour of Rain* pseudonymously in 1964. She went on to contribute articles and short stories to *The Listener* and *New Statesman* among other periodicals, and in 1975 founded *Bananas* – a literary newspaper specifically designed to extend the range of imaginative writing in print – which she edited until the summer of 1978. Emma Tennant has two daughters, and a son – Matthew Yorke, the grandson of Henry Green and himself a writer whose first novel has been extracted in *Vogue* and the *New Edinburgh Review*. She now lives with the writer Tim Owens in a comfortable and attractively bruised Victorian house off

Ladbroke Grove, London, where I talked to her in the autumn of 1983.

★   ★   ★

You come from a socially prominent family, you were brought up in the Borders of Scotland – I imagine your family was comfortably off – and your early career took you through the glossy world of fashion and magazines. Yet your novels, such as Wild Nights *and* Alice Fell, *show that your imagination insistently harks back to the world of your childhood.*

I was actually born in London, but just before the war broke out I was taken up to a house called Glen – near Peebles, about thirty miles south of Edinburgh – which is a Scottish baronial place built by my great-grandfather, though it had never been continuously lived in by anybody. I think I was the only person to have lived there for any stretch of time; I was coming up to the age of 2, and I was closeted in this freezing building throughout the war, much of the time with a retainer in the basement. My father ran the SOE in Cairo, and for much of the time he was away travelling on his important tasks. My childhood was therefore extremely beautiful and isolated, and filled with the most extraordinary animals and companions, many of them provided by my father when he came back. He would take me for long walks and invent animals which lived in the roots of trees, without being a fanciful person at all. I went to the village school, which had about eight pupils, and had the benefit of a Scottish education – meaning that you are taught to read within three weeks, and no nonsense about it. At the end of the war we came down to London, and I shall never forget the shock. I had never before left this extraordinary fake castle surrounded by huge and very ancient hills, in a *cul de sac* you couldn't and had no wish to get out of. Just the other day, in fact, I found some diaries I'd kept at about the age of 9 in which I'd written, 'This can't be true . . . I've never been so unhappy in my life. I sit on the tops of buses and the old men's spit runs down the wooden runnels.' That was the depression of the number 27 bus, since we lived in Regent's Park and I went to a crammer in Ravenscourt Park, which meant a journey of an hour-and-a-half each way. I think a kind of sadness settled on me then, and I could hardly wait for the holidays when we went back to Scotland.

So that your childhood really does stand out as an idyllic memory?

Yes, it was a complete Eden. One of the most interesting things I've recently read was Angus Wilson's *The Wild Garden*, his autobiography of his writing, and his discussions of the Edens which his parents had separately constructed for themselves. There are of course many other examples – such as Lord Cockburn's Eden in the Pentland hills outside Edinburgh – of writers who have indefatigably drawn a great spring of imagination from childhood Edens.

You were young enough to have no sense of loneliness, as many adults might have felt in that environment?

No, there was no question of feeling left out of things. The hills and valleys and burns were so rich, and I did have friends to play with. We used to do a lot of naughty things, which was very enjoyable.

Nor any sense of escaping from life to imagination?

No, not at all.

Were your parents ambitious for your education?

Yes, they were: my mother got me into St Paul's Girls School when we came to London. Because I was unable to settle down I insisted on leaving at the age of 15½, having taken three or four O-levels. My mother was and is very interested in literature, and her greatest aim was that her daughters should have a good education, but I was known as 'wilful'. I was then sent to an extraordinary establishment in Oxford run by a woman called Cuffy, a finishing school for young ladies of good family. Cuffy had been the governess of Lady Violet Bonham-Carter, and she eloped with Mr Bonham-Carter's private secretary, O. T. Falck, a man who had been a great economist, a friend of Keynes, and who had apparently made and lost three fortunes in his life. So Cuffy and Falck set up house together, to run this establishment of eight girls in Merton Street, and that became the most exciting and informative period of my life. It turned out that most of those girls talked about nothing but painting their nails and becoming debutantes, so I became Cuffy's pupil.

She was a woman of absolute brilliance – one of nature's teachers – and I read an enormous amount of German and French literature and history of art. Since that opened up my imagination in so many directions, I then went off to the École du Louvre, sat in the basement there with a torch, and followed the lectures on Flemish painting and so on. After that I did come back and become a debutante, which I once wrote about for the *London Review of Books*.

Were you a grim and dutiful debutante?

Not really, although I found nobody to match the young undergraduates who had taken me out in Oxford and were intelligent and interesting people. In Paris I was just very lonely, like someone in a novel by Anita Brookner, and I had never had such a good time as during that year in Oxford.

Did you then want to pursue a career in art, in some capacity?

Yes, I became fascinated by art and by the history of art, but I always knew I would write. The problem was that my way of carrying on had been completely oral. From the age of 2½ onwards I would unselfconsciously walk round and round the garden waving a twig or branch while stories poured out of my mouth, which my family used to refer to as my 'walking-about'. It came to an end when I was 15, because in wet weather I would walk about in my bedroom waving an old Penguin I'd split down the middle – I split the spine so that I could wave it – and one day some people listened outside my room while this was going on: it made me so self-conscious that I never did it again. But I became baffled because I had no idea how to translate this activity into writing. The only thing that made me feel better was reading that apparently Madame de Staël used to walk about waving a branch and speaking.

Were you making up characters, or describing scenes?

Some descriptions, but mostly characters; I think I had a great many people talking.

Most of the critics praise your novels for your powers of impressionistic evocation, sensuous description, and image-making, all of which would tie in with your appreciation of art, but then they also say that Emma Tennant has comparatively less sense of characterization. In other words, I think, reviewers at least like to type you one way or the other.

Yes, and I think I've just begun to bring those elements together in *Woman Beware Woman*. I think and hope that I have at last put together a strong evocation of place and characters too. I found it very exhausting to write, and it very much forced itself to be written.

What do you value in the novel as a form?

The space. I have tried – not very hard, and unsuccessfully – to write poetry, but I couldn't achieve that lovely feeling of elbow room . . . and the feeling that anything might happen next, as long as you can also keep control of what is going to happen next. I recently read Wilson's *Late Call* and thought it a marvellous novel: I was furious when it ended, because I felt I had lived with all the people. During the summer holidays I was so interrupted that I thought I couldn't read any novel properly, but one day when I had taken four 10-year-old girls into Bridport I picked up *Late Call* in a second-hand bookshop and began reading it in a bus. Three-and-a-half days later I finished it and looked up to find the same number of rather thinner children saying that they had so much enjoyed burning their fingers on the fish fingers. So I value irresistible narrative drive, and a feeling of real obsession with the characters, plus a distance from them which will not embarrass you with the feeling that the author has gone over the top.

I don't need a bizarre or exotic setting in a book. I love and can smell the Far Eastern setting of Graham Greene's *The Quiet American* – and I was once lucky enough to go out to Laos – but that is not what fascinates me about the book: it's something else in the author's sense of his characters. The other day somebody told me about how Rose Macaulay had asked someone to tell her about Evelyn Waugh's latest novel – it was *A Handful of Dust* – and the answer came that it was about adultery in Mayfair. Her response was that she certainly didn't want to read about such a thing, but then she corrected herself the next day and said that of course she would read the book, because what a book's *about* isn't the point – it's the way it's done. A book creates its own world, and it doesn't matter whether it's about Hampstead, South Kensington or Vietnam. I think I might be expected not to like Molly Keane's *Good Behaviour* – because it is set in upper-class Anglo-Irish circles – and I know that it was disliked by various pursuers of the fantastic whom I know quite well. But I did like it. Although I know its setting, I found *Good Behaviour* as strange and remote as Milosz's memoirs of his Lithuanian childhood – because of the writing.

People who come to your work by way of Wild Nights *and* Alice Fell *might well form the impression that you are less interested in plot than in eccentricity of perception. Would that be true as far as you are concerned?*
I think it was so then. *Wild Nights* was tremendously inspired by Bruno Schulz's *The Street of Crocodiles* and *Sanatorium Under the Sign of the Hourglass*. A tiny man who had never left his family, Schulz was shot in the Warsaw ghetto in 1942, and *The Street of Crocodiles* gives an extraordinary vision of his family. The thing is that, having led an isolated life – though in many ways unlike Schulz – in a strange place where members of the family would sometimes appear and then disappear, I thought I would feel very happy if I could capture the child's eye of the world. *The Street of Crocodiles* has no plot, or only a plot of weather and moods, and the arrival of relatives and the atmosphere they bring with them. When I was reading *The Street of Crocodiles* I happened also to be reading some Rilke, and I saw a line which goes something like, 'Why is it that those lights in the fen remind me of my great-aunts now and then?' and I thought: how absurd this must sound to the prosaic ear, but nevertheless it has a poetic truth. I thought *The Street of Crocodiles* a wonderful answer to anyone who might say to me that I shouldn't somehow merge relationships and nature and the supernatural, since Schulz was not a poet but an extraordinary prose writer.

I didn't feel happy with *Alice Fell*, which followed *Wild Nights*, because I couldn't get it right: I wanted to put it in the first person, but I couldn't because I couldn't have a girl describe her own fall. It wasn't meant to be myself, but the fall of a girl, using the myth of Persephone, and I realized later that what had kept *Wild Nights* alive was 'my' – the first person narrator's – child's eye, which homed right in on things. I now see that to do such a thing in the third person, as I tried to do in *Alice Fell*, can produce a much more dead sort of narrative, however good some of the imagery may be here and there.

Because the child's-eye view became too governed by the adult view of narrative, and you couldn't marry those opposing perspectives?

Exactly, though I couldn't think so at the time.

Would it none the less be true to say that up to about Queen of Stones *you weren't particularly absorbed by story but rather by states of temperament and sensation?*

No, I've always been tremendously absorbed by story. *The Time of the Crack* is very carefully plotted, and so are *Hotel de Dream* and *The Bad Sister*. I've only written two so-called poetic novels, *Wild Nights* and *Alice Fell*, and everything else was closely plotted. I think that in my writing-life so far people have rather fixed on those two, whereas six of my books have been plotted. *Wild Nights* and *Alice Fell* were intended to be short works of poetic prose. I will always stand up for *Wild Nights*: it doesn't actually imitate Bruno Schulz but it was wonderful for me to find in him something that responded to my childhood, even though he came from a totally different world.

Did you feel any sense of self-indulgence in capturing the child's vision of Wild Nights?

Not really, because it followed the seasons, which are a tremendously strong plot, if you like, and it followed the arrival and departure of relations who were so unlike each other that they set up different atmospheres. The child's eye registered incredible changes in environment as the relatives brought about winds and snowstorms. So I didn't think it was self-indulgent.

It might be said that in investing so much in sense-impressions you make style the thing which alone validates the novel. The critics have rightly observed – and mostly with a good deal of appreciation – that you are meticulous in conveying feelings, and yet that such a procedure can become a mannered end in itself.

I think it can't go on forever, though it is exciting to have tried to capture that childhood in *Wild Nights*. But certainly there would be no excitement if you carried on repeating metaphors. Virtuosity for itself would go dead.

Childhood has given you a theme for a large part of your writing.

The theme of childhood came from having two daughters who were growing up. *Queen of Stones* was my third book about childhood, and I won't do another one, because I've already forgotten how my daughters – who are now 14 and 10 – were looking at things at a certain age, and how it reminded me of how I had looked at things.

In terms of your writing career what had you done in the period before you came to write The Time of the Crack *and* The Last of the Country House Murders, *which you published in your 30s?*

When I was 24 I wrote a book called *The Colour of Rain*, which was published pseudonymously – partly because there were people in it who could (and instantly did) recognize themselves, and partly because of a young person's whimsical desire to be pseudonymous. My first great influence was Henry Green, whom I first met when I was 18 and who was my father-in-law for a period of time, and I was tremendously impressed both by him and by his wonderful novels. *The Colour of Rain* I wrote almost entirely in dialogue, and it concerned upper-class young people in London . . . which was the colour of rain. Weidenfeld submitted it for the Formentor Prize in 1964, and I was told by somebody that Alberto Moravia had said that it was a symbol of the decadence of English writing today, and that he'd hurled it into a wastepaper basket. I found that crushing, and hence the nine years' silence. I then wrote a novel about a young couple being corrupted by working on a glossy magazine (corrupted by the free gifts which were showered on them), and I lost it – sort of by mistake. After that I wrote two novels of 400 pages each, which I showed to nobody and kept under my bed . . . and then I lost them the last time I moved house. So that although I produced a large amount of wordage I couldn't find a way of working towards publishing another book, until I met the science fiction world of Michael Moorcock and J. G. Ballard: they told me that I must be professional, structure a book in four parts of 40 pages each, introduce and develop characters in situation, and then lead up to climax or catastrophe. Although it sounds *faux-naif*, it was true that up till then I was hardly able to write at all. It was then that I wrote *The Crack*, and by the time I wrote *Hotel de Dream* I found writing exciting and felt that something richer was coming out, and *Hotel de Dream* came to have more of that walk-about element in it.

I've read one profile of you which portrays you as being confident and impulsive, with a very secure sense of your social identity, and I wonder if you don't really experience some disequilibrium in writing?

I certainly have very little confidence as a writer, and disequilibrium is just about the word for it. I've just read a review of Buñuel's autobiography which quite rightly said that he had put his unexamined nightmares and dreads straight into his haunted and haunting films. The most interesting thing he said about his work was that it consisted of nothing but repetitions and interruptions, and that therefore the continual appearance of repetitions and interruptions means that he's never been able to live his life in a linear manner, which shows that his work consists of nothing but lack. I would in no way compare myself to Buñuel, but I do think that a lack of a feeling of linear life, plus a desire to rid myself of nightmares, have together produced my writing. I think 'lack' must also mean lack of confidence, and the only confidence I feel is when I think I am getting on top of my material: it lasts for a very short time, because I suffer from tremendous anxiety while plotting a book. I feel terrible when I start, I have a short buzz – of perhaps no more than four weeks – when I seem to be getting on top of it, and then I may finish with a sense of pleasure although I've become very tired and drained. The impression of impulsive, confident behaviour is a matter of social learning. It would be impossible to pinpoint exactly what the lack is, but after re-reading *Woman Beware Woman* I've noticed that the fact that I've kept going back and changing the time – as seamlessly as possible, I hope – had to do with a refusal to give a rather simple story any kind of linear life: I had to enrich it through that lack of linearity, so that it's really a book about memory. But of course I also do believe that in any one moment there are about 150 things going on inside a person. People were shocked by *Jekyll and Hyde*, but one of the things that meant a lot to me was Stevenson's comment that it was just the beginning: 'every human being is a polity of innumerable and incongruous denizens.'

But it is a paradox of art, particularly of the written word, of narrative, that it is actually impossible to present in one moment that multiplicity of levels of being and thought and sensation.

Yes, and I think it would be dangerous for writers to think they could slap down multiple personalities. The multiple schizoid personality has obviously been deeply explored by psychologists, but it would go against the discipline of art to write a character in a random way.

What do you think about appropriating Freud's analyses to the creative imagination? I think there would be no way in which you as author of Queen of Stones, *for instance, would endorse Freud's view of 'Dora' – which you draw on in that novel – because Freud's psychoanalytic equations, and his deterministic view, are inadequate explanations of character.*

Well, what I did in *Queen of Stones* was to present a dossier of quite a lot of rather stupid people's opinions, including a social worker, an ancient Freudian analyst, a journalist and a bishop – all done with a tongue in cheek which may not have been noticeable enough in the novel. Although Freud was certainly a genius, the Freudian passages in the book were actually meant to be rather funny.

I'm glad you say that, because I think you successfully parodied the smugness that comes over in Freud – or at least in English translations of Freud. Freud's presentation of his study of hysteria strikes me as maddeningly self-congratulatory.

Yes, but I don't think I made the fact it was parody clear enough to be picked up. Some people thought I was being portentous, but when the narrative says that it might comprehend 'the psychopathology of the developing female' and 'the mythology sustaining our concept of the feminine in society', it is said not by me but by a pretty stupid narrator: the very narrator who is collecting the dossier is somebody who is capable of making that kind of judgement. The narrator is a fictional person, and I think I did much the same thing in *The Bad Sister*, which ended with a perfectly convincing psychiatrist's report but which I wrote tongue-in-cheek. Life is too complicated for 'Jane Wild', as the girl was called in *The Bad Sister*, to be summed up as a paranoid schizophrenic.

What you evidently did in The Bad Sister *was to transpose James Hogg's* The Private Memoirs and Confessions of a Justified Sinner *into the modern world of sexual politics. Hogg's context was a pernicious religious logic, and yours is that of a radical and militant feminism. I think Hogg achieved a marvellously concentrated story of diabolic possession, and I don't quite believe in the ambiguities some critics like to find in him, whereas your contemporized version of the theme of the double personality invites numerous ambiguities. And you've translated the double from a male treatment to a female one: you've sophisticated Hogg, in a sense, in treating the question of masculine and feminine principles.*

I may have sophisticated Hogg, but the strength of Hogg's *Confessions* – a strength which my book lacks – is to do with Calvinism. Although it is a strong subject if you write about how militant feminism could be carried to its absurdist end in the murder of paternalist society, that is not as strong a theme as what happened with Calvinism in Scotland – because that actually happened in so strong a way. Nevertheless, I think the lack my book deals with is that to pursue the feminist position, to become aware of the loss of the masculine principle in you, and then to murder it – by murdering paternalist society – is no answer. It's self-defeating, just as in Hogg's *Confessions* it's self-defeating to go around murdering people in order to be told that you are one of the elect. I again felt inspired to write *The Bad Sister* because of my Scottish childhood, since Hogg actually wrote stories about the wood my bedroom window looked out onto – everyone continually being turned into three-legged stools and heaven knows what else – so that metamorphosis came into my mind at a very early age. Hogg lived about fifteen miles away, on the Yarrow, and I had early, very romantic feelings about his life, about the distant inn where he would meet Wordsworth and Scott after walking for 12 miles through snowdrifts. I was also fascinated by Stevenson's mother's snobbish reaction to Hogg's *Confessions*: she thought it couldn't have been written by one of 'us' because he was a working-class boy. I felt I could set a lot of *The Bad Sister* in that part of the world, and then follow through the girl's demented journal because of the alienation of a young woman transplanted to London – as indeed I was – along with the refusal to adapt to a life on a glossy magazine which seemed pointless compared to the extraordinary life in Scotland.

You mix definite sociological observation of a realistic kind with the fantasy-experiences of 'Jane Wild', interweaving levels of narrative and association.

It's a very complicated book to talk about, and I've noticed after finishing it that practically everything in it is a double. The double first came into the English language through Scotland via the German metaphysical writers and Hoffmann: it inspired first Hogg, then Stevenson; and since that time many other writers – including Edwin Morgan, and Karl Miller in *Cockburn's Millennium* – have written very interestingly on the split in the Scottish writer. I went to school in Scotland and spoke a broad Scottish dialect, and if you then come south there does exist a split as to whether you think you are Scottish or English. The concept of the split personality is particularly appealing to Scottish writers because the doubleness of national identity has been there for so long. I think I was also trying, as you say, to write a female double, which I think has not been attempted before. I'm looking at a situation where the male poet has a muse who is obviously female, and at Virginia Woolf's remark that it is very difficult for a woman poet or writer to coexist with another woman – because if the muse is female there are then two unpleasantly warring women in the same breast. That is very important for me in *The Bad Sister*: the girl 'Jane Wild' is desperately trying to invoke a male muse, which has never existed in history. *The Bad Sister* is perhaps even more concerned with the idea of the female double than with feminism. I think feminism works and has worked in a fantastic way, but I also think that a young and innocent person surrounded by propaganda can be corrupted, wherever the forcing comes from.

You mean that a young person can swallow a doctrine wholesale without any experience?

Exactly. The only thing which made it possible for me to write *The Bad Sister* was to use Hogg's structure in *Confessions*. I think that if someone is so leant on by the expectations of society and by a very frightening and rather occultish radical feminism it could only drive them to destroy themselves. But I do strongly believe in feminism, and I think that some of Virginia Woolf's extraordinary writings are among the best things that have ever been said.

In the first paragraph on page 63 of The Bad Sister *you write that 'a woman who thinks must live with a demented sister', and you go on to say that the 'subservient' sister will always win the battle – the 'terrible competitiveness' – because she is finite and never dreams. That would seem to be a statement you wanted to underwrite as the author of the novel.*

Yes, I wanted to underwrite that, because it's historically true. The important split which makes this wild person is only there because of the necessity to conform; if that necessity wasn't there, the wildness would have transformed into a proper sense of self-expression, without so many barriers.

Do you acknowledge in yourself the strong allegorical impulse critics see in your work? I think it is there in Alice Fell *at least.*

That book is allegorical, but in general my use of allegory has been to do with the fact that I couldn't see a point of view which made intelligent sense, such as an end to a novel narrated in the third person from the point of view of a middle-class man or woman, which is normally the case in novels . . . apart from novels like *Room at the Top* which have a definitely working-class point of view. I found it hard to imagine what kind of person I could make the narrator, and it's only very recently that I've turned on my heels, as it were, and realized that as far as I'm concerned the older you get and the more experience you have it is possible to make any kind of narrator and to get on with it. I think it's nonsense to talk about the post-imperialist state of the novel. Joseph Brodsky has observed that an enormous richness and diversity of cultures and languages have come together in someone like the West Indian poet Derek Walcott, and all that is true. But I also think that in terms of novel-writing the hardest thing of all is to write the traditional English novel, which is what the English have always been good at, the novel of character and feeling. It's only too easy to say that we've reached the end, the post-imperialist stage. If you allow into a novel random consciousnesses you don't end up with something that people really want to read, because of a lack of identification with the characters. This is something I would not have said before, because I felt that I could never achieve anything like

Angus Wilson's *Late Call*, for instance, but I do now feel that it is worth striving for a book of that kind.

It is a *volte face* on my part to say so, after producing *Bananas* in order to open up to a more 'imaginative' kind of writing, after striving to bring together writers of science fiction, writers of fantasy, and – in the case, for example, of Tom Nairn – political writers. But eight years later my feelings are very different. It's perfectly possible – if a writer has talent and experience – to show both the inner life and the outer life, and all the really good novelists, like Proust and Henry James, have always done so: the inner life of the characters, their feelings, together with the outer life and the *mores* of their times. I daresay it would be everybody's aim to merge those two things.

Yet what it might have seemed you were doing in your work up to Queen of Stones *was to enter the world of the inward and apparently fantastical experience of your characters, and to challenge the nature of 'reality' – such as the 'reality' of normal social intercourse – to offer new dimensions of experience by setting up a kind of fantasy life as a substitute for traditional plotting and characterization.*

I wouldn't agree with that, because I never saw a fantasy world. What I did was to stress what was going on inside people, and the interactions that would come about without anything necessarily being said, and I did it often in metaphor. In *The Bad Sister*, for example, there is a great deal of naturalistic description of Mrs Marten – her arrival, or her determination to have a gin and tonic – but 'Jane Wild' is driven increasingly mad by the unsaid antagonism which the mother-in-law brings. So from the point of view of the girl the trees outside the window will turn a particularly terrible shade of grey or red or green as Mrs Marten speaks. I'm using metaphor in that way.

All the same, your earlier novels do offer a sense of the numinous, and I wonder if you did actually believe in a psychic or magic dimension to life, not just as in the use of metaphor you've described?

No, I don't at all. I have a fear, which I think any right-thinking person should have, of any sort of theosophical or numinous way of thinking, because it could produce the kind of effect the occult-minded feminists have on 'Jane Wild'.

Do you think occultism is a sort of morbid escapism?

It is certainly that, and it's also extremely destructive to less strong-minded or less intelligent people. The Tantric belief that the figurative and the literal are identical is dangerous. None of us really believe that the figurative and the literal are the same, and in *The Bad Sister* I was interested in showing how the brain can become warped to such an extent that someone can believe that something said and inculcated can magically and then actually become the truth. I have always disliked the idea that I might be thought of as being somebody who believed in psychic powers, because if I had been a poet nothing of the sort would have been mentioned *vis-à-vis* my work . . .

. . . Because readers would have regarded it as being natural to the genre?

Precisely. On the other hand, I think there's been a muddle for about forty or fifty years about the so-called duties of prose literature – I mean the idea that it has a responsibility to be 'realistic', when in fact there has never been any such duty. I think the muddle has started to be cleared up by the appearance of such writers as Salman Rushdie, for whom the literal and the figurative coexist quite naturally. As far as I'm concerned, I would like to feel that I can go off in any direction that seems right.

That reminds me of what you once wrote about David Hockney [The Listener, 4 November 1976]. You praised his work for providing a 'marvellous feeling of freedom and relief', which I imagine is a phrase that could stand as a motto for your whole endeavour as a writer.

For me, a feeling of freedom and relief is certainly an important point of art. I used to think about the perfect book as being like Silenus' box: a cheap box which looked like fun – with a picture of a harlequin in gaudy colours on the outside – and when you opened it you found a perfect gem inside. I first read about that in the introduction to a selection of Rabelais' writings, and I thought it a wonderful description of art: something which should appear to be entertainment but would actually contain one perfect stone – the truth of whatever you are writing. That image certainly goes against didacticism or moral meaning in the novel. And yet I do think that a lot of my books have actually been a blend of Calvinism and romanticism – having to do with murder and morals – and that's something I don't really understand; it is what seems to have emerged.

Bernard Levin said in a very approving review of Alice Fell *[The Sunday Times, 16 November 1980] that the book didn't seem to be bitter or angry or even despairing, but that it conveyed a sort of elegiac sadness about England in the 1950s and 1960s. Did you ever think of that novel as a swansong?*

No, I just put in what was happening in England alongside her growing years, and my interest lay in the stages of the girl's growing up. The descriptions of infancy are what interest me most in that book, and then the idea of her fall at about the age of 16, which all parents dread. I didn't at all see it as an allegory of England, though I certainly appreciated Bernard Levin's review.

You felt no sense of social nostalgia in writing the book?

No, none at all; I didn't think of it as an elegy. I didn't treat what happens to a country house as a sign of the times: it would have been out of date.

Have you felt any need to justify the use of myth in the modern novel, the way you used the myth of Persephone in Alice Fell*? Is it simply a device which enables the novelist to fulfil a given pattern – usually, as Bruno Bettelheim points out in* The Uses of Enchantment*, a rather pessimistic pattern to do with superego control – or have you found a creative tension in fleshing out a character to fit an archetype?*

With regard to *Alice Fell* I think that a certain pessimism probably existed in me *vis-à-vis* the opportunities for female children, and I used the Persephone myth – as opposed to a fairy story – to show that it is still fantastically difficult not to have that kind of trajectory in life. I think that the horrors that lie in store for a girl beyond the age of 14 – unwanted pregnancy, for example, or rejection by the mother because of a threat to her sexuality – are very nearly as strong as they always have been, and that particular pessimism would make one want to use myth. But I think the fault of *Alice Fell* is that it does use a laid-out mythical pattern.

Some time ago I wrote a story called 'Philomela', set in Greece, which I think made an important point about Philomela and Procne being divided through jealousy by one man, Tereus, and it seemed to offer a way of looking at the new consciousness that was arising in women, including myself. I have noticed that quite a number of women writers went to myth to begin with. But I think that it was a certain stage in women's writing. Marguerite Yourcenar used myth in *A Coin in Nine Hands*, first written nearly fifty years ago but just published in England, and I found it had no resonance for me. So that I think the use of myth may be destructive to the imagination, and perhaps not much fun to read. If you use characters as archetypes, they can lose the right to be characters. Carol Rumens said about *Alice Fell* [*The Times Literary Supplement*, 7 November 1980] that the characters were like figures in a medieval tapestry, huge and yet very far away, and therefore without perspective. So that if you write a book in that way you lose any sense of the characters taking over from the author: you don't make three-dimensional characters. For *Alice Fell* I read a lot of art books – including Gombrich's work on order and on margins in medieval books – things of that sort which very much fascinated me.

Since you are happy to say that you have absorbed various models and influences for your books, how do you see the nature of 'influence'?

You realize that your imagination has been inflamed, or at least part of it that you didn't know was there, and a whole series of images and scenes will appear out of what inspired you. I don't think it's *voulu*. If you use a myth, then that *is* intended. But actually I have only used myth in *Alice Fell*.

Queen of Stones is concerned with the psychological turbulence and contests in a group of pre-adolescent girls, and it is also a kind of thriller climaxing in a murder or execution. The drama of the novel seems to lie so much in psychoneurotic conflicts that the finale could be taken as rather arbitrary; I think even Angela Carter found the conclusion de trop. Would you agree at all that the emergence of the one scapegoat–victim may be an artistically tidy but emotionally unsatisfying ending?

I can't say I agree with that, because I very consciously rewrote *Lord of the Flies* from a female point of view. I was very keen to keep to the idea of there being a certain kind of victim, which would certainly be the disadvantaged, plain and miserable little girl. I wanted to maintain a thriller narrative, and that it should resolve itself rather than become merely a dossier. My chief aim was to make the novel rather like a high-tech modern building, where all the plumbing is purposefully shown on the outside. The anatomy was put on the outside, to show all the things that Freudian analysts and social workers would think had happened, as well as all the things the girls had been indoctrinated with, and to lay them out in the form of a dossier.

The point at the end about the disadvantaged girl being killed is not arbitrary. The older girls have reached an age when they know very well that their Queen Elizabeth and Mary Queen of Scots fantasies *are* fantasies – they realize that they are acting something out – and the reason why the real violence happens with children of 10 or 11 is because they haven't come to that moment of near-adulthood, and they do react violently to the pressures put upon them.

Should it be taken as a didactic novel, a novel of ideas?

I think it is a didactic novel. I was trying to inform people about how girls are brought up to think of themselves and their expectations – through the early reading of fairy stories, through the way their mothers treat them, through Freudian or Adlerian analysis – showing both how society now reads those girls and how they have been indoctrinated. There is no adolescent girl who isn't indoctrinated, for example, by Elizabeth and Mary Queen of Scots, the royal fantasy of queenship. The novel shows those two things: what society now sees and what the girls have had pushed into their minds, so that it *is* didactic. The passages of male ratiocination are certainly sent up in the novel, and I intended that it should not be clear whether the narrator is male or female. In *The Bad Sister* the narrator is definitely a man, but it's deliberately unclear in *Queen of Stones*. The social worker in *Queen of Stones* is a woman using a man's language; it is very frightening to encounter women doctors, for example, who on certain levels deny their own knowledge of themselves – the way their minds work in certain circumstances which have been influenced by the body, such as childbirth or menstruation. It causes extreme misery and distress on the part of the patient when a woman doctor enunciates male doctrine.

Woman Beware Woman depicts the power structure and struggles of a family centred on the figure of the bereaved matriarch, Moura. It is all

*told through the first-person narration of an outsider, Minnie, who
implicates herself in that nexus of tensions because of her desire to be an
insider. It is a subtle and chilling psychological thriller, with every hint
and observation being totally relevant to the theme and story. How did
you come to write it?*

The novel is mainly inspired by *Colomba*, by Merimée. I say
'inspired' not in the sense of having copied Merimée's plot: I
mean literally inspired. *Colomba* is one of the most extraordinary
novellas ever written, and its theme of revenge by accident has
haunted me for years. About ten years ago I was commissioned
to write a filmscript based on it, but the film didn't get made. So
that for many years I have been thinking about how I could use a
theme of family honour despoiled and a forceful personality (in
Woman Beware Woman a mother, in *Colomba* a sister) getting a
son (in *Colomba* a brother) to enact a revenge which he has no
desire to enact at all. Going along with that was a thought that
came to me after reading *J'Accuse*, where you think of an
extremely dispassionate, lofty-minded and brilliant novelist
who – through wishing to protect someone – becomes involved
in local politics, petty crime and corruption. That idea has also
interested me for a long time, and the two ideas happened to
merge together. What then emerged was a story of strong
family tensions and conflicts, as you say, and the title *Woman
Beware Woman* seemed to be apposite because there are three
women in the story, each one of whom must beware of the
others. It was only because of the death and probable murder of
Hugo Pierce, the eminent novelist, that the whole chain of
women needing to beware of each other took place. The strong
loyalty Hugo instilled in people through his marvellous qualities
set up an atmosphere which enabled that sort of tension to get
out of control.

*We follow the story through the eyes and reflections of Minnie, whom
we tend to identify with, and we don't realize for some time that she is in
fact outwitted and highly suggestible . . .*

Are you sure she has been outwitted? She may be outwitted, but
you could say that she isn't. The powerful matriarch figure must
beware Minnie because you must beware someone who is
cunning and depressed. Minnie must beware Moura, who is

loyal and protective and driven almost to the point of insanity; Moura must beware Fran, the daughter-in-law who is a radical American film-maker, because the daughter-in-law throws a very cold documentary eye over a very private theme; Minnie must also beware Fran, who is going to break up her fantasies and tell her truths she doesn't want to know; and Fran has reason to beware Moura, who has not made life easier between Fran and her husband by being such a strong character. I see the book as an interplay between three very different women, as concerning treachery on public and private levels.

Would you be alarmed if the book is in any way taken as a text for our times – saying something about relationships between women?

I feel very strongly that it is not a text to do with women in our time. My feeling about *Woman Beware Woman* is that it might excite people to think so, but it would be completely untrue. That's not the point of the book at all, though Fran is perhaps a certain kind of American stereotype.

She seems to me not just an American stereotype but a stereotype of a woman who has taken on a kind of male attitude, seeing things externally, rationalizing, and refusing emotional response . . .

Yes, and refusing emotional responsibility. She is prepared to come into this family and lay it open to public speculation and interest with her camera, without respecting the feelings of anyone involved – despite the fact that she is related to them by marriage.

Are you then saying that families should maintain their privacy, and never be violated by outsiders – not even by an aspirant outsider like Minnie, who nourishes her fond fantasies of the perfect family and who is yet resolutely made to feel an outsider?

I think that everybody has the right to respect their privacy. Furthermore, there is a great difference between somebody like Fran, who is trying to make a film out of people's misfortunes, and a pathetic outsider who had been taken in by the family in the first place, in her childhood. Minnie had been encouraged to feel like a member of the family and is asked to come back ten years later, only to find herself a pitiable figure who still can't get in to this family which paradoxically no longer exists: the father has been found dead, and the sons have spent a long time in

America. The centre of power was actually Hugo Pierce, the father, and Minnie discovers that there's nothing left of the family but a very distraught widow. The thing that interested me about the book, as I discovered, was that it has to do with time and memory: that is what emerged as I was writing it. I was tremendously impressed by Márquez's *Chronicle of a Death Foretold*, and I thought that I had never seen time more brilliantly or extraordinarily presented. I hope that with *Woman Beware Woman* the reader won't want to race on to the end, because there is all the time something which should hold the reader down on to the page, so to speak. Minnie arrives ten years after she had first been part of this glamorous family, the whole of the action takes place in ten days, and – throughout those ten days – we return not only to what it was like ten years before but also to some of the memories Hugo Pierce had been talking about ten years before, which had happened to him twenty-five years before then. I may say that I took quite a lot of Dwight Macdonald's obituary to create Hugo Pierce's career.

The two sons, Gareth and Philip, are shadowy characters in the book, while Hugo Pierce is quite highly defined, but what we perhaps pick up about him is that in his younger days he had been an active adventurer and anarchist, and that he has lately become an anecdotalist. I have the impression of him as being a crusader who has made of himself a 'character'.

He was made into a 'character' by his many admirers – he was nominated for the Nobel Prize, after all, and was a legend of his time. But I think it's an oddly structured book because it goes on so much about Hugo, and yet the point is that the women are present together because he *isn't* there, *because* he died.

He therefore functions as a catalyst?

Yes, and that is what he was meant to be, a character whose end provides the start of the action. Minnie imagined that Hugo thought her an unsuitable wife for his son, but Hugo had never expressed any such thing. I hope the book does give out a feeling of women's weapons, which consist so often of secret knowledge passed on at bombshell moments, causing weakness and retreat on the part of another woman. There are always things which one woman knows and another woman doesn't know, and these are their arms.

Would you accept – in a general way – that the book shows the terrible claustrophobia that can arise in any family?

Yes, it's very much about the horrors of the 'perfect' family, and what in fact goes on underneath, the entrapments and tensions. But I just don't agree with the notion of it as being about women in our time. It's not a moralistic book, except in one important way which has to do with people dismissing other people and getting away with it. In this case, the revenge that Moura desires is carried out, but so is another revenge which Moura could never have expected – and that arises as a result of a sort of cruelty and dismissiveness. After Minnie realizes that she has been jilted and is not going to be able to marry Philip, Moura invites her back the next summer out of 'compassion and kindness' and gives her the most bloody awful summer, forcing her to go fishing and to do all the things she had formerly done with Philip. When Minnie is obviously on the verge of break-down, Moura then says with apparent kindness that the visit has done Minnie no good and that she'd better not come again. This then severs Minnie's links with a childhood place for which she had developed such deep affection, and she has to go back to her mother, whom she has never liked, while endlessly remembering that beautiful place and wonderful family.

I think every detail in this particular book is functional – even the tapestry of Diana the Huntress seems an appropriate image for Moura, the vengeful widow – whereas it might be thought that some of the free-floating and metaphorical association in certain of your earlier novels was more decorative in kind, or at least a function of a more open and contingent structure.

Wild Nights and *Alice Fell* are indeed odd poetic short pieces, not really novels, and *Hotel de Dream* is on purpose a comic apoca-lypse. It would be unsuitable in *Woman Beware Woman* to go off into any kind of free-floating imagery. There is nothing numi-nous at all in this book: if Minnie thinks or dreams something, she actually says 'I think I saw something' or 'I dreamt that . . .', and the fact that she gazes at a sixteenth-century French tapestry depicting something like Diana the Huntress is not meant to be a heavy analogy or symbol. I must have put in Diana the Huntress because Moura is being the huntress of her husband's murderers – but that actually never occurred to me until you mentioned it just now, and I think it would be a mistake to read it that way.

It would be a misconception for readers to take the tapestry as showing that you were allegorizing the idea of women against men?

Yes, totally. It was more that I wanted to present this very entrapped feeling with this large house, and that since Minnie is enclosed in her room she is bound to make some connection between the murder in a wood and what she sees in the tapestry. That's the way she images it, and she says so herself; it's not allegorical at all.

It is commonly felt that writers produce imaginative works because of a sense of dissatisfaction or unease or dissent. What do you fear . . . is life inadequate?

Everybody has nightmares and fears, and they're often remarkably similar. A sense of lack for me would mean not being able to go on writing. The fear is that one day you wouldn't be inspired or able to execute it. That is the greatest fear, and I don't consider my life to be inadequate in the slightest. I can't see that writing comes from inadequacy or unhappiness, but I think for me at least it may come paradoxically from the fear of not being able to do it.

You don't think that writing can provide a synthesis or resolution of existential problems?

I think that putting things in unexamined *is* a resolution in itself. I think diagnosis is a mistake. In my view, for example, Golding does diagnose rather too much . . . over-diagnose what he's writing. I like *The Inheritors*, but some of his other books are I feel too intended and analysed. I like to return to different things and thoughts, and that isn't linear, and perhaps that sort of thing going through one's mind does make a lack which has to be filled by writing it. If you were stopped from writing it, you might then feel very inadequate. The lack would come from an inability to answer the things which are coming in all the time, and they can only be met by knowing the right technique to deal with them. It is a question of hitting or finding the correct method to resolve the thing you are lucky enough to receive: the right method will resolve in the thing that has suggested itself. Every different thing demands its own expression.

· FAY WELDON ·

Author and feminist, funny and mordant, Fay Weldon is a
compulsively readable anatomist of human relationships in the
modern world. 'Art', she once wrote, 'is invention and distil-
lation mixed': it is 'fundamentally subversive' (*National Times*
[Australia], 11 April 1982). She has written several highly
acclaimed and best-selling novels including *Praxis* (1978) and
Puffball (1980), a volume of short stories, *Watching Me, Watching
You* (1981), and plays for both stage and radio (*Polaris* (1978)
won her the Giles Cooper Award for radio drama). Her numerous other credits include the first of the TV series *Upstairs,
Downstairs*, the TV adaptation of *Pride and Prejudice* and the
screenplay of Erica Jong's *Fanny*. Before becoming a full-time
writer she worked in market research, in journalism (answering
problem letters for the *Daily Mirror*), for the Foreign Office
('writing propaganda, really'), and then as a talented advertising
copywriter for Ogilvy Benson and Mather and other firms,
where the slogan 'Go to work on an egg' figured among her
successful devices.

Brought up in a family of women – grandmother, mother and
sister – she is now married to Ron Weldon, an antiques dealer ('I
consider it a testimony to the extraordinary qualities of both
men and women,' she has said elsewhere, 'that we are still
together – on and off – after twenty years' (*Image*)), and has four
sons. She divides her time between a small modernized terrace
house in Kentish Town, London, and a country house in
Somerset. She is indefatigable and totally professional in her
approach to the job of writing, never intimidated by a blank

sheet of paper, and amazingly productive. Her career and achievements exemplify her passionate conviction that a woman can achieve independence, self-confidence and self-motivation. 'As a writer,' she has said, 'I can free myself from the need to be liked and appreciated and not disapproved of by men. . . . I think happiness is a secondary goal to self-realization. I think a liberated woman is a woman who has freedom of choice' (*The Observer* colour magazine, 18 February 1979).

I interviewed her in London in 1982 – just before she flew to Australia to resume work on the filmscript of a novel by Christina Stead – and began by asking about her eighth full-length novel, *The President's Child* (1982).

* * *

You said to me on the 'phone that you think of The President's Child *as being three novels in one. What did you mean?*
That was the attitude with which I wrote it, though it shouldn't be apparent to the reader. It seemed to me that there were three separate skeins going through it: one was a domestic novel, the other was a literary novel, and the third was a kind of thriller in the middle of it. You try and wrap them all up into a singular view of the world instead of three separate views.
Which part do you think of as the literary novel, the story the blind woman, Maia, tells about her neighbour Isabel?
Yes, in a way, it's full of literary conceits and a slight bizarreness, and the reactions of the people up and down the street.
It's not in any way based on this street where you live?
No, not at all. I do make it up. I would to God that I lived in a street like that.
Did the three-ply concept come to you all at once, or did you start from Maia's narrative?
No, that was the last bit. First of all I had the thriller idea. Ideas are usually what come last in writing, not first, and they're very treacherous things. If you are to keep yourself out of your novel, which I thought I would try to do this time, you have to put someone in your place. It has to be somebody who is supposed or assumed or allowed to know better than other people –

someone who is wise in spite of themselves – while at the same time having some kind of character. Somebody who has become blind has to lead a life of contemplation, in spite of their nature. It seems to me quite interesting.

What do you mean by the idea in a story? Nothing to do with plot?

No, the plot is never the point. But in this particular novel the plot was so heavy that it was in danger of becoming the point. The point is a rather smart-alecky point that you can never trust men, or rather that nice men are only pretending. That's my thesis. I'd rather have a nasty man than a nice man any day.

So that all the while you were writing you knew that Homer, Isabel's husband, was a nasty secret agent?

Yes, I did. It's rather a sneaky trick and in that case it's rather a vulgar novel in the proper sense of the word 'vulgar'. Novels for me usually have a proposition which you examine in literary terms, without being quite sure of the answer.

Puffball is devoted to a proposition I don't necessarily believe in, you see: it's an examination of the degree to which women are victims of their biology, good and bad. The proposition, that is to say, is that a woman has something in her that she has to contend with. And having come to the end of that novel I was rather glad to realize how much I could disagree with what I began with. The book also required that the father should in some sense be a threat to the foetus, but at the end the father comes home.

I took in that in Puffball *Liffey's child is her only real ally.*

Well, any mother with a 3-year-old regards the child as in some sense an enemy, but it's an ally before it starts answering back. *Puffball* now seems to me a very complex book, far more complex than when I wrote it, a pattern of opposites and contradictions and polarizations.

The President's Child *is perhaps your most sober book to date – there seem to be fewer jokes, for example, less general lightheartedness – as if you didn't want to diminish the seriousness of the book as . . . what, a political allegory?*

Yes, it is a political allegory. It is, I suppose, about American involvement in Europe. It's also about the impossibility of pretending that there isn't a conflict between male power and female power.

Isabel is betrayed by the men in her life, but she in her turn is living a lie, isn't she?

Yes, she is, and the lie is engendered by the world she lives in. I suppose, in a way, the book could have been set up differently, but then it's too far removed from an observable reality. I'm repeatedly asked, in fact, to write a role model for women, which always seems to me an unfair demand to make of a writer.

I'm not sure I felt entirely convinced by Isabel's Australian childhood. I wonder why you decided that she should have been brought up in Australia, when the bulk of the novel is set in suburban London with flashbacks to Isabel's affair with an American presidential candidate? Isabel might well have begun as an English delinquent who slept around and found that she was later in a predicament with the past catching up with her.

I think I wanted her not to be from here. I didn't want the people to be English, but people from everywhere in a way, so that Isabel had no particular alignment except to the present. In fact, at the end, she's reconciled to her past and goes back to acknowledge it. But I don't know. If you knew why you did things, other people would also know why and write the books their way.

Am I right in thinking that Isabel's child is no more uncontrollable than any other child, and that it's only her bad conscience that makes her believe what all the men keep suggesting?

Yes, he's really behaving like any other child, but her guilty conscience makes her agree with what everyone else is suggesting. Her loving husband tells her that the child keeps biting people, and on the whole it's not true (though he bit somebody once), but it doesn't occur to Isabel to doubt him. It gave Homer the idea and he manoeuvred her.

Are you conscious of writing literature with intent?

Literature with intent to reform? I think so, yes.

You feel you're propounding a moral?

Most certainly.

Concerning how beastly men are?

No, that's not a moral, nor is there necessarily any condemnation implied. It's just an observation that women had better know it if they want to look after themselves. Once they know it, they can do what they want about it.

The moral is how to survive?

No, you can't say the moral *is*. And anyway, survival is the one thing in which no morality is involved. I don't think I'm giving lessons in survival, but perhaps I am. But you couldn't say *The President's Child* is a lesson in survival.

Some readers might judge that the whole story of Isabel is something – I'll call it a lesson – made up by Maia, the blind woman, that it's all her fiction.

Yes, it might well be. The difficulty of writing so much fiction is that you become rather uncertain of what you made up and what happened.

At the end of the book Maia starts to see again, and it's particularly ironic that she recovers her sight at the point where, like Mephistopheles perhaps, she decides that this is hell nor am I out of it.

Exactly. It is an hysterical blindness, and she's cured when she comes to acknowledge it. You could complain about all sorts of contrivances and coincidences in the book, and the only answer is either that you should write it yourself or, if you want real life, live it. But the thing is, as we all know, coincidences abound in real life, because of the peculiar synchronicity of events. But it is a kind of cheating to make fiction echo real life. Fiction on the whole is a great deal more believable than real life. It's perhaps why people turn to it . . . for peace, really.

Is Maia's rediscovery of her sight meant to be a small moral in the book?

Yes. It dawned upon me when I was very young that you produce the physical symptoms which suit your psychic state. I remember working in an office with the most irritating woman I've ever known; she'd been married for three weeks and said, 'It's very funny, but ever since the day my husband married me he's had a pain in his neck.' So you may go blind because you won't see. But it's something you can carry too far, to uncharitable lengths.

Most of your heroines begin life in extreme positions. Praxis, for example is underprivileged and has a mad mother; others are bastards . . .

I don't know that I always mean them to begin like that, it's how they end up. I suppose that fiction on the whole has to be about people who are open to change. Bad news is good news for writers. Books about happy, secure and stable people are not the kinds of books I write, I suppose. Or I would not know how to make such people interesting.

But stacking the deck in that way can provide a sort of comic absurdity which characterizes a whole book.

I think the lives of perfectly serious people are very often comic. They're not experienced as comic at the time, but people deal with them by making them comic. Certainly there is a bizarre element in a lot of them.

What sort of early life did you have?

I was born outside Birmingham. My father was a doctor. He worked in New Zealand, and I went out there when I was very small. Then I came back here after the war. I lived in fairly dire poverty, went to South Hampstead High School, then to university, and knocked about in a neurotic fashion.

You were a child of divided parents, then?

Yes, I was. My mother was supporting us all. She's a writer.

So that when you speak of difficult upbringings in your novels, you're actually speaking from experience?

Oh, yes, I don't make it all up. And I had a child to support when I was very young. Advertising was the only thing I could do in order to earn a decent enough living. But that wasn't why I did it; I knew someone who did it, and they got me a job. I did it for about eight years.

And you gave it up to become a writer?

I spent some time in analysis . . .

Before you started writing?

Yes, and I would probably not have written had I not gained some self-knowledge and decided I was capable of doing it.

What made you go into analysis?

I was thirty, inadequate and depressed and ignorant, and knew it. Analysis was dreadfully painful and very interesting. It was a painful and necessary thing.

Did analysis prompt you to make any resolutions or to take decisions about yourself and your life, your career?

Analysis does not induce states of decision or resolution: the acquiring of even minimal self-knowledge is practically helpful, however.

Did you feel embittered by your childhood?

Not particularly. It seemed no worse than many, or indeed most.

It wasn't a factor that took you into analysis?

I think anybody's childhood is what takes them into analysis: a mixture of childhood and personality. Two children with the same background will react totally differently to it. One of the things about analysis is that you recognize what went right. You lose your sense of grievance because you are actually prepared to take responsibility for your own personality.

Your novels are particularly strong on middle-class marriages, doctors, architects . . .

There is a difficulty in writing about the working class, if you're going to call it that, because if you're dealing with people who are not practised in dealing with abstract thought or see no virtue in it, or who aren't practised in expressing their thoughts with any subtlety, you have to spend your entire time with internal monologue, which I don't particularly enjoy writing, I suppose. In a way you can write women more easily than men. You get extremely vocal cleaning women, for example, who are highly intelligent but because of lack of education and opportunity have been kept to a certain level in society. Now it doesn't happen with men, who by and large find themselves in the situation in life that suits their ambition, their aspiration and their intellect. They will usually be socially mobile. Women, by virtue of having got married, will appoint themselves to a certain status in life forever. There are more differences between men and women in this way. The first part of my life was spent in a middle class without security, without money and without property. Being a young woman with a child to support and no father for it, you lived on what you as a woman could make, which wasn't much.

Do the distressed marriages in your books reflect your own life?

I think it might reflect my early life . . . but we're becoming too personal. I'm only personal in foreign countries, where nobody I know is going to read it.

Do you believe D. H. Lawrence's notion of shedding one's sicknesses in books?

I don't think so. The writing of fiction seems to be a function of a surplus of animation, rather than neurosis. Certainly, *I've* never found anything curative in it. More's the pity.

Critics have labelled you our most 'intelligent feminist novelist', which suggests that you have a campaign going.

I have a campaign going, yes. It's at a point between feminism and psychoanalysis. There are two prongs to it: one is that you had better know yourself, and the other is that when I started writing the structure of society was weighted very heavily against women and their lot was very obscure. Now it's not so obscure, and there are many women who are prepared to take a more political stance than I need do. I do feel that women have to fight as much against their own natures as against the world or against men's behaviour. I'm more content to involve myself in form; I mean, what I like about *The President's Child* is its structure, which was difficult and took a long time to do. Feminism is there if you wish to make it available to you.

Are there any feminist writings – fiction or non-fiction – which you regard as central to your experience and views?

No particular work: a whole body of opinion and comment, of course, has been fed into society over the last twenty years, and no doubt picked up by me.

What must women fight in their natures, a lapsing back into passivity and unawareness?

Yes, a lapsing back into the belief that you don't have to work and struggle because somebody will always be there to look after you.

Do you feel you have a prejudice against men?

It's in women's interests to change the way the world is, and it's not in men's interests. I think it's to men's disadvantage that they've had it so easy. Probably everybody is as bad as they're allowed to be. But I may well have a prejudice against men. When people ask me if I hate men, I usually reply, 'Yes, I do hate men,' because I think it's every woman's right to hate men if she wants. I say I do profoundly dislike men, but I don't actually think it's true . . . I'm just turning into a rather difficult interviewee. It's the same kind of question as when people ask if you're a feminist, and you immediately say 'yes' because there's an implied criticism, and you will therefore not regard it as a criticism. I am a feminist, but I would not describe myself as a feminist novelist because that would imply that the novels were written because I was a feminist. I am a feminist and I write novels, and because I believe feminism to be a true view of the world what I write is bound to come out to be feminist. You could advance the view that all good writing is bound to be feminist . . . it depends on how you're going to define feminist. *I wonder if we haven't reached a stage where there should be some post-feminist writing in which the men might be liberated?*

It's astonishing the way men depend on women to write it for them. Or men say, 'What about the women in Iran?', as if it was purely a woman's problem, not their problem. It's as though women are being held responsible to bring about a post-feminist literature in which men are included as human beings. Well, let men do it. To that extent I'm certainly a feminist. Let the men liberate themselves, it's time they did it. I'm pleased to see a novel or two coming out in which men are beginning to write like women, not here but in America. John Irving's *The World According to Garp* seems to be beginning to deal with human relationships and a bizarre reality . . .

What comes out of your novels for me is the idea that men are more to be pitied than despised.

I think *people* are more to be pitied than despised. The difficulty for women is that they've been treated as if they were not people. One wishes women to join the human race. But I don't think that in my novels my men are any worse than my women, you see. I do think that men are accustomed to seeing themselves in fiction as noble heroes carrying the action along, and in my novels they rarely do. So it appears to men that they are somehow discriminated against. In fact they're no worse than the women.

You don't offer any worthy men.

But are any of my women worthy? No. They're terrible creatures.

But you find yourself allied with them?

Yes, and so you should, just as you like your friends although you see their faults. But I don't think I judge the men as any worse than the women. Praxis behaves in the most appalling fashion.

Praxis remarks, 'Nature does not know best, or if it does, it is on the man's side . . . we must fight nature tooth and claw.' Is that just Praxis's opinion, or did you share it?

That's certainly me at the time. But fortunately in fiction there are this week's truths and next week's.

Praxis finds herself killing a child at the end of that book. Did you approve of that action or take it as the logic of her position and experience?

Not approve; I think what she did was practical. It was the logic of her position, yes. Better than the Falklands War, for example. What adults are allowed to do to adults, women are not allowed to do to imperfect children.

Why should she confess to the deed?

Because there should be no action of which one is ashamed. If she did it, let her say so.

I think it may be true to say that in most of your books the women begin as rather naive and unworldly and move on from that position, whereas the men are immovably egotistical and constantly act according to what might be called inalienably man-made laws.

I think that's what happens. Men on the whole don't change. Women change because they have children. The thing that children seem able to do for their parents is to change them. Where men are not responsible for their children, they don't change. It may be what happens to childless people, that they don't change.

In Praxis *you write, 'the rejected, the humiliated, the obsessive, the angry, live their lives by principle rather than by convenience.' It's a compelling thought, but is it not just as likely that rejection and humiliation might lead people to be blinkered, bitter and unjust in their attitudes, even perverse and bloody-minded?*

Principle isn't necessarily *good*. The principle may well be to hate everything, not just something. It might be convenient to accept a lift from an ex-husband, but more rewarding to be bloody minded and see his goodness and generosity as a

plot. You walk up the hill on principle: *mean*, but consistent.
Do you feel that people who've been subjected to intolerable situations just invariably become more wily?
I think they pass the intolerable situations on *if they can*. You just have to watch the way children behave . . . shouting gets passed on from one to another, or injury.
Is it your experience that people are incorrigible, that they become locked into their attitudes?
I suppose it is more likely – culturally – that men are more incorrigible than women at the moment. But I think it's a great mistake to say that men are always like this and women like that. The culture we live in has divided men and women so that they appear to have different qualities. Women are probably incorrigible if they're allowed to be, and men are incorrigible because they're encouraged to be.
I wonder what brief you actually have for the concept of sisterhood? It seems to me that you might sometimes be sceptical of it. Women do betray one another in your novels.
It seems a safer bet than any other. Sisterhood is a relatively new concept, and I think it does work. My characters don't betray each other once they've gained a concept of sisterhood. In the fifties it was a kind of convention that women were the enemies of other women, that they'd be catty about each other, and it is not nearly as true now as it was. When women can survive by themselves, and have a man as a matter of choice, an optional extra, women are far less ready to see men as possessions or other women as competitors or rivals.
I think men who read your novels will find an irresistibly knowing quality which they might happily assent to without feeling too threatened.
It may tend to be so here, but men are very nervous in Australia and New Zealand, and I get very different reactions. I know someone in Belgium who reads my novels while shut in the loo because her husband forbids her to read them. There are still countries where men think for women, and this is regarded as subversive literature. I think fiction does make minute alterations in people's lives; people get their view of the world to an amazing extent from novels.

I think one or two reviewers have decided that you are essentially romantic, whether or not that's a pejorative word. What they perhaps mean is that you display a fairly hideous social world but that you either end on a high note or sustain an essentially positive impetus.

I think that's a fairly true reflection of the world. If your actual position is appalling, you need to have some positive reaction, or some positive spirit left. The practical, rational position is to have no experience at all, and then you might as well be dead.

It sometimes happens that you adopt a coolness, almost a cynical posture, towards the characters in your novels, as though you might just enjoy displaying their paradoxical lives and ridiculous attitudes. I think I wonder how seriously you mean the reader to take them?

I feel quite fond of them. But I don't know any other way to write novels, you see. I think the nastier they are, the fonder I feel of them, though it may not come over like that.

What I'm really asking, I suppose, is whether there's a danger that a satirical novel might at times become simply sarcastic?

I don't see why that should be a danger. You're supposing there's a world in which there's a right way to do things, where satire is all right and sarcasm isn't.

Well, satire may stem from a saeva indignatio *in the novelist, while sarcasm might show a certain condescension towards characters, a manipulation . . .*

But what else do you do, if you write novels, but manipulate your characters? What are you supposed to do? If you want to make distinctions between satire and sarcasm, you will have to do it, and I will not be involved in it.

What makes you write novels, then? Is it the terrible comedy of human life?

I am quite frequently moved by a sense of outrage and indignation; otherwise I wouldn't do it in the first place. But on the other hand I suppose it tends to wear thin every now and then, and one may find pleasure in what is outrageous: you deal with it by presenting it in a palatable form. Or work it out on the page at the expense of one's readers, which may well be the case.

And at the expense of your characters?

I suppose I have a certain loyalty to them in that I invented them, but I don't particularly feel I have to look after them. I wouldn't want them to get above themselves. They're tossed here and there as plot and passion drives them.

Do you ever fear that readers might think you complacent in your view of human betrayals and hypocrisies?

I wouldn't wish them to, nor would I wish to think that I stand outside human folly and wasn't a prey to it. It never occurred to me that I was anything other than *in there* with *them*. But it is very difficult, you see, to be in charge of a novel and to appear *not* to be in charge.

It must be equally difficult to write novels which have a high entertainment value and which are at the same time – more or less earnestly, as the case may be – concerned with the serious matter of feminism?

Yes it is, but so far as I am concerned there is no point in doing one without the other. There's no point in being so serious that nobody wants to read you or can't respond, and no point in writing only for people who agree with you anyway. So you have to make it accessible to the people who don't agree with you. Now it's quite easy to write books with no funny lines in at all, and you get taken more seriously if you do. I took out about a third of the funny lines in *Praxis*, because it's actually quite a serious book. I fear that my instinct, which I shudder against all the time, is always to trivialize everything. That's a weakness, because it's such a temptation to be funny; you can go too far and you have to struggle against it, or balance it.

Do you believe in the magic and supernaturalism that figures in some of your works, in Remember Me *and some of the short stories?*

Well, I take *New Scientist* weekly, and it's much easier to believe in magic than it is to believe in current cosmology or particle physics, I can tell you. So the answer is that I believe in magic as much and as little as anything else. The nature of reality is so totally absurd. If you have a slight difficulty with accepting the reality of the world, then you can write a ghost story . . . Do you know about naked peculiarities? Naked peculiarities are a form of black hole, a cosmic implosion of matter that has got so minute as to have opened out on the other side, and they're so small that you can have them in your brain. So they say that it's all inner space anyway, and the whole thing becomes quite absurd . . . Compared to that, magic seems quite ordinary.

So do you read New Scientist *to multiply your sense of the weirdness of the world?*

On the whole, yes, for the actual pleasure of discovering these extraordinary things. You have to keep reading, because it's like a soap opera.

Do you particularly admire any contemporary writers, and are you friends with any?

Some of my best friends are writers. Some writers are not my friends. We rarely talk about writing. I don't admire anyone; it doesn't stop me liking or indeed loving them. Do you like or love people for their qualities? Or do you respond to them, and then attribute to them all kinds of qualities which they probably don't have?

You're about to go back to Australia to continue working on the filmscript of a Christina Stead novel. Which novel is it?

For Love Alone.

Did it come to you as a commission or did you know the book?

It came out of the blue, but I've been reading Christina Stead for some time. I hadn't read *For Love Alone* before, and it was a daunting task since it's such a very verbal book.

There's not much dialogue in that novel, is there?

Well, Jonathan Crow talks quite a lot. But it can be done. You can very rarely use the original dialogue when adapting for the screen. Films and television are very different, for reasons which I never quite understand, and I started out as a dramatic writer. Novels, television, stage and films are all different ways of communicating, and they require different techniques which you have to learn. Once you have learned the form, you can throw the switch, but it takes some difficult and painful time while you acquire the form. Films are not novels, and I find the novel a far, far higher form. I write screenplays because I wish to learn how it's done; it's another experience and challenge.

Part of the difficulty with *For Love Alone* is that the characters are really all descriptions of real people. Real people on the whole make bad novels, and they require novels to confine them; they're indestructible and multifaceted, whereas fictional characters are often very crude.

Did you find that you have to commit yourself to the story of Teresa,

who is depicted as a romantic idealist in Christina Stead's novel?
No, you have to be dispassionate, it's somebody else's character. You honour it and enter into the spirit of it, but you're not committed to it. The great pleasure of adaptation is that you're not responsible; you use a craft and a skill – a slightly medium-istic approach – but it's not your idea. Teresa is a rather shocking young woman, I think, pig-headed.

Jonathan Crow, who's a kind of anti-hero, is a rather tiresome character, don't you think?
I rather liked him. He was trying to be honest. He had a view of himself and of the world which was very uncharitable, and he was trying to face it and come to terms with it, to change the world, and to make her and himself acknowledge the truth of the matter. What I like about the book is that it actually deals with people, not with heroes, villains or heroines. They are flawed, and they approach the realities of life. It is disconcerting that the heroine marries the goody and then rushes off with his best friend, so you're not quite sure what that has to do with this romantic story of dogged devotion. So it's really a tale of sexual emancipation, you see; Teresa discovers a kind of male freedom, being married but sexually free. It was what men were supposed to do, but women weren't, and that's what she achieved.

Your own style of writing depends on events and dialogue, whereas Christina Stead's perhaps depends on rich interior activity, and I wonder if you react against her style of writing?
No, I like that sense of overflowing . . . a language at the end of its tether. I really like it. It's just another way of doing it, and I don't think I could do it like that. I'm accustomed to discipline, and after writing so much for television where something has to happen all the time, it makes me feel that I want something to happen. And, really, I want something to happen; you write the kind of book you'd like to read.

You don't feel impatient with Christina Stead's searching psychology?
I think a searching psychology is implicit in what you write, you don't need to spell it out on the page.

Did you feel that working in advertising was meretricious, as some of your characters suggest, or are there any particular advertising campaigns you were especially proud of?

Of course advertising is meretricious. I was never *proud* of what I did, though occasionally gratified by the effect a particular advertisement had on sales. Or indeed on people's lives. 10,000 home-made Christmas puddings, when opened up on Christmas Day 1963, were *green* because I'd forgotten to put sugar in the *Woman's Own* Add an Egg for Christmas recipe, in October. Advertising gives you a sense of power. Write in a TV commercial 'it's a cold arctic night' and the whole crew goes to the North Pole. Well, they used to, in the good days.

Did advertising help to form the style in which you write?

Designers and typographers actually teach you the look upon the page. Words are given resonance by their positions, they must be displayed properly. If you wish to give something emphasis, you surround it by space. Of course it develops a sense of language and an economy of style, the practice of any allied craft is helpful to the writer. You've got to do *something* while waiting to have something to say: and it's probably better to be a copywriter than a general, say, or chief of police. You spend a lot of time having what you've written fed back to you, so that you learn what people respond to. It was a kind of crash course, not in language as written but in language as received by readers, which can only be helpful though it may make you kind of slippery. Style seems to me in the end a matter of economy, of how to get down rapidly and exactly, with precision, what you wish to say. If you have enough to say, you want to get it down as quickly as possible, without losing any of its subtlety, and that is what develops an individual style. Style in advertising depends on cost; there are no ideas in particular, there are products, so that you're always dealing with a craft. It's the pressure of money which creates an advertising style, and the pressure of content which creates a writer's style.

· SELECT BIBLIOGRAPHY ·

Place of publication is London, unless otherwise indicated.

· MARTIN AMIS ·

The Rachel Papers. Cape, 1973.
Dead Babies. Cape, 1975.
Success. Cape, 1978.
Other People: A Mystery Story. Cape, 1981.
Money: A Suicide Note. Cape, 1984.

Non-fiction

Invasion of the Space Invaders. Hutchinson, 1982.

· MALCOLM BRADBURY ·

Eating People Is Wrong. Secker & Warburg, 1959.
Stepping Westward. Secker & Warburg, 1965.
The History Man. Secker & Warburg, 1975.
Who Do You Think You Are? (stories and parodies). Secker & Warburg, 1976.
Rates of Exchange. Secker & Warburg, 1983.

Non-fiction

Evelyn Waugh. Edinburgh: Oliver & Boyd, 1964.
The Social Context of Modern English Literature. Oxford: Blackwell, 1971.
Possibilities: Essays on the State of the Novel. Oxford University Press, 1973.

(ed.) *The Penguin Companion to Literature 3: USA* (with Eric Mottram). Harmondsworth: Allen Lane/Penguin, 1971.

(ed.) *Modernism* (with James McFarlane). Harmondsworth: Penguin, 1976.

(ed.) *The Novel Today: Contemporary Writers on Modern Fiction*. Manchester: Manchester University Press, 1977.

(ed.) *The Contemporary English Novel* (with David Palmer). Edward Arnold, 1979.

'Trouble in the Funhouse: The Writer and the Critic', *London Magazine* (New Series), 18, 12, March 1979, pp. 34–42.

(ed.) *An Introduction to American Studies* (with Howard Temperley). Longman, 1981.

Saul Bellow. Methuen, 1982.

The Modern American Novel. Oxford University Press, 1983.

Plays

The After Dinner Game: Three Plays for Television. Arrow, 1982.

· ANITA BROOKNER ·

A Start in Life. Cape, 1981.
Providence. Cape, 1982.
Look at Me. Cape, 1983.
Hotel du Lac. Cape, 1984.

Non-fiction

Watteau. Hamlyn, 1971.
The Genius of the Future: Studies in French Art Criticism. Phaidon, 1971.
Greuze: The Rise and Fall of an Eighteenth-Century Phenomenon. Elek, 1972.
Jacques-Louis David. Chatto & Windus, 1980.

· ANGELA CARTER ·

Shadow Dance. Heinemann, 1966.
The Magic Toyshop. Heinemann, 1967.
Several Perceptions. Heinemann, 1968.
Heroes and Villains. Heinemann, 1969.
Love. Hart-Davis, 1971.
The Infernal Desire Machines of Doctor Hoffman. Hart-Davis, 1972.
Fireworks (short stories). Quartet, 1974.

· SELECT BIBLIOGRAPHY ·

The Passion of New Eve. Gollancz, 1977.
The Bloody Chamber (short stories). Gollancz, 1979.
Nights at the Circus. Chatto & Windus, 1984.

Non-fiction

The Sadeian Woman: An Exercise in Cultural History. Virago, 1979.
Nothing Sacred: Selected Writings. Virago, 1982.

Plays

Come unto these Yellow Sands. Newcastle upon Tyne: Bloodaxe, 1985.

Translation

The Fairy Tales of Charles Perrault. Gollancz, 1977.

· WILLIAM GOLDING ·

Lord of the Flies. Faber, 1954.
The Inheritors. Faber, 1955.
Pincher Martin. Faber, 1956.
Free Fall. Faber, 1959.
The Spire. Faber, 1964.
The Pyramid. Faber, 1967.
The Scorpion God (short stories). Faber, 1971.
Darkness Visible. Faber, 1979.
Rites of Passage. Faber, 1980.

Non-fiction

The Hot Gates. Faber, 1965.
A Moving Target. Faber, 1982.

Play

The Brass Butterfly. Faber, 1958.

· RUSSELL HOBAN ·

The Lion of Boaz-Jachin and Jachin-Boaz. Cape, 1973.
Kleinzeit. Cape, 1974.
Turtle Diary. Cape, 1975.
Riddley Walker. Cape, 1980.
Pilgermann. Cape, 1983.

Books for children

Bedtime for Frances. Faber, 1963.
Tom and the Two Handles. World's Work, 1966.
The Mouse and His Child. Faber, 1969.
Best Friends for Frances. Faber, 1971.
A Bargain for Frances. Faber, 1971.
Emmet Otter's Jug-Band Christmas. World's Work, 1971.
Herman the Loser. World's Work, 1972.
The Sea-Thing Child. Gollancz, 1972.
Harvey's Hideout. Cape, 1973.
How Tom Beat Captain Najork and his Hired Sportsmen. Cape, 1974.
Dinner at Alberta's. Cape, 1977.
The Dancing Tigers. Cape, 1979.
La Corona and the Tin Frog. Cape, 1979.
The Twenty Elephant Restaurant. Cape, 1980.

Non-fiction

'Thoughts on a Shirtless Cyclist, Robin Hood, Johann Sebastian Bach and one or two other things', *Children's Literature in Education*, 4, March 1971; reprinted in Geoff Fox *et al.* (eds) *Writers, Critics and Children*, Heinemann Education, 1976.

'Stories that Grew up with Me', *English in Education*, 13, 1, Spring 1979.

· DAVID LODGE ·

The Picturegoers. MacGibbon & Kee, 1960.
Ginger, You're Barmy. MacGibbon & Kee, 1962; reissued, with Introduction, Secker & Warburg, 1982.
The British Museum Is Falling Down. MacGibbon & Kee, 1965; second edn, with Afterword, Secker & Warburg, 1981.
Out of the Shelter. Macmillan, 1970; second edn, revised, Secker & Warburg, 1985.
Changing Places: A Tale of Two Campuses. Secker & Warburg, 1975.
How Far Can You Go? Secker & Warburg, 1980.
Small World: An Academic Romance. Secker & Warburg, 1984.

Non-fiction

Language of Fiction. Routledge & Kegan Paul, 1966.
Graham Greene. New York: Columbia University Press, 1966.
The Novelist at the Crossroads. Routledge & Kegan Paul, 1971.
Evelyn Waugh. New York: Columbia University Press, 1971.

· SELECT BIBLIOGRAPHY ·

(ed.) *Twentieth-Century Literary Criticism: A Reader*. Longman, 1972.
The Modes of Modern Writing: Metaphor, Metonymy and the Typology of Modern Literature. Edward Arnold, 1977.
Working with Structuralism: Essays and Reviews on Nineteenth- and Twentieth-Century Literature. Routledge & Kegan Paul, 1981.

· IAN McEWAN ·

First Love, Last Rites. Cape, 1975.
In Between the Sheets. Cape, 1978.
The Cement Garden. Cape, 1978.
The Comfort of Strangers. Cape, 1981.

Others

The Imitation Game: Three Plays for Television. Cape, 1981.
Or Shall We Die? (words for an oratorio set to music by Michael Berkeley). Cape, 1983.

· IRIS MURDOCH ·

Under the Net. Chatto & Windus, 1954.
The Flight from the Enchanter. Chatto & Windus, 1956.
The Sandcastle. Chatto & Windus, 1957.
The Bell. Chatto & Windus, 1958.
A Severed Head. Chatto & Windus, 1961.
An Unofficial Rose. Chatto & Windus, 1962.
The Unicorn. Chatto & Windus, 1963.
The Time of the Angels. Chatto & Windus, 1966.
The Nice and the Good. Chatto & Windus, 1968.
Bruno's Dream. Chatto & Windus, 1969.
A Fairly Honourable Defeat. Chatto & Windus, 1970.
An Accidental Man. Chatto & Windus, 1971.
The Black Prince. Chatto & Windus, 1973.
The Sacred and Profane Love Machine. Chatto & Windus, 1974.
A Word Child. Chatto & Windus, 1975.
Henry and Cato. Chatto & Windus, 1976.
The Sea, The Sea. Chatto & Windus, 1978.
Nuns and Soldiers. Chatto & Windus, 1980.
The Philosopher's Pupil. Chatto & Windus, 1983.

Non-fiction

Sartre, Romantic Rationalist. Cambridge: Bowes, 1953.
The Sovereignty of Good (essays). Routledge & Kegan Paul, 1970.
The Fire and the Sun: Why Plato Banished the Artists. Oxford University
   Press, 1977.

Plays

A Severed Head (with J. B. Priestley). Chatto & Windus, 1964.
The Three Arrows, and The Servants and the Snow. Chatto & Windus,
   1973.

Poetry

A Year of Birds. Tisbury, Wiltshire: Compton Press, 1978; Chatto &
   Windus, 1984.

· V. S. PRITCHETT ·

The Other Side of the Frontier: A V. S. Pritchett Reader. Robin Clark,
   1984.

Short stories

Collected Stories. Chatto & Windus, 1982.
More Collected Stories. Chatto & Windus, 1983.

Novels

Nothing like Leather. Chatto & Windus, 1935.
Dead Man Leading. Chatto & Windus, 1937; reissued, with Introduction
   by Paul Theroux, Oxford University Press, 1984.
Mr Beluncle. Chatto & Windus, 1951.

Memoirs

A Cab at the Door. Chatto & Windus, 1968.
Midnight Oil. Chatto & Windus, 1971.

Literary criticism

The Living Novel. Chatto & Windus, 1946.
The Working Novelist. Chatto & Windus, 1965.
George Meredith and English Comedy. Chatto & Windus, 1970.

· SELECT BIBLIOGRAPHY ·

The Myth Makers. Chatto & Windus, 1979.
The Tale Bearers. Chatto & Windus, 1980.

Travel

The Spanish Temper. Chatto & Windus, 1954; reissued, with new Introduction, Hogarth Press, 1984.

· SALMAN RUSHDIE ·

Grimus. Gollancz, 1975.
Midnight's Children. Cape, 1981.
Shame. Cape, 1983.

· DAVID STOREY ·

This Sporting Life. Longman, 1960.
Flight into Camden. Longmans, Green, 1960.
Radcliffe. Longmans, Green, 1963.
Pasmore. Longman, 1972.
A Temporary Life. Harmondsworth: Allen Lane, 1973.
Saville. Cape, 1976.
A Prodigal Child. Cape, 1982.

Plays

The Restoration of Arnold Middleton. Cape, 1967.
In Celebration. Cape, 1969.
The Contractor. Cape, 1970.
Home. Cape, 1970.
The Changing Room. Cape, 1972.
The Farm. Cape, 1973.
Cromwell. Cape, 1973.
Life Class. Cape, 1975.
Mother's Day. Cape, 1977.

· EMMA TENNANT ·

(as Catherine Aydy) *The Colour of Rain*. Weidenfeld & Nicolson, 1964.
The Time of the Crack. Cape, 1973; new edn, as *The Crack*, Faber, 1985.
The Last of the Country House Murders. Cape, 1974.
Hotel de Dream. Gollancz, 1976.
The Bad Sister. Gollancz, 1978.

Wild Nights. Cape, 1979.
Alice Fell. Cape, 1980.
Queen of Stones. Cape, 1982.
Woman Beware Woman. Cape, 1983.

Uncollected short story

'Philomela', in *Bananas* (ed. Emma Tennant). Quartet/Blond & Briggs, 1977.

· FAY WELDON ·

The Fat Woman's Joke. MacGibbon & Kee, 1967.
Down Among the Women. Heinemann, 1971.
Female Friends. Heinemann, 1975.
Remember Me. Hodder & Stoughton, 1976.
Little Sisters. Hodder & Stoughton, 1977.
Praxis. Hodder & Stoughton, 1978.
Puffball. Hodder & Stoughton, 1980.
Watching Me, Watching You (short stories). Hodder & Stoughton, 1981.
The President's Child. Hodder & Stoughton, 1982.

Plays

Words of Advice. Samuel French, 1974.
Action Replay. Samuel French, 1980.